THE LIE OF THE LAND:
JOURNEYS THROUGH LITERARY CORK

The Lie of the Land:
Journeys through Literary Cork

Mary Leland

To my three travellers:
'If you love your child, send him on a journey ...'

Published in 1999 by Cork University Press
Cork, Ireland

© Mary Leland 1999

British Library Cataloguing in Publication Data
A CIP catalogue record for this book is available from the British Library.

ISBN 1 85918 231 3

Typeset by Janet and Roger Hall
Printed by ColourBooks Ltd., Baldoyle, Dublin

Contents

Illustrations

The Publishers wish to thank Laurence Pollinger Ltd for permission to use
Robert Gibbings' illustrations and the Crawford Municipal Art Gallery, Cork for the
remainder of the pictures that are used herein

Acknowledgements

In expressing my gratitude to all those friends and acquaintances who reminded me of possible inclusions for this book, I must thank especially Gerald Y. Goldberg who put his library, his scholarship and his genial alacrity at my disposal; Tim Cadogan, Niamh Cronin and Denis Murphy of the reference room at the Cork County Library, are knowledgeable, efficient and above all reliably patient. Thanks are due too to the staff of Cork City Library at Douglas and the Grand Parade.

I am grateful also to Cork University Press for agreeing to consider this proposal and then to see it through. And to The Revd G.H. Jerram Burrows, Pat Cotter, Gearóid Ó Crualaoich, Theo Dorgan, Nessa Durcan, Trish Edelstein, Patricia Egan, Brian Fallon, Cal Hyland, Áine Leland, Alec Morrogh, Patricia Morrogh, John A. Murphy, Maighréad Murphy, Patrick Murray, Peter Murray, Mary Porteus, Pádraig Ó Rian, Michael Twomey, Camille Wheeler and Richard Wood, my thanks.

The publishers gratefully acknowledge the following for permission to quote from their work: Theo Dorgan, 'A Nocturne for Blackpool' and 'Lover's Walk'; William Trevor, *Excursions in the Real World* (1993); Eileán Ní Chuilleanáin, 'Old Roads'; Eibhlín Dhubh Ní Chonaill, 'Caoineadh Airt Uí Laoghaire' (1981); John Montague, 'The Point'; Patrick Galvin, 'Plaisir d'Amour'; Eilís Dillon, 'In the Honan Chapel'; Seán Ó Tuama, 'Besides, Who Knows Before the End What Light May Shine'; Paul Durcan, 'The Late Mr Charles Lynch Digresses'; Roz Cowman, 'The Annunciation'; Anvil Press for Tom McCarthy, 'Love Like Trade' and 'Gardens of Remembrance'; Catholic Book Club, London for Ethel Mannin, *Two Studies in Integrity* (1954); Chatto & Windus, London for Patricia Cockburn, *Figures of Eight* (1985); Christopher Somerville for Somerville and Ross, *Irish Memories* and *The Real Charlotte*; Coisceim, Dublin for Colm Breathnach, 'Stiúrthóir Cúir'; Dedalus Press for Gerry Murphy, 'Poem in one Breath'; Dolmen Press, Portlaoise for Thomas Kinsella 'An Duanaire' and 'Tonn Cliona'; Gallery Press, Dublin for Seán Dunne, 'One Day in the Gearagh'; Geography Publications, Dublin for Diarmaid Ó Catháin, *Cork, History and Society* (1993); Greene's Library, Dublin for John Brophy (ed.), *The Voice of Sarah Curran* (1955); Gill & Macmillan, Dublin for Daniel Corkery, *The Hidden Ireland* (1925) and Frank O'Connor, *My Father's Son* (1968); Irish University Press, Dublin for Anne Fogarty (ed) *Spenser in Ireland* (1989); Laurence Pollinger Ltd for Robert Gibbings, *Sweet Cork of Thee* (1952); Lilliput Press, Dublin for Terence Brown, *Ireland's Literature* (1988) and Lady Mary Carbery, *West Cork Journals* (1995); Macmillan, London for W.B. Yeats, 'The Green Helmet', Frank O'Connor, *Kings Lords and Commons* (1962), Frank O'Connor, *The Backward Look* (1967), Frank O'Connor, *An Only Child* (1961), W.B. Yeats, 'September 1916'; Mercier Press, Cork for Eric Cross *The Tailor and Anstey* (1964); Michael Joseph, London for Lennox Robinson, *Curtain Up* (1941); O'Brien Press, Dublin for Kevin Corcoran, *West Cork Walks* (1991); Peter Davies, London for *Rural Rides* by William Cobbett, (1930); Phoenix, London for Richard Hayward, *Munster and the City of Cork* (1964); Rogers, Coleridge & White for Sean O Faolain, *An Irish Journey* (1940) and Sean O Faolain, *Vive Moi!* (1993); Routledge, Chapman & Hall for Seamus Murphy, *Stone Mad* (1950); Sáirseal agus Dill, Dublin for Sean Ó Riordáin, 'Adhlacadh mo Mháthair'; Sinclair-Stevenson, London for Conor Cruise O'Brien, *The Great Melody* (1992); Virago for Elizabeth Bowen, *Bowen's Court* (1942); Wolfhound Press, Dublin for Sean Lucy, *Unfinished Sequence and Other Poems* (1979).

Every effort has been made to trace the copyright holders of the works quoted herein. If there are any omissions Cork University Press will correct them in reprints or future editions of the book.

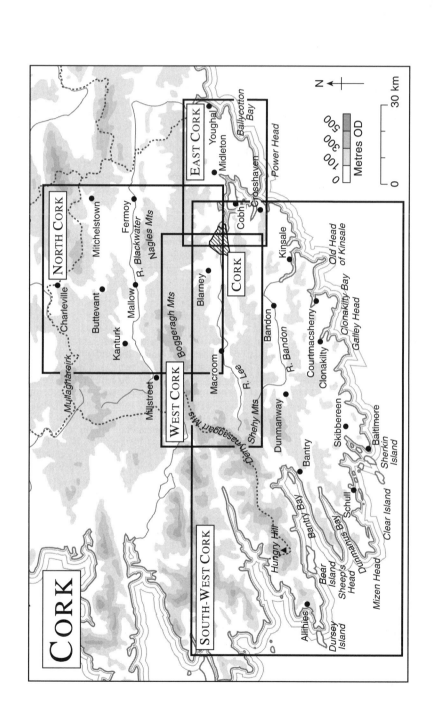

I NTRODUCTION

You might have called the country a magic mirror,
reflecting something that could not really exist. [1]

*L*ooking at evening across the landscape of North Cork from the steps of
a house which would eventually be destroyed, novelist Elizabeth
Bowen consoled herself in 1941 with the illusion of peace at its most ecsta-
tic. Writer and proprietor, she recognised that the undue joy with which she
welcomed this picture of peace offered by 'an island of quietness in the
south of a country not at war' was itself a reaction to what was only a nega-
tive calm.

> Wave after wave of war news broke upon the quiet air of the room and,
> in the daytime when the windows were open, passed out on to the
> sunny or overcast lawns ... Yet, at the body of this house threats did
> strike – and in a sense they were never gone from the air. The air here
> had absorbed, in its very stillness, apprehensions general to mankind.

There must be a reason why this book, *Bowen's Court*, above all else com-
mendable and memorable that she wrote, has kept for Elizabeth Bowen so
enduring a place in the Irish, as opposed to a British or European, literary
canon in which her status is anyway secure. I suggest that it is because – in a
way as yet undefined – the house and its history provide a metaphor: a syn-
onym of something not yet understood? Against this suggestion must be set
the long Irish experience; as a building Bowen's Court is surrounded by a
history in which, to recall a phrase of Dickens', the house is no more than a
dewdrop in an ocean.[2]

It is uncomfortable, and therefore unfashionable, still for us as Irish writ-
ers or critics to accept the Elizabeth Bowens, the Somervilles and Rosses, the
Wildes, Shaws, Swifts and Yeats as wholly Irish. As Irish in literary terms as
Kate O'Brien or Frank O'Connor or Brian Friel, let alone as truly Irish as
Ó Bruadair or Máirtín Ó Cadhain. That discomfort flamed into bitter dispute
at the opening of this century when the reaction to the Anglo-Irish-led Literary Revival provoked a doctrine of national culture which asserted, as
Terence Brown has written that 'the only authentic national life was cer-
tainly Gaelic, and possibly Catholic as well.' [3]

In a book such as this, what can be done about that awkwardness, springing from the thesis that, in Brown's phrase, 'the Anglo-Irish Literary Revival

was an exotic flowering of the colonial mind in which the true concerns of the Irish people did not find any adequate expression'?[4]

The truth is surely otherwise; in deference to that possibility here visitors, invaders, settlers as much as any native-born green-blooded Gaelic-speaking commentators are to be numbered not for their birthright but for their words.

Is the suggestion of a metaphor, then, mere impertinence, or can it act for this book as a whole? In *Bowen's Court* we have an edifice with its principal inhabitants; we have its landscape, its languages, its tenants and neighbours. We have its walled garden and its stables, its arable acres, its church. We have its legends, its battles, its defeat. We have news from abroad creeping across the pastures like a mist. We have its journeys, its ghosts, its beginnings and endings, its letters and its visitors. Its failures. Above all we have its literature.

Literature is both revelation and chronicle. Reminiscences are matched to a landscape whose use has changed; a novel's description of the beating flight of a curlew, complaining and afraid, across an ashen sky unites land-lord and author through centuries; biographies claiming ruins as warm and hospitable homes; political tracts posed with such skill that fiction itself could not outpace them; savage national disasters fictionalised into volumes and serialised in magazines read to family gatherings in firelit Victorian parlours – these all carry an aura of hinterland.

Just as a poet's tramp across sodden territories to attend the funeral of another poet, immense to one another but doomed to national obscurity (an obscurity subsequently known and chosen by later poets loyal to their tongue), this too brings with it the smell of the hedgerow, the reek of sodden leather, voices in an unknown but not forgotten language. Some or all of these were the shadows darkening the crystal of Bowen's Court.

That darkened crystal, 'in which, while one was looking, a shadow formed' is true enough of Ireland to suit this book. It is an image stemming from a viewpoint, from the steps, in the evening, looking across the coun-tryside but in this case looking without surprise, knowing that the shadow has its right to be there, that a landscape is thick with shades, of people as much as of trees.

A country can be like a house in whose quiet rooms great or little events took place, in which family myths were born and legends took flight as lit-erature. But literature is neither a lament for, nor an exculpation of, the past. It keeps pace; the contemporary landscape has its singers too, fresh-voiced because their vision, like their territory, is new and therefore young to them.

So:

I am Stephen Dedalus. I am walking beside my father whose name is Simon Dedalus. We are in Cork, in Ireland. Cork is a city. Our room is in the Victoria Hotel. Victoria and Stephen and Simon.[5]

Or:

Up in the north-east corner of County Cork is a stretch of limestone country – open, airy, not quite flat; it is just perceptibly tilted from north to south, and the fields undulate in a smooth flowing way. Dark knolls and screens of trees, the network of hedges, abrupt stony ridges, slate glints from roofs give the landscape a featured look – but the prevailing impression is, emptiness.[6]

Written in 1941, that description is still true today of the land around Farahy, Kildorrery, Bowen's Court. True except for its single qualification: whatever the impression, it is not empty now nor was it then.

The picture of peace was thronged. The shadowed crystal was peopled. Elizabeth Bowen said there were no ghosts in her home – but her engaging topography echoes the description by Edmund Spenser of the land around Doneraile, a few miles from Bowen's Court.

This is North Cork, a territory which begins outside Cork city on the hilly spine of Carrignavar; Carrignavar for a century was the homeland of families of poets and scribes working in what remained of the bardic tradition of ancient Ireland. The distance between *Colin Clout's Come Home Again* and *My New Curate* and *The Last September* spans 400 years of history.

In Co. Cork, as elsewhere in Ireland, that distance is bridged not by geography but by literature – which is itself a magic mirror: 'Out of reach, the windows down to the ground open upon the purple beeches and lazy hay, the dear weather of those rooms in and out of which flew butterflies ...'[7]

Is that the lie of the land? Or is it wishful thinking?

Wondering for the purposes of this book what is the nature of a literary landscape I find an unexpected image: a garden in East Cork, in summer, where a young Dutch woman, light-haired among the woven garden greenery, is carving words on stone: the limestone slab is to mark the grave of Liam Hourigan, a journalist born in Dublin and buried in a churchyard on the Kerry coast. The phone rings and it is a call from his widow at home in Brussels. She commissioned the carving. She recites from memory the lines William Butler Yeats recast from an Irish legend: these give the phrases to be cut on the limestone.

I choose the laughing lip
That shall not turn from laughing, whatever rise or fall;
The heart that grows no bitterer although betrayed by all;
The hand that loves to scatter, the life like a gambler's throw;
And these things I make prosper, till a day come that I know,
When heart and mind shall darken that the weak may end the strong,
And the long-remembering harpers have matter for their song.[8]

The sun glints on the honed blade of the chisel flashing as it slants to incise the characters. Holland, Belgium, Castlegregory in Kerry and Castleredmond in Cork: all gathered to catch in stone the words that establish a man's vanished presence.

This is no idyll. It is merely a particular witness to a general truth: words are the marks we leave on the stone of life. Whether we borrow them or fashion them for ourselves, where they outlive us they weight and sometimes enrich the places they describe, the passage they commemorate. Above all and at their best – which does not mean their most accurate or their most enduring – they give us back something of myth, some sense of the heroic or at least the memorable.

To bring this down to earth – if the pun can be forgiven – poet Tom McCarthy writes after twenty years in Cork:

> ... Cork's sense of itself is heavily dependent upon the assembly of memory. Memory rather than art is the major contrivance that writers depend upon. I am guilty of it myself ... [these books] tell us, more urgently than art, that Cork life is viable, and *significant* because it can be remembered so completely. [9]

Memory is not always exclusive, but it is very personal. That is the only excuse to be offered for the choices made here. The writers and books included are not always of great prominence or importance; they enter the pages because of the lie of the land, and sometimes because of the truth of it. In 'Morning in Beara', for example, the poet Bernard O'Donoghue remembers how 'Angled houses through glassless frames/Overlook the sound where the gannet/cuts out and falls ...' and where the listener hears '... the shingle's scramble/As the escaping pebbles lose their footing.' O'Donoghue defines something of this search for meaning in landscape as 'the architecture of the spirit'; in the title poem of his new collection *Here nor There* a journey back to Ireland from England reminds him that '... the whole business/Neither here nor there, and therefore home.'

In order to avoid, if at all possible, any accusations of wilful neglect of one of the most important facts in literary Ireland today: I draw attention here to the significant health of modern writing in the Irish language; more easily indicated in poetry, this is also particularly vigorous in prose: vividly alive, contentious and confrontational. It is as if a declining audience has conveyed new freedoms to writers who no longer have to court popularity, obey conventions or observe mutual obligations. I cannot analyse that bright revival here but hope that by indicating it at least its best exponents will be reassured that there is no intention to ignore or diminish them or their work and, above all, no lack of respect for either.

Inevitably, there are omissions from this patchwork of writers' lives. In townland after townland throughout Ireland, villages and rectories produced their diarists, the composers of sermons, the compilers of collections of family letters and family records, botanic observations and antiquarian researches. Priests, teachers, unmarried daughters and unoccupied sons wrote to one audience or another and sometimes to one and the same audience. The Beamish family of Cork, for example, counted among its members North Ludlow Beamish (1798–1872) who was a military historian and who also published translations of Norse sagas.

Florence Beamish contributed to *The Ballads of Ireland* in 1855, James Caulfield Beamish and Richard Beamish collaborated on a memoir of Sir Marc Isambard Brunel, and Henry Hamilton Beamish (d. 1872) published his religious lectures. Bill Evans of Aghada wrote reminiscences of life from his public house. Mrs Emma Moore (d. 1916) was the wife of George F. Moore, manager of Guys' Printing Works in Cork city; a contributor to *The Munster Journal* and a compiler of the famous *Guys' Directories* for the city and county she published, as E.M. Lauderdale, the novel *Tivoli* in 1886. Guys' Printing Works have a resonance for the contemporary poet Greg Delanty who uses his father's employment there as a source for much of his own work.

The Victorian journalist and editor Thomas Crosbie of Cork published various sketches and a novel, and another Victorian, The Revd Denis Crowley of Castletownbere who lived mostly in America is anthologised in *Poets of America*. Joseph Hillary (*fl. c.* 1814), the son of a silversmith in the North Main Street of Cork, was a poet and novelist who published his collection of *Poems, Lyrics, Tales and Elegies* in 1794. Anthony Edwards, compiler of a *Cork Remembrancer*, died at Hop Island near Passage in 1832.

The composer Paul MacSwiney (1856–89?) left his birthplace in Cork for London where he wrote operas; in New York he published the novel *Nirvana* in 1888. The journalist John Francis Maguire (1815–72) was a barrister, MP for Dungarvan, founder of *The Cork Examiner* and four times mayor of Cork as well as writing as an historian and essayist and publishing, in 1863, a biography of the temperance reformer Fr Theobald Mathew. His wife Margaret Bailey (d. 1905) was a playwright and published a book of stories on Fr Mathew and his times in 1903.

Mary Chavelita Dunne (1859–1945) was born in Australia to an impecunious Irish army officer who was eventually cashiered. Educated in Ireland she married, during a riotous romantic career, the Canadian George Egerton Clairmonte and later the agent Reginald Golding Bright. She lived for some years in West Cork before becoming a literary agent herself, her clients including George Bernard Shaw. Her short stories were published under the pseudonym George Egerton, the most celebrated as the harbinger of the New, Ibsenite woman being *Keynotes* (1893) (re-issued by Virago 1993).

From such a catologue who is to say who were minor figures and who major? James O'Shea of Ballinhassig (1850–1925), for example, is mentioned by bibliographer Patricia Egan as having sold over 1,000 copies at half a crown of his novel *Felix O'Flanagan, an Irish-American* (1902), a hugely popular account of the trials and triumphs of an Irishman's adventures in America. Clerical figures of some local importance in their time must include the essayist The Revd Arthur O'Leary (1720–1802) of the Capuchin Order of St Malo who was chaplain to the Irish Volunteers in Cork from 1782–84 and to the Spanish Embassy in London from 1789; his grand-nephew was Daniel Florence O'Leary (*c.* 1800–54) who left for South America at the age of seventeen, rose through the ranks of the Bolivian army, became British consul to Venezuela and *chargé d'affaires* in Bogota and wrote his memoirs and recollections as tracts on national liberty.[10]

There is the Gaelic scholar The Revd Daniel O'Sullivan who resigned his professorship at Maynooth to minister as curate of Bandon and Enniskeane, publishing his translation into Irish of *The Imitation of Christ* by Thomas à Kempis in 1822. There is The Revd Charles Herbert Orpen (1791–1856) of Cork city, the philanthropist who devoted himself to the spiritual and temporal needs of those who were both deaf and dumb, founding the Clermont Institution in 1816.[11] And there is The Revd Timothy Mahony (1839–1917) the last surviving nephew of Sylvester Mahony (Fr Prout) who published verse widely at home and abroad as well as contributing to several popular Catholic journals.

A noted folklorist was An tAthair Pádraig Ó Laoghaire (1871–96) whose collection of old Munster folktales was published as *Sgealaidheacht Chuige Mumhan* (1895).

It is with some temerity that the literary archaeologist selects from the artisans uncovered in a dig of this kind those who are now most worthy of attention or of notice. The revelation is how many of them exist beneath a surface which seems to bear a harvest rich enough in itself. Perhaps in some, even many cases, their current obscurity is deserved, perhaps it is merely that the reading world has such a wealth of material and choice that only a very few – and not always the most deserving – can hold their place in the field of literature.

Of the visitors, those who from Wordsworth to Thackeray, Anthony Burgess, Robert Graves and John Heath-Stubbs came to Cork for a day, a week, a lecture or a holiday, only one – Dickens – has left a name on the city – and at that the connection may be spurious.

Giving readings at the Athenaeum in August, 1858, Charles Dickens drove from the harbour village of Passage to the city: on the Rochestown Road near the suburban village of Douglas stood Monsfield House, traditionally the scene of a fatal wedding breakfast.

There are rivals to Monsfield for this distinction: there are at least two such breakfasts recounted in Cork. In the most persistent the bride, returning from the wedding ceremony to the reception in her father's house, is accosted by the lover rejected earlier for want of money. His fortune made, he has come back to claim his love, who instead kills herself and falls dead across the breakfast table which, apart from the removal of her corpse, is left undisturbed for a generation. The coincidence of Dickens' journey along this road and the subsequent publication of *Great Expectations* in 1861 is too good to be wasted by Cork; a hotel nearby is called 'Havisham House', although Monsfield itself is long gone.

Visiting readers may need to be reminded that the careers of people such as statesman and orator Edmund Burke which span both Ireland and Britain were typical for generations of the personal accommodation to the political relationship between Ireland and England. Up to the opening of the Victorian universities, further education was available only at Trinity College, Dublin, or the English universities. From there the path led to the law (and often parliament), the church and the services, but rarely homeward.

Obviously, what was geographic as well as economic necessity changed with the spread of college education and easier travel, but it remains a fact of artistic life, perhaps of cultural life in general, that there is a chosen duality for Irish writers, who often select English publishers as their first option, and for English writers, who sometimes prefer to live in Ireland.

History too has its dictatorial influence on the connections made here; certain events, and how they have been reported, celebrated and interpreted, affect the process of selection. A common language also provides a common readership. The presumption of this book is that the major writers and titles in its pages will be known to many visitors either in the original or in translation. The hope is that where this is not the case, an opportunity to meet these and other writers more or less at home will shorten the road for the reading traveller.

Home can mean many places; the modern Irish poets included here no longer indicate a sense of placelessness, of exile, of inhibited geography. With an ease they may not recognise themselves, they lay claim to all the territories of their own countryside. This restoration is a reclamation of landscape more appropriate to poets than prose-writers, for it was the poets who first felt displacement and who made exile their matter, their climate, and their song.

Note: where quotations are taken from Irish (Gaelic) sources the spelling is that of the source material. In all other cases the spelling will be the current usage which also has its variations. An example is the patron Saint of Cork City who may be named Bairre of Cork, St Finn Barre, Finbarr, or variants of all three styles.

Notes to Introduction

1. Elizabeth Bowen, *Bowen's Court* (1942).
2. Charles Dickens, *Bleak House*.
3. Terence Brown, 'After the Revival: Sean Ó Faolain and Patrick Kavanagh' from *Ireland's Literature, Selected Essays* (1988).
4. Brown, ibid (1988).
5. James Joyce, *A Portrait of the Artist as a Young Man* (1916).
6. Elizabeth Bowen, *Bowen's Court* (1942).
7. Elizabeth Bowen, *A Day in the Dark* (1965).
8. William Butler Yeats, 'The Green Helmet'.
9. Thomas McCarthy, 'Gardens of Remembrance' (1998).
10. See Manuel Perez Vila, 'Vida de Daniel Florencio O'Leary, Primer Edecion del Libertador' (1957), in J.C. Healy, 'Daniel Florence O'Leary', *Journal of the Cork Historical and Archaeological Society*, series 2, vol. LXIV (1959).
11. See Emma L. Le Fanu, *Life of Rev. Charles Edward Herbert Orpen M.D.* (1860).

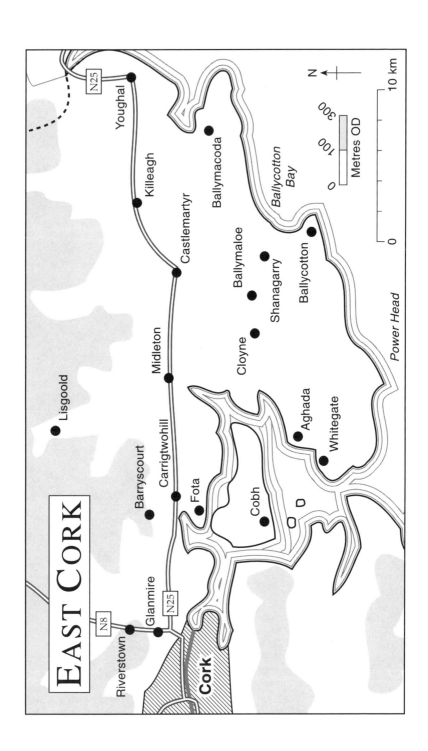

EAST CORK

**Glanmire, Carrigtwohill,
Midleton, Castlemartyr, Killeagh, Youghal;
Youghal, Ballymacoda, Shanagarry, Ballycotton,
Whitegate, Aghada, Cloyne, Fota, Cobh**

It pleased your excellency, invincible king of the English, duke of Normandy, count of Anjou and Aquitaine to send me from your court, with your beloved son John, to Ireland. And there, when I had seen many things not found in other countries and entirely unknown, and at the same time worthy of some wonder because of their novelty, I began to examine everything carefully: what was the position of the country, what was its nature, what was the origin of the race, what were its customs; how often, and by whom, and how, it was conquered and subjugated; what new things, and what secret things not in accordance with her usual course had nature hidden away in the farthest western lands? For beyond those limits there is no land, nor is there any habitation either of men or beasts – but beyond the whole horizon only the ocean flows and is borne on in boundless space through its unsearchable and hidden ways.[1]

Giraldus de Barri, also known as Giraldus Cambrensis or Gerald of Wales, first arrived in Ireland in 1183. His elder brother Philip had already taken part in the Norman invasion and begun the acquisitions between Youghal and Cork city which were to establish the Barry family as overlords of most of this part of the county. As an employee of the crown and a relative of one of the conquerors Giraldus was hardly unprejudiced; his observations have been fervently challenged by Irish and other historians ever since, but in relation to music there is no dispute:

> they seem to me to be incomparably more skilled ... The melody is kept perfect and full with unimpaired art through everything – through quivering measures and the involved use of several instruments – with a rapidity that charms, a rhythmic pattern that is varied, and a concord achieved through elements discordant ... They glide so subtly from one mode to another, and the grace notes so freely sport with such abandon and bewitching charm around the steady tone of the heavier sound, that the perfection of their art seems to lie in their concealing it, as if 'it were the better for being hidden. An art revealed brings shame.'

It is not far-fetched to apply those last lines to much of the territory of East Cork, a region which marches so closely with West Waterford that it is almost a hindrance to have to observe where one county ends and the other begins. The countryside which is truly east in a line from Cork city onwards to Youghal via Carrigtwohill and Midleton seems flat, quaking with the lure of the sea. But the hinterland, the hidden villages and their streams and castles and the rich pastures lying along the Blackwater and its tributaries the Tourig and the Bride, the hillocky fields with their dense hedges, their copses, their old barns and new farmhouses – among these there is a sense that Giraldus might find some things still recognisable were he to return.

Our territory is lowland, south of the Blackwater, north of the sea, bounded by the river's mouth at Youghal and the estuary of the Lee at Cobh. The chief exit routes north and east from the city of Cork cut into the land-scape, but looped and tunnelled though they are, these highways also provide glimpses of the hinterland which is explored in this chapter.

Here are the villages of Conna and Bridebridge, of Aghern and Britway and Dungourney and Lisgoold; the Glashaboy river winds down from Car-rignavar, at Youghal the Blackwater meets the sea, the countryside is laced with little rivers like the Glendine and the Togher, the Dissour and the Wom-anagh, while south of Midleton the eastern edge of Cork harbour is necklaced with villages like Rostellan and Aghada and Farsid. Small, almost secret, they hold their history in broken graveyards, ruined towers, vanished romances. The fifth Earl of Inchiquin, first Marquess of Thomond, enter-tained the celebrated actress Mrs Siddons at Rostellan Castle; nothing remains of the great house but the folly built to commemorate the actress can still be seen. Sir Walter Ralegh rested at Rostellan before returning to London to give an account of his last, failed and fatal voyage.

At Midleton the college established in 1696 by Lady Elizabeth Villiers, mistress of William of Orange, is a thriving modern institution with a fine academic reputation. It is out of our jurisdiction to note another Villiers con-nection – that with Barbara Villiers, mistress of Charles II, a connection of the Villiers-Stuarts of Dromana House, wonderfully perched on a rock over the Blackwater near Youghal, but on the Waterford bank.

There is a fifteenth-century tower house at Belvelly which gives an excuse to visit the inner shores of Cork harbour, the areas known as Marlogue and East Ferry; there is a wedge tomb at Castle Mary, a FitzGerald tower house at Castle Richard built in 1592. Ballinacurra to the east of Midleton was the birthplace of the Antarctic explorer Edward Bransfield, and also of P.N. FitzGerald, a founder member of the Gaelic Athletic Association, the sporting organisation which, commonly called the GAA, has an immense cultural significance in modern Ireland. In Cloyne another GAA connection is celebrated with a bronze figure of Christy Ring, Cork's most famous expo-nent of the art of hurling (even those who are not devotees admit that hurling at its best is performance art), who was born in this town.

Ballymaloe may now be renowned for its restaurant and country house hotel, but it was first a FitzGerald tower; one of the most famous of the FitzGeralds, the old Countess of Desmond (d. 1604), who is believed to have survived to the age of 140, lived in the thirteenth-cen-tury castle at Inchiquin.

In the gentle uplands behind Midleton, where Dungourney hides among the spreading hills gladed by the Owenacurra river, Spaniel Cross still speaks of the little dog whose cries betrayed the murderers of his family at beautiful Ballyvolane House. In Midleton itself a heritage centre has been provided from the transformation of the town's mighty distilleries; a coaching inn was designed by Pugin, architect of the cathedral at Cobh. The Pain brothers produced the church of St John the Baptist.

Carerra, Midleton and Castlemartyr marble decorate the Church of the Most Holy Rosary in the town. Midleton is a bustling centre developed on the site of the Cistercian foundation of Chore Abbey and later designated by its modern name, geographically accurate in relation to the distances between Cork and Youghal. Buildings and memorials here record the Brodricks, Viscounts Midleton since the time of Alan Brodrick (1660–1728), solicitor general for Ireland, speaker of both Houses of the Irish Parliament and a supporter of Jonathan Swift.[2]

The castle at Castlemartyr was held by the FitzGeralds, seneschals of Imokilly, and controlled the ancient pass between Cork and Youghal, then an important maritime town. Through centuries ferocious battles were fought over the ground which with the confiscation of the Desmond estates and the plantation of Munster fell at last (although there were yet more battles to be fought) to the heirs of Richard Boyle, styled the Great Earl of Cork. Boyle created Castlemartyr as a royal borough out of the two small medieval villages which had grown around the castle. Henry Boyle, the first Earl of Shannon, had a thousand acres around his mansion landscaped; some of this remains: the house is now a Carmelite college and retreat centre.

In Aghada the ancient cemetery contains something not often seen in Irish graveyards – a headstone in the Irish language; although if not here, where? For all this countryside was wealthy in words, beginning with those ubiquitous Ó Dálaigh poets, whose origin was traced by Gofraidh Fionn Ó Dálaigh back to the sixth century and Dálach, a pupil of Colmán Mac Lénéni, the patron saint of the cathedral town of Cloyne.

By the twelfth century all these much-disputed territories were designated under the title of the Uí Mac Caille family, now loosely given as Imokilly. When the Normans arrived off the east coast of Ireland late in that century the lands east of Cork city were taken by Robert FitzStephens, whose nephew Raymond le Gros is believed to be buried at Molana Abbey, an island monastery on the Blackwater a few miles above Youghal.

Gerald of Wales had ancestral links through his maternal grandmother Nesta with many of the Normans who invaded Ireland. His family links included the FitzGeralds who were shortly to become intensely Hibernicised, his uncle Robert FitzStephen, and of course the Barrys. An ambitious cleric,

Gerald was a credulous explorer, easily convinced of amazing folktales and heresies lingering from the days of Ireland's druidic past. But he was the first foreigner to write about Ireland: he produced two books, *The Topography of Ireland* and *The Conquest of Ireland*, and as someone who heard him read his own writing noticed, he 'spoke much evil well'.

'The very value of the "Conquest" is that it is plain, clear and easy of apprehension', writes F.X. Martin. 'Not that it is without defects as a historical piece. It sets out the story of the invasion without sympathy for the Gaelic Irish, whom Gerald describes as "the fierce and barbarous Irish nation". He is not only the apologist for the Norman invaders; he sets out to glorify the part played in the invasion by his own kinsmen of whom he exclaims, "O family! O race! Indeed it is doubly noble; deriving their courage from the Trojans and their skill from the French."'[3]

At Barryscourt Castle, between Carrigtwohill and Fota, (which eventually would be the last Barrymore demesne in Ireland), Gerald of Wales sat down to write while his brother Philip went to war. The castle was given to Philip by his uncle Robert FitzStephen, who had taken it from the native Uí Liatháin family; Robert's son Ralph had been killed as he travelled to Lismore with Milo de Cogan, who also died when they were set upon by a group of the MacTire clan of Imokilly. From this holding Philip's family developed the Barrymore lordship, ruling with various degrees of success estates throughout Cork, from Buttevant to Timoleague. Eventually they deserted the tower house (now impressively restored and open to the public) at Carrigtwohill and lived instead in their new mansion at Castlelyons. The last of the Barrys were three brothers affectionately known as Hellgate, Cripplegate and Newgate (after the only prison he is reputed never to have entered).

The demesne at Fota where the garden and acclaimed arboretum are open to the public remained with the Smith-Barry branch of the family until the 1970s. Originally a shooting-lodge, Fota House was recreated by the architect Sir Richard Morrison as a charming Regency centrepiece to an ornamental demesne in which farm buildings, folly, orangery, kennels and the extensive greenhouses were all part of an idealised overall picture. Now giraffes sway over many of these acres which have been transformed into a reputable wildlife park with dedicated breeding programmes for endangered species; a golf course covers some of the splendid, tree-bordered pastureland.

Sir Richard Morrison who, with his son Vitruvius designed many of the finest houses in Ireland, is buried at Ballyoughterra, near the demesne of Castlemartyr. The ruins of Castlelyons stand close to the churchyard with its Barrymore mausoleum; also nearby are the remains of the Carmelite friary founded by John de Barri in 1307.

And at Kilcredan, four miles south-east of Castlemartyr, are the remains of the church built in 1636 by Sir Robert Tynte of Ballycrenane Castle. Unroofed and left derelict a hundred years ago, the church still holds the Renaissance tomb of Sir Robert Tynte; weeping at his effigy is the figure of his second wife, Elizabeth Boyle of Youghal, widow of Edmund Spenser.[4]

Glanmire

The modern main road from Cork to Dublin pushes northwards shortly after passing handsome Dunkettle House, a route introduced only a few years ago. The earlier road skirted the estuary of the Glashaboy River, threading between densely wooded hills on both banks and through the village of Glanmire. Now almost obliterated by swarming housing developments, the village still retains some evidence of its earlier charm: the hills are steep, some woods at least remain (most generously at the Dunkettle side), and the older houses are villas set among trees or deep in the glens reaching to the river or on sloping lawns above the roadway.

The river cuts through this valley from its source beyond Carrignavar to the north. The links with the court of poetry which once distinguished that whole area, drawing it into a tenacious cultural tradition shared with Blarney and the northern outskirts of Cork city, are glimpsed here also in Glanmire, which was chosen as the setting for the seventeenth-century text, composed in both Irish and Latin, known as *Parliament na mBan*, or The Women's Parliament.[5]

Written *c.* 1697 by Fr Dónall Ó Colmáin of Cork, it consists of a sermonising textbook of advice for James Cotter, or Séamus Mac Coitir, of Ballinsperrig, near Carrigtwohill. James was the son of the Royalist Sir James Cotter, and Ó Colmáin was his tutor. Sir James Cotter had been rewarded by the Stuarts not only for his loyalty to their cause but for his pursuit and murder of the regicide John Lyle (or Lisle) at Lausanne in Switzerland. His Jacobite allegiance did not interfere with his ownership of estates in East Cork, where his neighbours were the Brodricks of Midleton.

The 'Parliament' is based on – parts of it are in fact translations of – the *Colloquia familiara* of Erasmus, and Breandán Ó Buachalla writes that this is the last text of Renaissance origin to be provided in the Irish language.[6]

Its great interest today however arises from its relation to one of the most celebrated injustices of East Cork's history. Ó Colmáin was ignorant of this connection because the text was written (with a preface added in 1697) before Cotter's tragic end in 1720 could be anticipated. Instead the work was based on the whimsical notion of thirty-two 'noble, honourable, wise, sensible, prudent, exemplary, well-intentioned ladies' of the Kingdom of Ireland with the habit of meeting regularly to discuss matters affecting the common good.

They summon a parliament of 500 women to Glanmire and issue their findings in the form of a report on their discussions, largely consisting of a sermon on topics such as political representation, education, precepts of religion and the uses and abuses of fashionable dress, each sermon ending in a verse:

Is é an raingce do ghríosann cuisleanna an chuirp,
san ringce so smaointear turrainn gach uilc,
san ringce so cítear buile & bruid,
's lé ringce théid mílte go hifrionn dubh.

In dancing the pulses of the body beat,
In dancing many an evil thought doth heat,
In dancing madness we see here and woe,
And by dancing thousands down to hell do go![7]

Ó Colmáin used his introduction to his composition as an opportunity to sing the praises of his patron, the father of young James. Shorn of its hyperbole, it reveals Sir James as a redoubtable personality, astute and confident of his role within the contradictory politics of his day:

Moreover as everyman is known by his acts, and a tree by its fruit, it is unnecessary to observe that it was not by any sinister means that he acquired the large estates he possessed between the Blackwater and the sea. If it be praiseworthy in the estimation of the world, to merit and obtain the love and esteem of kings and princes, observe what confidence King Charles reposed in his strength, valour and performance when he gave him orders and authority to proceed with a small military force in quest of the traitor Lisle, and to cut him off, an action which Sir James executed with success, as a compensation for and to avenge the death of King Charles. And therefore it is not proper for any man to say or think that it was assassination or wilful murder he committed, in killing a proscribed traitor by the King's special command, but that it is rather to be considered so distinguished an action, that it seems to me and to other learned men, to deserve to be written in chronicles, in characters of gold, as a warning to the regicides of other ages.

Ó Colmáin reminds his pupil that King James, too, valued and rewarded Sir James, after being with him through seven naval engagements:

For neither the voice of the cuckoo, nor the harmonious music of the harp sounded sweeter in his ears, than the sound of the trumpet, the whistling of the harsh-sounding bullets, or the bellowing of the wide-mouthed cannon. The days of Glanworth and Kanturk can bear testimony to this, in which princes, field-officers and many hundred of horse and foot fell by the valour and magnanimity of Sir James.

His services to the Catholic faith, 'the great service he did the Irish language in bestowing gold and silver to the learned, to performers on stringed and other musical instruments and to eminent poets', his compassion for the poor and liberality to his friends and his reputation as 'a protector of science' all make Sir James the ideal example for 'you, son of my heart ... which you may draw the lines of your conduct. There is for you the points of your compass by which you may steer your course through this turbulent sea of the world ...'

Ó Buachalla decodes much of this encomium for its social and political relevance – a relevance which is not carried through the main body of the 'Parliament' text. Having explained the context in which this classically based manual of advice was composed and read, Ó Buachalla (using the Irish form of its subject's name), adds: '... Sir Séamus Óg Mac Coitir, like his father, remained loyal to the Catholic Church and patronised Irish learning, and ... he also took up, on his father's death, the cause of their king – with tragic consequences.'

Somewhat in the manner of Art Ó Laoghaire in Macroom, young James Cotter flaunted his independence of the ruling class and laws in Ireland and earned the enmity of his powerful neighbour Baron Brodrick of Midleton, a reckless indulgence at a time of extreme Whig-Tory tension in both England and Ireland, with Catholics largely supporting the Tories in the hopes of a Stuart restoration.

Although married, Cotter had a reputation as a ladies' man; Brodrick himself was reputed to have been jealous of Cotter's attraction for Lady Brodrick. His association with political activists campaigning for the Stuart restoration and his own involvement in minor but frequent challenges to the Penal Laws eventually contributed to his conviction, and sentence of death, on a charge of abducting and raping the Quaker Elizabeth Squibb.

The arrest, trial, and execution have been described as easily the most traumatic political event of the first half of the century in Ireland. So immediate was the Catholic recognition of this as either a trumped-up or inadequate charge that the Quakers of Cork went in fear of their lives for months.

Convinced that the charge could not stand Cotter delivered himself up to the sheriff of Co. Cork; although granted bail he was kept in prison until his trial – at which the presiding judge was Sir St John Brodrick. After his conviction attempts to obtain a pardon seemed to have succeeded when a reprieve was sent from Dublin (another member of the Brodrick family had befriended him), but the execution was hurriedly brought forward and the messenger arrived too late. Cotter was hanged in Cork city on 7 May 1720; he was waked in his birthplace, Ballinsperrig (also called Anngrove) and buried beside his father in the family tomb at Carrigtwohill.

This was not the course marked out by that idealised compass described by Ó Colmáin. 'Justice', said Maria of the Parliament, 'keeps the people together and binds them peaceably in communion and love with one another?'

Let justice be thy chief and constant care
Nor ever think against it to declare
But in your hearts let godly fear abide
And you'll not sin, while you on earth reside.[8]

The tombstone marking the graves of Sir James Cotter, father and son, has been removed; what remain are the manuscript elegies – some made by the poets of East Cork – the historic record, and the epitaph of a Cork broadsheet of 1720:

Beneath this stone, his body now doth rest
Whose Soul enjoys converse of death,
Just, Prudent, Pious, everything that's Great
Lodg'd in his Breast, and formed the Man complete,
His Body may consume, his Virtues shall
Recorded be, till the World's Funeral.[9]

The fact that Cotter's solicitor in this case was Richard Burke, father of Edmund Burke is a reminder of another, if somewhat indirect, link with Glanmire. At the beginning of the nineteenth century Cork was diverted with the trial following the abduction of an another Quaker, the heiress Mary Pike, who was taken from the home of her friends, the Penroses of Woodhill at Tivoli, in Cork, by Sir Henry Brown Hayes.

Sentenced to death at the Cork Assizes in 1801, Hayes was reprieved and sent instead to Botany Bay where he established himself in comfortable circumstances until his daughter convinced the Prince Regent that he deserved a pardon and he returned to Cork in 1820. (Poor Mary Pike, in the meantime, had become deranged and spent the rest of her life in confinement.)

The prosecution against Hayes was led by John Philpot Curran, a friend of the Penrose family. It was with the Quaker Penroses of Woodhill that Curran's daughter Sarah (1782–1808) took refuge after the execution of her lover Robert Emmet in 1803, and it was at the parish church of St Mary and All Saints at Glanmire that she married Captain Henry Sturgeon in November 1805. With Henry, who was devoted to her, Sarah travelled to Sicily, from where she wrote to her friends Elizabeth and Anne Penrose at Woodhill:

We expected the Equinoctial Gales and we have had them ... I was not frightened much ... on board a ship there are certainly a thousand ridiculous circumstances to counteract fear. Oh, how you would have laughed could you have peeped in on us in the Cabin while we dined all sitting on the floor, every moment inclining all at the same time to one side or other as the ship rolled; an unhappy goose literally *nailed* down to keep it steady. I was *lashed* on with Henry's sash, having no strength to hold myself fast, my plate in my lap, all the gentlemen sliding against each other. I never laughed more in my life.[10]

In the Irish pantheon Sarah Curran is not supposed to have a sense of humour, but in this collection of her letters she emerges as a woman of strong feelings, considerable wit, musical, sensitive, well-read and eager to improve herself, and unable to forgive or deny the emotional hardships endured in the family deserted by her mother and dominated by her father.

'I have already experienced the healing power of your affection and friendship,' she later writes to Anne Penrose.

You found me once, I may say, laid low by a cruel storm, and you raised my head and spoke comfort. But, dear Anne, I often think the effects of that period on my mind are not to be done away radically. I have read somewhere that in youth a long succession of violent griefs and strong emotions are as likely to corrode as to correct the heart. I fear it is so. It creates a leaven of bitterness in our nature which breaks out now and again in spite of ourselves. Reflect only on what has been the lot of myself ... and, I will add, Amelia. What have been the days of youthful carelessness or pleasure we cannot reckon up. What little kind encouragement to improve ourselves have either ever received. What was our portion, to bear tyranny and injustice, to submit, to bear as well as we could a melancholy home and confined circumstances, which latter had the additional weight of being *unnecessary* parsimony towards us ... for myself I think all the better traits of my disposition were stifled and lost.

Even in such a letter, however, Sarah attempts humour: 'So, my dear Anne, the sum total is, I think, we are all equally bad, but have all nearly equal excuse.' In her letters she writes also of explorations of ancient ruins, of meetings with mutual friends, of engagements with the enforced society of her husband's postings at several of which she is made produce her harp for the delight of the party:

'... the mice inhabit my harp noon and night. In the daytime they stay at the bottom, but at night range the strings and get to the attic story via the top of the pillar.' She describes her groans on being asked to sing and play the harp in a large company, rendered more awful by your knowing that it consisted (with the exception of one *very anxious friend*) of people willing to find out that you had no merit; finding on sitting down every motion of the pedals answered by a responsive squeal from within; and during the course of your performance (as the adagio had given them time to breathe) seeing the company amused by the efforts of an entire family of mice to make their escape.

In fact an accomplished musician with a sweet singing voice, Sarah promises her friends that she is trying to practise more often:

But when one is at the very lowest ebb of idleness and abomination and (as Kate Wilmot would say 'tumbled into the very coal-hole of one's own contempt') I have known of a resurrection and sudden elasticity being restored by hearing that a friend was practising, and improving, in the very thing in which you were falling off.

Before returning to this mention of Kate Wilmot the story of Sarah herself must be ended. Her letters send news of her pregnancy and of her longing to see her friends again. Then in January 1808 in a letter written from Portsmouth, comes news of the premature birth of her son; her labour began while she was on board ship travelling back to England:

The day after Christmas Day I was (just as a heavy storm was raging round us) taken in labour. No boats could be hoisted for assistance for me. (Judge of Henry's feelings.) There I lay on the floor of a cabin where no fire could be made, and the freezing cold paralysing us all (two strange gentlemen *within hearing* of me) I was taken ill at 11 and at ½ four was delivered of *your* little Godson. I lay in *imminent danger* till next day at one, when a Physician came during a calm interval. *Luckily* then the storm encreased, for he could not return to his ship for five days after ...

Sarah succumbs to fever:

My poor baby was then for the first time removed from me, down between the decks among the soldiers and sailors. Bitter cold, storms still blowing, threatening at every blast his tender frame ...

The letter ends in a fervent plea to Anne: '... come to me for some time. A refusal I do not expect from you ... Come, my best beloved friend, to your poor Sarah.'

Although by now Anne herself is in England, she does not go to support Sarah. She is staying with her friend Miss Elliston, daughter of the archdeacon of Lincoln, a woman who seems to have had remarkable and inflexible influence on Anne. Three days after Sarah's beseeching letter comes this:

My darling child is lying dead ... Henry will buy the little coffin and shroud this day for my dead Johnny. Oh Anne, pity me and come to help my Henry to bear his griefs. He has *no* friends to comfort him ... Oh Anne, Heaven seemed to promise Happiness, I had made cloaths for my boy but a shroud will do all for him ... If you are my own Anne, I have said enough ...

Again, although telling Anne where she can now be reached in London, Sarah is left alone. A few days later she writes:

In vain have I waited for one line from you, one line to ease my poor broken heart, to say you would come to Henry and me in London. My boy is gone to his little grave, my darling is wrapped in his shroud and the little cap I made for him ... Henry went up to see Johnny laid out and returned weeping and said he looked *very* pretty. My little angel was pretty perhaps to no-one but us, but oh, Anne, my heart will know peace no more ...

    I cannot think you do not mean to come to me ... For Heaven's sake and mine, my darling, I conjure you on my knees to come ... Farewell. Remember me. This is my third letter to you, and one besides to Ireland. Enquire for us at No. 3 Wimpole Street.

Sarah's next letter is dated 20 March, from Hythe, and it is her last. Obviously Anne has written, although she did not visit. Sarah is now fully aware that she has been replaced in Anne's loyalties, if not affection, by Miss Elliston – Kate Wilmot has assured her of this.

She explains her delay in answering Anne's letter by her illness and by the move to Hythe where Henry is stationed:

The change in my mind is too obvious to be overlooked. The instances are too various for me now to detail in which we have found disappointment of some *well founded* hope (as I thought), and have had reason to see the hollowness of human friendships and human promises ... Do not imagine, dear Anne, that I am cold because I have said no more, I am really *unable* now. You may indeed truly think me changed in some respects, but those who live at ease surrounded by kind friends and every comfort know not what it is those wretches tossed about the world, as I have been, suffer in mind and body. No wonder one is altered ...

Altered indeed, Sarah Curran died aged twenty-six on 3 May 1808 in Hythe. Major Charles Napier, who served under Sir John Moore and was wounded during the retreat to Corunna, rode to Hythe to see

poor Sturgeon, who has lost his little wife at last, the betrothed of Emmet ... they are going to take the body to Ireland. Mrs Sturgeon was past hope when she first came; she seemed a perfect ghost, and could not speak without stopping to get breath at every word.[11]

Although they took the body to Ireland, where Sarah had requested that she be buried with her sister Gertrude in the grounds of the Curran home at Rathfarnham in Dublin, her father refused to let her corpse sully the Priory landscape. She is buried with her grandmother in Newmarket, Co. Cork.

'Poor Sturgeon' died in 1813 during the Peninsular Wars, where Charles Napier also served. And with the army of Wellington for part of that campaign was The Revd William Bradford, Chaplain of Brigade to the British expedition, who said the prayers over the grave of Sir John Moore in January 1809. Three years later he married Miss Martha Wilmot, born and brought up in Glanmire, sister of that Kate Wilmot mentioned by Sarah Curran in her letters.

Katherine Wilmot (1773–1824) was one of the daughters of Edward and Martha Wilmot (who had been married in the little church at Rathcooney, near Glanmire, in 1771) and lived with her family in a large villa at Glanmire. She was for a few years the travelling companion of the restless Lady Margaret Mount Cashell and while in Paris encountered Robert Emmet before his love-affair with Sarah Curran had even begun. Following Emmet's tragic death she met Sarah in Cork through her friendship with the Penrose sisters; she knew of Captain Sturgeon and kept in contact with Sarah, writing with news of her own travels and the doings of the Mount Cashells.

In the matter of Anne Penrose and Miss Elliston it seems she took Sarah's part, noting some time later that she looked on the name of Elliston as 'my natural enemy'.

Warm-hearted, witty and high-spirited, Kate was not robust, yet she went on her family's instructions to bring her sister Martha home from Russia. For the sake of her health following the death of her brother Charles, Martha Wilmot (1775–1873) was permitted to follow Kate's example by going abroad. Kate's accounts of her travels were enticing, and it was arranged that Martha would be the guest of Princess Dashkov (the spelling of whose name varies throughout Martha's correspondence and is given as Daschkaw in some publications) at the princess's country home near Moscow. The princess was also known to Martha's sister-in-law, Anna Chetwode.

Begun in 1803, the 'visit' was to last for five years; the princess grew to depend on Martha's affection and made increasingly generous gifts of money, clothing and jewels, demanding in return only the company of the young woman. The relationship aroused the suspicion of relatives of the princess, but also gave her young visitor an unprecedented opportunity to travel through Russia and to meet its aristocracy. This social passport was not always reliable, for the princess had been a significant agent in the palace *coup* by which Catherine the Great had overthrown her husband, Czar Peter. By now the Czar Alexander was not exactly comfortable about the princess, and Martha encouraged her to write her memoirs, more or less while the going was good.

Released by the Mount Cashell party, Kate, writes Elizabeth Mavor, 'arrived in Russia at about the time the Czar Alexander had signed a treaty with Great Britain against Napoleon. [She] left in 1807 two months after he had signed another with Napoleon against Great Britain.'[12]

But just as Kate and Martha were about to go the Princess was stricken by the death of her only son, and Martha found it impossible to leave her. Kate started on her own in the summer of 1807, and Martha followed her a year later, posting from Moscow to St Petersburg to catch a boat – on which she was shipwrecked off the coast of Finland. Even before leaving port she was in trouble, the customs officials, possibly alerted by the princess's family, insisting that she might be smuggling state papers out of Russia. In a way she was, carrying with her the memoir she had encouraged the princess to write. Panic-stricken at the possible consequences if this were discovered she burned the pages.

The original, however, had been copied by the resourceful Kate who had brought her manuscript out of Russia without trouble. The Princess Dashkov died within a year of Martha's departure, but lives in history and in Kate's word-pictures:

An old brown greatcoat and a silk handkerchief about her neck, worn to rags is her dress, and well may it be worn to rags for she has worn it 18 years ... she helps the masons to build walls, she assists with her own hands in making the roads, she writes for the press, she shells the corn, she talks out loud in the Church and corrects the Priest if he is not devout, she talks out loud in her little theatre and puts in the performers when they are out in their parts, she is doctor, and apothecary, a surgeon, a carpenter, a magistrate ...

It was not long after this that Kate began to have symptoms of consumption; she moved to the more suitable climate of France in 1817, by which time Martha had married William Bradford, naming her first daughter Katherine.

William was appointed chaplain to the British Embassy in Vienna in 1819; it is from this period that Martha's additional journal and letters are dated.[13] Curiously, although Martha visited Kate twice in Paris before 1819, she never saw her again once she moved with her husband to Vienna, Kate dying in Paris in 1824.

Among those whom Martha did see, however, was Metternich; among those with whom her little son played was the young Duke of Reichsdtadt, called the Prince of Rome by his doting father Napoleon Bonaparte. Virtually imprisoned until his early death in Vienna by his grandfather, the emperor of Austria, the prince was given riding lessons in the Imperial Riding School, and there he was joined by the politically unthreatening little Wilmot Bradford.

Glanmire today seems a far cry from the Schönnbrun Palace, almost as far as from the gathering of fair and noble ladies who constituted 'Parliament na mBan'; but with that last tradition at least there are still vigorous connections kept alive in Glanmire, where a small Irish-speaking community was set up thirty or so years ago. One of its prominent citizens is Tomás Ó Canainn (1930–), former lecturer in engineering at University College Cork, musician and writer. A founder member of the traditional music group Na Fili (his own instrument is the uileann pipes), he has written several books of poetry, the autobiographical novel *Home to Derry* (1986), *Traditional Music in Ireland* (1978/93), collected and introduced *Songs of Cork* (1978) and published his autobiography *A Lifetime of Notes* (1997).

The Miller of Glanmire is the title of a novel (1895) written by Cornelius T. Murphy of Cork, who was brought to America at the age of six and became there a very popular actor and dramatist. Glanmire is near Riverstown, where the early eighteenth-century Riverstown House still displays the exquisite plaster work of the Francini brothers dating from *c.* 1734, copies of which decorate the residence of the president of Ireland in Dublin.[14] Formerly the residence of Dr Jemmet Brown, bishop of Cork, it was also the home of his descendant, barrister J. Jemmett Browne (b. 1832), poet and author of *A Lone Lassie* (1886).

Behind Riverstown the old Dublin road meets the new one close to Rathcormac, where a turn to the right indicates Conna and Lismore. Hidden among the trees is Ballinterry House, most recently the home of the film and stage actor Hurd Hatfield (1917–98) who restored and saved this Jacobean premises which was once the home of Bishop John O'Brien (1701–69).

A scholar and lexicographer, noted patron of Irish poets and scribes (especially those living at or near Carrignavar), John O'Brien was born at

Glanworth, Co. Cork, and studied for the priesthood in France, working for some years after his ordination with distinguished expatriate Irish families in Spain, London and elsewhere. Appointed parish priest of Castlelyons and Rathcormac in the diocese of Cloyne in 1738 O'Brien went to live at Ballinterry.[15] He was appointed bishop of Cloyne and Ross in 1748.

A linguist who wrote in Irish as well as in several continental languages O'Brien published his English-Irish dictionary in 1768. Important though this was it paled into public insignificance when compared with his contro-verial attack on the publication by James Macpherson (1736–96) of his Ossianic ballads – 'Fragments of ancient poetry collected in the Highlands' – which Macpherson claimed to have translated from the Scots Gaelic tradition. That tradition was a heritage shared with Ireland through the common cultural language of the bardic order. A native speaker of Scots Gaelic, Macpherson mined the sagas and cycles for his characters of Finn Mac Cumhaill or Oisín or the Sons of Uisneach; his ballads were instantly and immensely popular abroad, especially in Germany (inspiring Mendelssohn to write *Fingal's Cave* and giving Goethe ideas for *The Sufferings of Young Werther*) where they were widely translated.

Not without some academic caution, according to Diarmaid Ó Catháin writing in *Cork History and Society*:

As was immediately suspected and has since been proved, however, Macpherson in general changed his materials almost beyond recognition. His *Ossian* rarely approaches what would nowadays be termed a translation and, of course, there was no pre-existing epic. Doubt about the authenticity of the poems arose almost as soon as Macphersons's first book was published, but it was long drowned out by the reception accorded them. Bluffer though he may have been, Macpherson obviously had antennae for what the literary public all over Europe wanted to hear.[16]

In Paris the critical *Journal des Scavans* commissioned, and published in 1764, a series of articles on the Ossian poems in the form of a 'Memoire' by M. de C., which took them to pieces in terms of history, geography, language, distinctions between oral and written tradition, rhythmic structure, usages and conventions, and above all the authenticity or otherwise of the source material.

M. de C. was identified as John O'Brien of Cloyne no earlier than 1933 by Alexander Gilles in his study 'Herder und Ossian' and subsequently by Cormac Ó Cuilleanáin, professor of Irish at University College Cork in 1947. The memoire was taken seriously both on the continent and in England but Germany was slow to accept the fallibility of Ossian;

both Goethe and Herder determined to learn Irish in order to read the original material – Herder using O'Brien's English-Irish dictionary in the process. While eventually it became obvious that there were no original Gaelic sources to be studied, the Ossian debate at least produced one hugely significant and sustained benefit for Ireland: it aroused the interest of German scholars in Celtic history, archaeology and language and began that whole school of Irish studies to which Germany has contributed so much.

Kilshannig, near Rathcormack, is the birthplace of United Irishman Thomas Russell (1767–1803). A friend of Wolf Tone, and confidante of Robert Emmet, Russell was convicted of high treason and hanged. He has been immortalised in the poem by Florence Wilson, 'The Man from God Knows Where'.[17]

Carrigtwohill

Ballinterry is a diversion from a route which takes the traveller in a rough orbit of East Cork, from Glanmire to Midleton and Youghal, after which a sweep south-westwards takes in Shanagarry, Cloyne and Cobh on the way back to the city. Before Midleton is Carrigtwohill, and from the motorway swooping towards the town can be seen the restored roofs of Barryscourt Castle, built by those Barrys who followed Philip and Gerald de Barri on the site of the castle they would have known in the closing years of the twelfth century.

Open to the public, the castle is being refurbished in medieval style, the garden recreated according to old records and an orchard planted with cherries, apples, pears and climbing roses so as to present to the public as much as possible of the atmosphere and appearance of what was one of the finest tower-houses in Ireland.

A bloodthirsty and riven dynasty, the Barrymore branch of the family at Barryscourt was taken over by the Barryroe branch of West Cork, itself shattered a few years later during the Desmond Rebellion. The castle was burned by David Barry rather than let it be taken by Sir Walter Ralegh on his avaricious swing through Munster; what remains now is the castle David rebuilt between 1603 and 1617. It stood almost astride the medieval route from Glanmire to the cathedral town of Cloyne and was of great strategic importance, yet with the death of David in 1617 it was abandoned by the Barrys, who moved instead to Castlelyons.

The birthplace of poet Dáibhí Ó Bruadair (*c.* 1625–98) is uncertain but the consensus seems to accept the neighbourhood of Carrigtwohill. Described by Séan Ó Tuama (in *An Duanaire*, 1981) as the first of the well-known seventeenth-century poets to try to live completely out of verse – at which he failed in the end – Ó Bruadair was educated at a bardic school just as such institutions were finally extinguished by the Confederate Wars, the Cromwellian expeditions and the defeat of the Jacobites.

His ardent and sarcastic poetry took these great themes as its material; the disappearance of the old order and the patronage by which he would have hoped to live, the habits and powers of the new rulers, the destruction of the Gaelic aristocracy and the adoption by the few remaining members of the Irish nobility of the manners of their usurpers produced some of his most powerful work. Moving to Cahirmoyle in Co. Limerick in 1660 he was supported by prominent Catholic families there but his life and his work were dominated by political events; one of his most powerful poems is 'An Longbhriseadh' – The Shipwreck – a metaphor for the condition of Ireland after the departure of its Wild Geese, those last members of the old noble houses who were exiled after the Treaty of Limerick in 1691.[18]

Another poet from Carrigtwohill although from a less classical tradition was Dáibhí de Barra (1757–1851), a small farmer who had been educated in a hedge school and who also worked as a scribe; closer to Castlemartyr the poet and schoolteacher Labhrás Ó Séagha worked like his contemporary de Barra on more local themes.

Lisgoold lies a little to the north of Castlemartyr on the banks of the Owenacurra river; Maurice Riordan (1953–) was born here; now working in London he won the National Poetry Prize in 1991 and his first collection *A Word from the Loki* was published in 1995.

At the other side of Slieve Corran is Dungourney, and here lived poet Eamonn de Bháll, a contemporary of Seán Clárach Mac Domhnall (1691–1754) who befriended him – perhaps because de Bháll may have come from Seán Clárach's own home town, Rath Luirc (Charleville) in North Cork.

Drumcollogher, Co. Limerick, seems to have been the birthplace of Tadhg Gaelach Ó Súilleabháin (1715–95), but this poet is associated mostly with East Cork, having lived in these townlands around Midleton, Rathcormac and Cobh for more than thirty years before moving to Dungarvan in Co. Waterford, where he died. Religious conversion made a devotional writer of Tadhg Gaelach; one of his most famous pieces is this 'Poem to the Heart of Jesus', its assonance in the original a linguistic litany indicated by the first verse:

Gile mo chroí do chroí-se, a Shlánaitheoir,
is ciste mo chroí do chroí-se a dháil im chomhair;
ós follas gur líon do chroí dem ghrá-sa, a stóir
i gcochall mo chroí do chroíse fág i gcomhad.

The light in my heart, O Saviour, is Thy heart,
the wealth of my heart, Thy heart poured out for me.
Seeing that Thy heart, Love, filled with love for me
leave Thy heart in keeping, hooded in mine. [19]

Midleton

Midleton is the fine market town of East Cork, situated at the junction of the Owenacurra river and a deep inlet of Cork harbour. Fr Edmund Barry (1837–1900), parish priest of Rathcormac, was born here; he was noted as a scholar of the ancient Irish alphabet known as *ogham*. This form of writing was cut into stones along the side, to be read upwards on one side and downwards on the other; possibly originating in the use of the tally-stick as means of recording transactions, the identification of the different characters was based on tree and branch-like references and further defined by accents. The earliest usage was for commemorative stones, but *ogham* later was refined by the poets of the bardic schools as an element in traditional education.[20]

Also born in Midleton was the architect Sir Richard Morrison (1767–1849). Moving from marble halls to gilded salons, creating in Ireland mansions as exquisite as any stately home in England, architects such as Morrison surely must have noticed, if not relished, the facts of native peasant housing so graphically described by the radical economist, reformer and farmer William Cobbett (1763–1835) after a visit to Ireland:

> I went to a sort of hamlet near to the town of Midleton. It contained about 40 or 50 hovels ... They all consisted of mud-walls, with a covering of rafters and straw. None of them so good as the place where you keep your little horse ... The floor, the bare ground. No fire-place, no chimney, the fire (made of Potato-haulm) made on one side against the wall, and the smoke going out a hole in the roof. No table, no chair ... There was a mud-wall about 4 feet high to separate off the end of the shed for the family to sleep, lest the hog should kill and eat the little children when the father and mother were both out, and when the hog was shut in. No bed: no mattress; some large flat stones laid on other stones, to keep the bodies from the damp ground; some dirty straw and a bundle of rags were all the bedding ... *All built their own hovels*, and yet have to pay this rent. All the hogs were in the hovels today, it being coldish and squally, and then, you know, hogs like cover ... There is a nasty dunghill (no privy) to each hovel. The dung that the hog makes *in the hovel* is carefully put into a heap by itself, as being the most precious. This dung and the pig are the main things to raise the rent and

get fuel with. The poor creatures sometimes keep the dung in the hovel, when their hard-hearted tyrants will not suffer to let it be at the door! [21]

From Midleton the roads splinter the countryside, one going sharply east and south towards Cloyne and the harbour villages, another north to Tallow and Lismore in Co. Waterford, another heading east to Castlemartyr, Killeagh and Youghal.

Castlemartyr

Ruins of the FitzGerald castles record the domination and dissolution of that great family; their last stand was made at Castlemartyr. Through the centuries control of this area had moved from the Earls of Ormond (whose centre was at Kilkenny) to the expansionist Earls of Desmond, through whom the important office of seneschal to the courts of the barony of Imokilly was passed to the Geraldines in the fifteenth century. That ended at Castlemartyr in engagements which heralded the supremacy of Richard, Earl of Cork. Despite the clamour of its past Castlemartyr today claims local attention as the home of Richard Alfred Milliken (1767–1815).

A solicitor who published plays, poetry and fiction, Milliken's fame in Cork rests with his verses in praise of that early MacCarthy fortress, Blarney Castle. His lines hymn the civilities of its current owner, the Lady Arabella Jeffreys:

'Tis Lady Jeffers
Owns this plantation;
Like Alexander,
Or like Helen fair;
There's no commande
In all the nation,
For regulation
Can with her compare ...

And so on until Fr Prout adds his ditty to the end.

Milliken began his literary career as editor of *The Casket* magazine, which ceased publication when he joined the Cork Royal Volunteers at the outbreak of the rebellion led by the United Irishmen. He lived most of the rest of his life in Dublin but is buried in Douglas, a suburb of Cork.

Revd Tomás Ó Gallchobhair (*c.* 1894) was parish priest of Ladysbridge. Born in Conna, and educated at St Colman's, Fermoy, he translated material into Irish, including Standish O'Grady's *The Coming of Cuculain*.

Killeagh

Killeagh, famous in Ireland for its production of hurleys, the stick or bat made from ash for use in the sport of hurling, has a delightful hinterland. Laden with woods, boasting a ringfort and souterrain at Lisnaraha, with castles on the banks of the Womanagh river and the ruined remains of Castletown House, the village was the birthplace of Richard John Uniacke, for thirty-three years the attorney general of Nova Scotia. Risteard Ó Foghlú (1871–1957), critic and writer of essays, poems and translations was born here.

Youghal

A secluded road from Killeagh leads to the village of Inch on the river Tourig, and a reminder that it was through these winding byways that the great territorial marches were made, with the accents of Wales and France and London scouring the air. Later Cromwell tramped up here from Dungarvan, and through the ages the lanes groaned under the weight of armies and adventurers. Preceding Cromwell (whom his son was to serve well) came a man who, from his home in Youghal and later in Lismore, left his mark all over Munster.

> I arrived out of England into Ireland, where God guided me first hither, bringing with me a taffeta doublet and a pair of velvet breeches, a new suit of laced fustian cutt upon taffeta, a bracelet of gold, a diamond ring and twenty-seven pounds three shillings in monie in my purse ...

The Great Earl of Cork was no earl at all when he arrived on these shores although within a few years he was designing towns and creating industries: that first arrival of Richard Boyle of Canterbury (1566–1643) occurred when he was twenty-two years old and at the very threshold of a career which in any age would be called brilliant.

How much his sartorial elegance had to do with this is hard to tell, but from the beginning of his life in Ireland his elegance of dress and management of money brought him among the loftier – or more reckless – colonists; perhaps he made his own luck, yet there can be no doubt that it was his relationship with the colourful adventurer Sir Walter Ralegh which settled him in Munster and especially in south-east Cork.

In Smith's *History of Cork* there is an account of a letter written in 1631 by the earl to Mr Carew Ralegh, Sir Walter's surviving son; it explains how, the day before Ralegh set out from Youghal on his last desperate voyage in 1617, they had dined together at the house of Sir Randal Clayton and Ralegh had spoken as if he were not fully financed or equipped for the

The Clock Gate, Youghal by Brian Coughlan

expedition. The earl had already supplied money, food and stores and now offered an additional £100, but this Ralegh refused, and called his son and his friends to his side:

> And taking his son by the hand, told him and the gentlemen, how that the Earl had kept a continual open house for three weeks, to entertain him and all his company ... And addressing himself to his son, said, Wat, you see how nobly my Lord Boyle hath entertained me and my friends, and therefore I charge you, upon my blessing, if it please God that you outlive me and return, that you never question the Lord Boyle for any thing that I have sold him ... And thereupon the Earl accompanied him to the boat, where taking leave, Sir Walter repeated all the Earl's civilities. And this, says Lord Cork, was the last time I ever saw him ...

Prominent though Ralegh may have been he was not to prosper; the earl paid him £1,500 for his Munster estates – 'at a time when it was utterly waste and yielded him no profit' – when Ralegh was under attainder and in great distress. It may be that the earl felt some subsequent guilt at the comparative ease of his own undertakings compared with Ralegh's catastrophic end (although few in Ireland, aware of Ralegh's enthusiasm as an Elizabethan soldier, have much sympathy for him). For thirteen years Ralegh, his wife and children were kept in the Tower of London at the pleasure of James I; in 1617, charged with a mission to rediscover a goldmine in Guiana, he left Youghal on this last voyage which was to bring disaster to all involved, including the death of Ralegh's son Walter; on his return to England Ralegh was executed.

Boyle's first years in Ireland were subject to the same difficulties of indecision and place-making experienced by everyone trying to serve Elizabeth in the declining years of her life. The Tudor influence on Ireland was in its last, defining decade and Boyle fell foul of men who saw his ambition as a threat; imprisoned for a time in London he was rescued by no less a person than the queen herself and sent back to Ireland as clerk of the Council of Munster.

At last Boyle was in a position to take advantage of prominent or prosperous friends; his own prosperity culminated in his appointment as lord treasurer of England in 1631 by which time he controlled vast estates in Ireland (and substantial holdings in England) and bore the title of Earl of Cork, the first and the 'Great'.

His first wife, Joan Apsley, died with the birth of a still-born son; both are buried in Buttevant. But the marriage brought Boyle land and money and this was his working capital. His second marriage to Catherine Fenton brought him 'one thousand pounds in gold', but the girl herself was the crown of all God's blessings: 'for she was a most religious, virtuous, loving and obedient wife unto me all the days of her life, and the happy mother of all my hopeful children.'[22]

Some of them, as well as Joan Apsley with her dead baby curled in sleep at the hem of her skirts, can be seen on the tiered tomb in St Mary's Collegiate Church in Youghal, where Richard Boyle is buried with several of his fifteen children.

It must be admitted that Boyle was a hugely significant force in the development of Cork's urban character. His writ ran across the county, from Youghal at its eastern extremity to Ballydehob in the west. 'Magnate' is the term most often and accurately applied, and in a sense, in Ireland at least, he was its first personification. He was a lawyer, speculator, improver, manufacturer; he opened mines and schools, he built towns and mills and churches, he sent his sons to war (at Liscarroll five were in arms together; Lewis, Lord Kinalmeaky, died there) and his daughters to careful marriages.

His seat was finally at Lismore; his children were titled (Cork, Orrery, Broghill, Shannon and Kinalmeakey) or married to titles. One was the wife of David, first Earl of Barrymore, and lived at Castlelyons; viscounts, earls, barons and baronets pepper the family tree from Richard down. The children of his daughter Katherine, Lady Ranelagh, were taught by John Milton in England.

Early in his Irish career he arranged the marriage of one of his orphan sisters to Edward Smyth of Ballynatray, the house on the Blackwater near Molana Abbey; his other sister married Pierce Power of Lisfinny Castle, near Tallow. He arranged the appointment of his brother John as bishop of Cork. A man who took family matters seriously, his burial vault is crowned with the effigy of his mother-in-law wearing a wide Elizabethan straw hat as though arrested in the work she devoted to Boyle's gardens in Youghal.

Included in that Renaissance monument is the little figure of Robert (1627–91), the youngest surviving son; born in Lismore, Co. Waterford he trained as a scientist and philosopher and lived in England where he was a founder member of the Royal Society, as he was of the Royal Philosophical Society in Dublin. He is the originator of 'Boyle's Law', and his work includes *The Sceptical Chymist* (1661) and *Occasional Reflections* (1665).

His elder brother Roger (1621–79), Lord Broghill and first Earl of Orrery, was both poet and soldier; born in Lismore he was able to interpret the Irish language but was dedicated in his opposition to Catholicism. His published works range from his *Treatise on the Art of War* (1677) to his dramatic tragedies *Mustapha* (1668) and *The Black Prince* (1669), and he is also accepted as the author of *Altemera, or The General*, the first heroic verse play written in English.[23]

Another Boyle has his name in the literary annals: Lord John, fifth Earl of Cork and of Orrery (1707–62) biographer and translator and friend of Swift who described him as 'a most deserving person, a good scholar, with much wit, manners and modesty ...' He is best-known now for his *Remarks on the Life and Writings of Dr Jonathan Swift* (1752).

We shifted from one decaying mansion to another, never buying one as my parents knew that one day my mother would inherit Myrtle Grove, a charming and mysterious place. It was a manor house built in 1461, for the warden of the Ecclesiastical College of St Mary's, and was the home of Sir Walter Raleigh [sic] when he was Governor of Ireland in 1588.[24]

Patricia Cockburn (1914–89) who with her husband the journalist and writer Claud Cockburn (1904–81) would live in Youghal for many years after her marriage, moved with her family into Myrtle Grove in 1916. Her grandfather had acquired the house from Sir John Pope-Hennessy and here in the panelled rooms and within its ancient garden (still containing some of the yews from which the town of Youghal derives its name – Eochaill – meaning a wood of yew-trees) Patricia Arbuthnot spent most of her happy childhood:

It was a delightful place to grow up in, with its secret gardens and ruins and summer houses. When Sir Walter Raleigh acquired it he must have thought that he was going to spend a great deal more time in Ireland than he actually did because he made extensive alterations and repairs himself, installing the beautiful oak panelling on the first floor amd the elaborately carved mantlepieces. He was in some ways a civilised man and he preferred the airiness and brightness of the large windows of Myrtle Grove – which being inside the walls of the Town of Youghal had no need of defence – to the darkness of the arrow-slits of Lismore Castle, eighteen miles away, which he also owned.

Patricia Cockburn began life as the pony-mad hunting daughter of Myrtle Grove, moved on to debutante status, became a traveller, explorer and writer and then as wife and mother grew more and more absorbed in the uncompromising political journalism of which Claud Cockburn was the mischievous master. 'The Years of the Week' (1968) is her version of this career.

Cockburn wrote a two-volume autobiography and several novels includ-ing *Beat the Devil*. Of their three sons – Alexander, Patrick and Andrew – Alexander includes in his book *Corruptions of Empire* (1987) a reminiscence of his childhood in Youghal. He recalls the publication of *Beat the Devil*, his father's meeting with film director John Huston – who had just completed *The African Queen* – at Luggala in Co. Wicklow, and the subsequent visit by the Hustons to Youghal to discuss Cockburn's screenplay for the filming of *Beat the Devil*.

Written under one of Claud Cockburn's numerous pseudonyms (Jack Helvick) and filmed with a sumptuous cast – Humphrey Bogart, Peter Lorre, Gina Lollobrigida, Jennifer Jones and Robert Morley – this eventually became something of a cult movie for Huston fans:

> One aspect of this cult caused some irritation to my father and indeed to the rest of the family. The film's credits announced a screenplay by Truman Capote, from a novel by James Helvick. Admirers of the film professed to find evidence of Capote's mastery in every interstice of the dialogue and over the years Capote did nothing to dissuade them from this enthusiasm. But in fact his own contribution was limited to some concluding scenes, for it had chanced that during the final days of shooting in Italy the end had suddenly to be altered; as far as I can remember, the locale of the scenes had to be changed in a hurry. In the emergency, with my father back in Ireland, Capote, who happened to be visiting the set at the time, was drafted to do the necessary work and his name – more alluring then the unknown Helvick or the ex-Red Cockburn – scrambled into the credits ...

More credits were to come for Youghal at least, because it was as a result of the collaboration on *Beat the Devil* and his visits to the Cockburns that Huston transformed the town's waterfront to the New England setting of his production of *Moby Dick*.

Patricia Cockburn was also an artist, a gardener of skill, a warm hostess who is remembered to this day in Youghal and elsewhere. She and her husband eventually moved to Ardmore, over the next headland from Youghal bay on the Waterford side where they lived in a cliff-top house: 'after all these years I live close to the place where I was born, and in the same kind of house ...'

As for her husband (whose grave is marked with a fine tombstone by the Cork sculptor Ken Thompson), Patricia's funeral was held in St Mary's Collegiate church in Youghal, a church so closely built into the town's medieval walls that they form the boundary of its churchyard.

Friaries and abbeys dating from 1231 and perhaps earlier have left their traces in the town, but of them all the most intriguing and beautiful is this ancient building. The official guidebook suggests that an eleventh-century Romanesque church was built here on the site of an existing church; some small parts of this remain in the newer Anglo-Norman foundation begun by the Anglo-Norman de Clares and FitzGeralds in 1220, which in 1464 was re-created as a collegiate church by Thomas, eighth Earl of Desmond.

In 1579, however, the sixteenth Earl of Desmond ransacked Youghal and with it most of the college's property, including the church which was used as stables. On the arrival of Walter Ralegh the church was reconsecrated, but it was his successor Richard Boyle who repaired it, restoring the tomb of the founders and several other memorial catafalques and building his own monument in the chantry.

Cromwell stood within these walls; George Berkeley, later Bishop of Cloyne, was warden of the college in 1734, John Wesley preached here in 1765. The antiquarian and architect Edward FitzGerald (1820–93) conducted the restoration of the interior of the church, not to general satisfaction, but this also has by now taken on an acceptable atmospheric patina. Richard Boyle built New College House as his own residence in Youghal; although largely rebuilt in the eighteenth century this retains the defensive flanking towers essential during the wars with which Boyle's life in Ireland began and ended.

In St Mary's church on this damp afternoon a film crew are setting up their gear. In the vestry there are photographs of previous rectors, among them Canon Darling, good at tennis in 1934, who accidentally ignited a box of matches when meaning only to light a cigarette, whose cat sipped whiskey from his glass and staggered drunkenly about. The camera crew wear bright anoraks, but speak in low voices, as is fitting in these surroundings. A coffin rests on a trolley in front of the altar steps, a candle in a massive candlestick at each corner. The varnish of the coffin gleams, high-lighting the yellow wood. Such hefty candles, in this Protestant church, do not look right ...

'An uphill struggle', the clergyman complains, referring to the problems of old buildings and keeping everything up. He's dressed to take a service, and I wonder who has died. In fact, no-one has; the yellow coffin's empty. 'Some kind of documentary', the obliging cleric explains, his tone of voice suggesting there has been a fee. 'I wonder if I should tell them those candles shouldn't be there?'[25]

In *Excursions in the Real World* William Trevor, who lived in Youghal as a child, remembers the town for its long, misty beach, its 'stubby little lighthouse', the Moby Dick bar commemorating another film crew and the town's brief cinematic fame, and the annual arrival of the 'Amusements' or the 'Wall of Death'.

Patricia Cockburn suggested the possibility that Shakespeare was among the group of players from London who came to Youghal on an Irish tour arranged to keep away from the plague-stricken capital. There may be another Shakespearean link, possibly with *The Merchant of Venice*: Shakespeare's friend and patron the Earl of Southampton was a close friend of Robert Devereaux, Earl of Essex. Essex was instrumental in the destruction of Rodrigo Lopez, the Marrano Jew who was doctor, at one time, both to Essex and Queen Elizabeth and some believe the man on whom Shakespeare modelled Shylock. Lopez was married to Susan Anes or Anyas, sister to Francis Anyas, a soldier of fortune distinguished in his defence of Youghal during the Desmond risings, and mayor of the town in 1583. A Francis Anyas, perhaps his father, was mayor three times in 1569, 1576 and 1581.

Another soldier to bivouac in Youghal was the father of the dramatist William Congreve (1670–1729), who was stationed in the garrison here from 1674 to 1678. The Cork-born short story writer and novelist William Buckley (*fl.* 1905) set his novel *Cambia Carty* (1907) in Youghal. His most famous novel is *Croppies Lie Down* (1903) an account of the Rising of 1798. The poet and academic Richard Kell (1927–) was born in Youghal, and among the several distinguished clerical authors living in or born in the town was The Revd George Cotter (*c.* 1754–1831) who published poems and essays (his son James Laurence Cotter of Castlemartyr was also a poet).

> Like many self-made men he felt an urge to throw down roots, and this he did in Co. Cork first by buying Sir Walter Raleigh's house at Youghal (where he wrote an elegant, imaginative book, *Sir Walter Raleigh and Ireland*) and then by selling Youghal and buying the former seat of the Earls of Inchiquin, Rostellan Castle, overlooking Queenstown Harbour. As a boy in Cork he had tramped through its demesne and made a vow that he would one day own the house and land …

The 'he' is John Pope-Hennessy (1840–91), Catholic MP and follower of Disraeli and the origin, it is believed, of Trollope's eponymous hero 'Phineas Finn'; his name is also invoked in the brothel scene in Joyce's *Ulysses* – a distinction Pope-Hennessy might not have welcomed. His career as a colonial administrator included the governorships of the Bahamas, Barbados, Hong Kong and Mauritius; his wife Katherine remarried after his death and mortgaged Rostellan so that it was never inherited by either of his sons Richard and Hugh.

It is Richard's son, art historian and curator Sir John Pope-Hennessy, who presents the family portrait quoted above in his book *Learning to Look* (1991). Richard's wife was Una Birch, whose father was lieutenant-governor of Ceylon where Sir William Gregory was governor, and through this connection Una spent many holidays at Coole Park, the almost legendary house in Co. Galway where Lady Gregory entertained W.B. Yeats among others.

In 1932 Yeats sent my mother an emotional letter describing Lady Gregory's death ... but she could never forgive him for the complacency with which he allowed Coole to be destroyed. One of her last pieces of writing was a review in 1949 in *The Spectator* of the autobiography of Sean O'Casey in which she described how Yeats 'after he had become a Senator and one of the leading men in Ireland, made no effort to save Coole as a shrine of culture, but permitted it to be razed to the ground and degraded to a nettlebed.'

Dame Una Pope-Hennessy wrote several biographies (her subjects included Dickens and Sir Walter Scott) and was a well-known literary reviewer. Her son James was a successful writer – his first book *London Fabric* won the Hawthornden Prize in 1939; in 1960 he published a biography of Queen Mary and he also wrote biographies of Anthony Trollope and Robert Louis Stevenson. Born in 1916 he was brutally murdered in London in 1974.

Sir John Pope-Hennessy himself, however, although he wrote a great deal, is best known for his service to the fine art institutions of Europe and America. He was for six years the director of the Victoria and Albert Museum in London and later of the British Museum; for ten years after that he was chairman of the department of European paintings at the Metropolitan in New York and during all those years he was also living part time in Florence, the city to which he retired in 1986.

Something of the difference between himself and his brother James can be gleaned from the paragraph in which he describes the few years during which they shared a house in London: '... I in my study writing on Fra Angelico and he entertaining Guy Burgess and Derek Patmore downstairs.'

Among Sir John Pope-Hennessy's titles are *Sienese Quattrocento Painting* (1947), a three-volume *Introduction to Italian Sculpture* (1955) and several catalogues and introductions to collections such as that of the Frick museum in New York or the Samuel H. Kress collection and to the works of Nicholas Hilliard. Sir John Pope-Hennessy died in Florence in 1994.

William Cooke Taylor (1800–49) historian and pamphleteer was born in Youghal but lived later in London and Dublin; in a relatively short life he produced a great deal of work on aspects of French and Irish history, on manufacturing and religion and the British in India. His many-claused titles suggest a ponderous style (as in his *History of the Overthrow of the Roman Empire and the Foundation of the Principal European States* (1836)) but he also produced the catalogue of the National Portrait Gallery in London.

Maurice Kennedy (1925) writer of short stories was born in Youghal, and so was Liam Ó Laoghaire (1910–1992) writer of radio plays and director of Gaelic drama at the Abbey Theatre. Founder of the Irish Film Society, the critic and film historian was a son of Donncadh Ó Laoghaire

(1877–1944) of Ballyvourney in West Cork, a Gaelic scholar, poet, musican and teacher and translator into Irish of the stories of Hans Andersen and the Brothers Grimm.

The Revd Monsignor Bickerstaffe-Drew (1858–1928) spent much of his childhood on visits to his grandfather, Pierce Drew, Rector of Youghal; Bickerstaffe-Drew later converted to Catholicism at Oxford and wrote several novels under the pseudonym of John Ayscough. Bishop William Coppinger (*c.* 1740–1831) formerly parish priest of Youghal wrote essays and sermons as well as a biography of the Cork educationalist and religious foundress Nano Nagle; The Revd George Sackville Cotter (*c.* 1754–1831) lived most of his life in Youghal and, as well as writing poetry and translating Terence and Plautus, became a well-known essayist on agriculture and the production of food. Most of the literary publications of Canon Samuel Hayman concentrated on the town of Youghal and the river Blackwater; they included a guide to St Mary's Collegiate Church and *The Annals of Youghal* (1848).

The town is an attractive one with old shop-fronts still maintained along narrow winding streets, the main thoroughfare passing under the clock tower built in 1777 on the site of an earlier town gate. At the western end of Youghal, where the main road curves over the shallow cliff above the tide and drives into the heart of the town, itself built between the sea and the hills, stands the white lighthouse. This stands at the side of the street at the site of St Anne's Tower, a twelfth-century beacon managed by an order of nuns until the middle of the sixteenth century.

Ballymacoda

The long promenaded strand which forms the coastline at Youghal can be followed westward for miles, leading around Knockadoon Head towards Ballycotton Bay. The village of Ballymacoda sits at the inner edge of this peninsula: here again the traveller meets the Gaelic hinterland, for Ballymacoda holds the grave of the poet Piaras Mac Gearailt (1700–91) who was born at Ballykinealy a few miles away in a house which is still standing and which was once the focus of the Cúirt Éigse or court of poetry established around him. The village is also the birthplace of the poet Pádraig Phiarais Cundún (1777–1856), a farmer who emigrated to America with his wife and children and settled in Uttica, New York State.

Cundún never became fluent in English, his adopted tongue, but he continued to write poems and songs which were circulated in Ireland in manuscript form. MacGearailt was born to different circumstances, a member of the Ballycrenane branch of the FitzGerald clan, whose two brothers (and possibly he himself) were educated in Spain:

Long before Piaras had grown to manhood and come into possession of Ballykineally [*sic*] he knew that only for the fortunes of war Ballykineally, instead of being the whole of his possession, would have been merely the home farm of a huge region. To lose Ballykineally now would, therefore, be to lose even the very name of property. In that was the sorrow of his life, for a moment came when he had not the strength to say: let Ballykineally go with the rest. To retain it, he must take the hilly road to Kilcreddan Church, to enter it as a Protestant, to become, in his own words, 'an innocent child of the Reformed Church'.[26]

To a fellow poet, Mac Gearailt defends his decision to turn from Catholicism to Protestantism in order to protect his family farm:

O gossip, O friend, O Barry, most cultured in behaviour,
'Tis sad for me to cleave to Calvin or perverse Luther,
But the weeping of my children, the spoiling them of flocks and land,
Brought streaming floods from my eyes and descent of tears.[27]

A long life and a substantial body of work offer a good deal of material to the scholar, but it is as Jacobite poet that Mac Gearailt has kept his place in Ireland's modern educational schemes. It is from this category of work that 'Rosc Catha na Mumhan' (Munster's Rallying Battle-Song), written to celebrate the imaginary return to Ireland of a Jacobite prince, has survived:

D'aithnígheas féin gan bhréag ar fhuacht
'S ar anfhaithe Thétis taobh le cuan,
Ar chanadh na n'éan go seiseach suairc,
Go gcasfadh mo Sheasar glé gan ghruaim
Measaim gur subhach do'n Mhumhain an fhuaim
'S d'á maireann go dubhac de chrú na mbuadh
Torann na dtonn le sleasaibh na long
Ag tarraint go teann 'n-ár gceann ar cuaird.

I knew it well by storm and cold,
The waves which lash the shore foretold,
The birds' sweet notes in forests tell
Our Prince comes over ocean's swell.
'Tis time for Munster now to cheer,
'Twill glad our wasting clans to hear
The dash of the wave 'gainst the ships of the brave
And gallant hearts that are drawing near.[28]

Mac Gearailt is buried in the hill cemetery at Ballymacoda, while in the Catholic graveyard lies Fr Peter O'Neill, a hero of the rising of 1798, and of Peter O'Neill Crowley, the Fenian who died in Kilclooney Wood near Fermoy and inspired *The Graves of Kilmorna* by Canon Sheehan.

Padraig Stundun (1825–1903) born Curraheen, Ballymacoda, county court interpreter for non-English speakers, was the scribe who translated the Life of St Finbarr into modern Irish from ancient sources.

Shanagarry

Here and there along this coastline the littoral swells into beaches, one of the longest being at Garryvoe, another at Ballindreen near Shanagarry. Shanagarry is now famous for the pottery established here by the late Philip and Lucy Pearce and for its successor run by their son Stephen Pearce. The village has also won international renown as the location of the Ballymaloe Cookery School and gardens at Kinoith House; here Darina Allen produces, among other delights, extremely popular cookery books which combine her own communicative flair with the splendid reputation achieved by her mother-in-law Myrtle Allen at Ballymaloe House.

Shanagarry was the home of the Penn family for many generations and was visited several times by William Penn, sent from England to settle his father's estates in Ireland. The castle whose remains are seen behind the Catholic church in the village belonged to the Poers, or Powers, who gave their name to Poer Head, the eastern extremity of Cork Harbour. The Penns, given Shanagarry after the Restoration when their estate in Macroom reverted to the MacCarthys of Muskerry, built Shanagarry House in the village and their connection with the place survived until the 1950s.

Ballycotton is a distinctive fishing village from which cliff-top walks can be made across the headland to Ballybrannigan and from here a maze of little roads wend to the harbour villages of Guileen, Trabolgan and Rostellan.

Cloyne

Between Rostellan on the water's edge and Ballymaloe's long pastures and hillside woods is the cathedral town of Cloyne, where one of Ireland's finest remaining round towers is found. The town has the reputation as the last ministry and home of philosopher and bishop George Berkeley (1685–1753). Born near Thomastown in Co. Kilkenny, Berkeley was for many years student and fellow of Trinity College Dublin where he established his status as an intellectual observer and commentator, with publications such as *A New Theory of Vision* and *A treatise concerning the principles of human knowledge* appearing between 1707 and 1713.

His Utopian scheme for the establishment in Bermuda of an ideal community where native young men would be trained as candidates for the

Anglican priesthood won attention and support when he began to promote it in 1722. By then his reputation as a scholar and writer was made; a friend of Swift, of Pope and Addison, encouraged by parliamentarians, well travelled and influenced by all that he saw, read and heard abroad, Berkeley won permission from King George I and a grant of £20,000 from the House of Commons towards his Bermuda foundation.

Before setting off he married Anne Forster, daughter of the speaker of the Irish House of Commons and lord chief justice; he also found himself richer by £2,000 from the estate of Esther Van Homrigh, the close friend of Jonathan Swift but estranged from him after a violent disagreement. Esther deleted Swift from her will and installed Berkeley, whom she had never met; she then very promptly died.

Swift (as has been mentioned in the chapter on South West Cork) rode to seclusion in Glandore for a few months while Berkeley, delighted with what he regarded as a sign of divine approval for his plan, set sail for America.

He spent three years there, mostly in or near Newport, Rhode Island. He did not get to Bermuda – the money from parliament never materialised – but was influential in the educational debates of the day, preached often, wrote and studied. His American visit is commemorated in Harvard, Yale, Columbia and other educational institutions including the University of California.

The explanatory titles of his many publications inhibit listing (*The Analyst, or a discourse addressed to an infidel mathematician* is one of the shorter examples) but they reveal his intense interest in and quick perceptions of the major issues of his times and also in the minutiae of daily life.

Religion, agriculture, domestic and political economy, medicine, literature, theology, banking, government – everything came within his power of critical analysis. *The Querist* is one of his most famous publications (1735) and in *A Word to the Wise* he encouraged harmonious relations between the Church of Ireland and Catholicism.

On his appointment to the See of Cloyne he addressed himself to rural poverty, hygiene and ill-health and produced a best seller, *Siris, A Chain of Philosophical Reflexions and Inquiries concerning the Virtues of Tar-Water* (1744); with his wife he decided to move to Oxford in 1752 to be closer to his son George, but died there six months later. He is buried in Christ Church, Oxford. Smith offers this contemporary picture of his life in Cloyne:

> His present Lordship has successfully transplanted the polite arts, which heretofore flourished only in a warmer soil, to this northern climate. Painting and musick are no longer strangers to *Ireland*, nor confined to *Italy*. In the episcopal palace of Cloyne, the eye is entertained with a great variety of good paintings, as well as the ear with concerts of excel-

lent musick. There are here some pieces of the best masters, as a *Magdalen* of Sir *Peter Paul Rubens*, some heads by *Van Dyke* and *Kneller* besides several good paintings performed in the house, an example so happy, that it has diffused itself into the adjacent gentlemen's houses, and there is at present a pleasing emulation raised in this country, to vie with each other in these kind of performances. The great usefullness of *Design* in the manufactures of stuffs, silks, diapers, damasks, tapestry, embroidery, earthen ware, sculpture, architecture, cabinet work, and an infinite number of other arts is sufficiently evident.

There was some evidence of the arts in Cloyne long before the benign bishop's residence here – the 92-foot-high round tower across the street from the cathedral is an indication of treasures worth protecting against the marauding Vikings. And Cloyne's first church of Cluain Uama was founded by Colmán Mac Lénéni, (530–606) a religious poet and patron of the poet Dálach, from whom the Ó Dálaigh bardic family claimed descent. Colmán's surviving work – some dated from 564 – is among the earliest examples of Irish writing using the Latin alphabet; it is examined by James Carney in 'Three Old Irish Accentual Poems' in *Eirú* 22 (1971). The noted astronomer John Brinkley (1763–1835) was bishop of Cloyne and is commemorated in the cathedral with a monument by Tallow sculptor John Hogan. The Revd Richard Hodges (1862–?), historian, was born in Cloyne. Other Cloyne writers included The Revd Robert King (1815–1900) Irish scholar and religious historian who wrote *The Little Red Book of the History of the Catholic Church in Ireland* (1848) and William Kenealy (1828–76) who wrote as 'William of Munster' for the *The Nation* among others.

Cobh

Ballyvaloon, Great Island, Barrymore, the Cove of Cork, Clonmel, Queenstown: all are among the names applied through the ages to the prominent harbour town now known as Cobh. As it stands today, built in terraces above the sea – the main street is called The Beach – it reflects its name, 'the haven'. The large and sheltered harbour was crucial to the prosperity not only of the town itself but of the wheat, butter, and cattle-growing regions between it and Cork city and far beyond that again. In this harbour, for centuries, lay the might of the British navy, and Cork – city and county – produced the food, fodder, sailcloth and timber with which both navy and army were supplied.

Tradition insists on a Phoenician landing here, but later ownership lay with the Uí Liatháin or O'Lehane tribe which was succeeded by the Barrys who gave their name to Barry's Great Island or the Island of Barrymore. The harbour, as a walk along the rampart-like roads of Cobh will reveal, is plated with islands: Spike, Haulbowline which is now a national naval centre and steel-works, and, closer to the city, Fota (which was also a Barrymore estate) and Little Island, now heavily industrialised. And apart from Spike, none are islands any more, all being accessible by road and causeway.

One of these causeways is at Belvelly, where the philosopher and mathematician Philip Ronayne (*fl. c.* 1760) lived at Ronayne's Grove on an estate which spread from the now industrialised site of Marino to Cuskinny at the other side of the island.

As an entrance to the Great Island Belvelly is fortified with two characteristic defences: the strategic importance of Cobh is indicated by the presence of the many castles and the later Martello towers. In these extensive and deep waters lay the British Atlantic fleet during the American War of Independence; the Napoleonic wars and the First World War (American naval forces for European action were based here) brought fleets here for marshalling and provisioning, and it was the major post-Famine port of emigration. The first steamship to cross the Atlantic was the *Sirius*; it left from Cobh in 1838 under Captain Richard Roberts, later lost with his ship *The President* but remembered at the family grave at Marmullane near his home at the other side of the harbour. The grave of Captain Roberts carries this inscription:

> The thousands that shall follow in his track must not forget who it was that first taught the world to traverse with such marvellous rapidity that highway of the ocean, and who in thus connecting by a voyage of a few days' duration the eastern and western hemispheres, has for ever linked his name with the greatest achievement of navigation since Columbus first revealed Europe and America to each other. [29]

While the great Pugin cathedral is Cobh's most obvious public building, the street-scapes of this town are wonderfully characteristic and, where not defaced with inaccurate improvements or replacement windows in plastic or steel, are persuasive of its maritime history, economy and society. Both the Barrys as Lords Barrymore or Smith-Barrys, and the Brodricks as Lords Midleton provided improvement in the shape of quays, churches and housing schemes. The graceful former Royal Cork Yacht Club which has been restored and transformed into an art gallery, the offices for the liner and shipping companies which were once so important to the town (and may be again, now that liner traffic of the most sophisticated kind includes Cobh as a destination), the many graceful official buildings surviving from the days of naval glory and above all the steep layered streets and their winding alleys and steps, all shining with reflected light from the tide at the quayside –

these are among the elements of Cobh which remain to charm visitor and resident alike.

They range from the dockyards at Rushbrooke to the villas of Cuskinny. From the hillsides the harbour opens out, to the west the estuary narrows, through the roads come the ships great and small, tankers and cruisers, freighters and ferries – and glittering through them all at any opportunity of sun or wind yachts by the score or by the hundred, stencilled on the horizon.

Cobh for many was a tragic port, the last of Ireland for the departing thousands following the Great Famine of 1846; this emigrant traffic continued to drain the young life from rural Ireland and its small towns up to the later years of this century, but took on renewed impetus after the famine of 1879–80. Neither famine brought out the best of those Irish who did not suffer from it: famine fever especially was dreaded by the local populations and country people moving through the towns towards Cork and other ports were cruelly treated by their fellow-countrymen.[30]

It was to minister to these emigrants that poet and novelist Charlotte O'Brien (1845–1909) came to Cobh. Her work in setting up decent hostels for those awaiting departure, and her achievement of significant improvements in shipboard conditions in terms of accommodation, food allowances and hygiene, especially for women, have obscured her literary status. Born at Cahirmoyle in Co. Limerick, the daughter of William Smith O'Brien, she moved to Dublin for a while but later returned to Cahirmoyle.[31]

The Jesuit Edmund Hogan (1831–1917), born on Great Island, was the first professor of Irish at University College Dublin, a noted scholar and translator and author of *Distinguished Irishmen of the Sixteenth Century* (1894) as well as of *Onomasticon Goedelicum* (1910) on Gaelic tribes in Ireland and Scotland. Another scholar associated with Cobh was Anthony Raymond of Derry (1675–1726), educated in the town by a Mr Jones and subsequently in Trinity College Dublin, after which he was ordained in Cork and worked as Vicar of Trim in Co. Meath, where he became a friend of Jonathan Swift.

Also from Derry was Edward Walsh (1805–50) one of the most important – and also one of the first – translators of Irish folk poetry from Gaelic to English. A contributor to *The Nation*, Walsh also taught Catholic children in local hedge schools, and was appointed schoolmaster to the convicts on Spike Island. He was subsequently a teacher in the workhouse in Cork, where he died, after a life which seems to have been devoted exclusively to the underprivileged and destitute.[32]

Spike Island is a fortified rock in the harbour. Formerly the chief penal centre in Ireland, it is still a jail. Up to the end of the last century prison hulks were anchored in the harbour and the island was used as a holding-area for felons awaiting transportation. Other prisoners worked on the naval dockyards or on the fortifications for the surrounding headlands.

Among them for a time was John Mitchel (1815–75), the Derry-born solicitor and journalist who founded *The United Irishman* in 1848. The editorial mixture (including the excited poetry of James Clarence Mangan which, with that of Thomas Davis Mitchel was to promote successfully) was so inflammable that Mitchel, advocating a 'holy war' against the English, was convicted of treason and sentenced to transportation.

He escaped from Australia in 1853 and settled in America where again he became an editor and again was imprisoned – this time, oddly enough, for supporting slavery. Elected MP for Tipperary he returned to Ireland but died shortly afterwards. His *History of Ireland* (1868) was written in his usual incendiary style, but his *Jail Journal* (1854) is regarded as a classic of prison literature.

The Revd Charles Bernard Gibson (1808–85) who began his clerical career at Mallow was later Chaplain to the Presbyterian convicts on Spike Island; he then went to London where he worked with the inmates of the Shoreditch workhouse. His two-volume historical romance *The Last Earl of Desmond* was published in 1854, and his *History of the County and City of Cork* – also in two volumes – in 1861.

An altogether different kind of school was opened at Ballybrassil near Cobh around 1774: this was the Reddington Academy which was established by the Jesuit Michael Harrington. It was the first Catholic boarding school in Ireland after the Reformation and its pupils included the poet J.J. Callanan. Daniel O'Connell (1775–1847), father of Catholic Emancipation in Ireland, was educated here for a time before studying in France.

A flamboyant and charming personality with impressive oratorical and political abilities, O'Connell organised the Catholic Association in 1823 and from that country-wide campaign which united people and clergy grew the irresistible movement which resulted in Catholic Emancipation in 1829. An agitation carried on through the unprecedented spectacle of 'monster' – and completely peaceful – meetings was O'Connell's approach to the question of repeal of the union between Ireland and England; this was to be ultimately unsuccessful, and O'Connell's perceived inadequacy in the face of the Great Famine added to his sense of failure. He died in Genoa while on pilgrimage to Rome but his legacy as the father of Irish democracy has been an enormously powerful influence on political thought and activity ever since.[33]

The Revd Francis Orpen Morris (*fl.* 1810–80?) was born at Merton in Cobh and wrote on a wide selection of subjects, from religion to natural history to education. Some of his material suggests the dilettante or the simply daft – the detection of thefts in letter carriers, or records of animal sagacity and character being among his many subjects. But he was a serious and well-trained naturalist and produced *A History of British Butterflies* (1864) and a *Catalogue of British Insects* (1865) as well as studies of moths and birds. His twin themes of faith and evolution came together in his examination of *All the Articles of the Darwin Faith* (1875) and other similar works, and his range extended to a dialogue about fox-hunting, a study of the rights and wrongs of women, his view of experiments on living animals, a listing of ancestral homes and numerous sermons and catechisms.

Also born in Cobh was Cecil Vivian Usborne, whose naval career reached the pinnacle of vice-admiral; as a writer his novels (including *Malta Fever* 1936) were coloured by his sea-going experiences. Cobh-born John Ward (1781–1837) shipwright and shoemaker was present at the Battle of Copenhagen in 1801; a mystic known as 'Zion Ward' he is commemorated in *The Writings of Zion Ward on Shiloh, the Spiritual Man* (1874).

Its situation and climate were supposed for a while to make Cobh a particuarly hopeful resort for those suffering from pulmonary diseases, which really meant tuberculosis or consumption. The Revd Charles Wolfe was a curate in Co. Down but came to Cobh suffering from TB from which he died here in 1823. His poems are read rarely now except for his one outstanding piece of work, his imagined account of 'The Burial of Sir John Moore' – that hurried interment in Corunna over which William Bradford read the prayers.

His body lies in Clonmel cemetery in Cobh, near the grave of John Tobin (1770–1804) the dramatist from Salisbury who died on board ship in the harbour while en route to the West Indies – again for his health's sake. Tobin's only successful play was his last: *The Honey Moon*, staged a few weeks after his death.

This graveyard is now widely known as the place in which bodies of the victims of the *Lusitania* disaster were buried in 1915; the Cunard liner was torpedoed off the Old Head of Kinsale, and both victims and survivors were brought back to the town. Clonmel was also the home of Robert Marshall, co-beneficiary with George Berkeley in Esther van Homrigh's will. At nearby Templerobin graveyard is buried John P. Leonard (1812–89), a native of Spike Island who was sent to France for his education and who remained there, working as a writer and translator, until his death. He was awarded the Ribbon of the Military Legion of Honour for his services during the Franco-Prussian War.

Antiquarian, engineer, poet and nationalist Charles Doran (1835–1909) was born in Carlow but spent most of his life in Cobh, where he designed the interior of the cathedral. George M. Atkinson (*c.* 1850–1908) was a member of the family of marine painters and was himself an archaeologist with an expertise in ogham. The Revd P.P. Dennehy, administrator of Queenstown (?1825–1902) worked in the town for twenty years, wrote treatises on religious and political topics as well as a *History of Great Island* (first delivered as a series of public lectures) and two historical novels – *Alethea, or The Parting of the Ways* and *The Flower of Asia*; his 'History' has been subsequently annotated and published with some appendices by James Coleman, (1925).

Coleman, who died in 1938, was the author of several guides and the editor of Windele's *Cork* (1910).

Cobh as a place, almost as a symbol in Irish history, has many eulogists in song, poem and story; it is like a lock on Cork's door, a portal hinge on a gateway to Ireland. For several centuries its population had the marks of mingled ancestries; sailors from all countries were left behind in its fever hospital and not every one of them rejoined their ship when it next called to the harbour. Those who stayed married, settled, reared families. Economic developments and changes in shipping routes as well as the departure of the British navy in 1937 ended that assimilation but still in Cobh there are features, colourings, names which hint at more exotic origins than the ordinary.

> I visited the Cove which is the port of Cork, ten or twelve miles lower down at the mouth of the river – it is one of the prettiest bays and one of the safest in Europe. There I was well and kindly received by the brave General Vallency ... The researches of the General in Irish antiquities are known throughout the whole literary world; perhaps he has pushed a little too far his enthusiasm for the Irish language. He asserts, or pretends to believe, that it is as old as the world, and is perhaps the same which Adam and Eve made use of in the Garden of Eden, the general mother of all languages of the universe from the Huron to the Chinese. He quotes in his grammar singular examples of its agreement with about thirty living languages in all parts of the world.

Chevalier De Latocnaye was describing, in *A Frenchman's Walk Through Ireland 1796–1797*, (1798) his meeting with the military engineer who arrived in Ireland in 1762 and discovered a new enthusiasm. The builder and improver of fortifications such as the mighty Charles Fort in Kinsale or Fort Camden in Cork Harbour, Vallency (1721–1812) never learned the Irish language despite his painstaking research on its behalf. His *Collectanea de Rebus Hibernicis* (1770–1804) included observations by several antiquarians, but this, according to De Latocnaye, was not his only claim to fame:

> General Vallency has travelled all over Ireland for fifteen years, and has made surveys for maps of the different counties. The Government in the end, as a reward for his labours, has given him the post which he occupies at the moment, that of Commandant of the Port of Cove, which is now so strongly fortified that there is no danger that any hostile vessel can enter. It cannot be denied that he is a man of value to the State in more than one way, seeing that he has twelve children of a first marriage, ten of a second, and twenty-one of a third. There are very few men who have done their duty so well.

Notes to East Cork

1. Giraldus Cambrensis, *The History and Topography of Ireland* (translated from the Latin by John J. O'Meara) (1951, 1982).
2. For more on these districts see Falvey, *The Chronicles of Midleton* (1998).
3. F.X. Martin, 'Gerald of Wales, Norman Reporter on Ireland', *Studies*, Autumn 1969.
4. For a brief guide to many of these places see *Historic East Cork* published by Midleton and Area Tourism.
5. Breandán Ó Buachalla, 'The Making of a Cork Jacobite' in *Cork – History and Society* (1993). Ó Buachalla also refers to Brian Ó Cuiv (ed.) *Parliament na mBan*, 1952 for his quotations; Ó Cuiv's study of the text is a valuable source for further reading, while Ó Buachalla widens the text into references for further reading on the Cotter family.
6. Ó Buachalla, op. cit.
7. *Parliament na mBan.*
8. ibid.
9. Ó Buachalla, op. cit.
10. John Brophy (ed.), *The Voice of Sarah Curran* (1955).
11. Quoted in Brophy, op. cit.
12. Elizabeth Mavor (ed.), *The Grand Tours of Katherine Wilmot* (1992).
13. Marchioness of Londonderry and H.M. Hyde (eds.), *The Russian Journals of Martha and Catherine Wilmot* (1934) and *More Letters from Martha Wilmot* (1935).
14. See Mark Bence-Jones, *A Guide to Irish Country Houses* (1988).
15. Diarmaid Ó Catháin, 'An Irish Scholar Abroad: Bishop John O'Brien of Cloyne and the Macpherson Controversy' (*Cork, History and Society*, 1993).
16. Ó Catháin, op. cit.
17. See Desmond Ryan, 'Threshold', (1958).
18. See Michael Hartnett, introduction and translations, *Ó Bruadair* (1985).
19. Thomas Kinsella, tr. in *An Duanaire* (1981).
20. For more on ogham, see Damian McManus, *A Guide to Ogham* (1991).
21. G.D.H. and M. Cole (eds.), *Rural Rides* by William Cobbett (1930).
22. Boyle's own *Remembrances* were edited by A.B. Grosert in 1986; see also Brian FitzGerald, *The Anglo-Irish: Cork, Ormonde, Swift* (1952) and *The Upstart Earl* (1982) by Nicholas Canny.
23. Wm S. Clark, *The Dramatic Works of Roger Boyle, Earl of Orrey* (1937).
24. Patricia Cockburn, *Pieces of Eight* (1985).
25. William Trevor, *Excursions in the Real World* (1993).
26. Daniel Corkery, *The Hidden Ireland* (1925).
27. Tr. Corkery, op. cit.
28. Tr. Dr Robert Dwyer Joyce in Corkery, op. cit.; for more on Mac Gearailt see Risteard Ó Foghlúdha (ed.), *Amhráin Phiarais Mhic Gearailt* (1905).
29. See Daphne Pochin-Mould, *Captain Roberts of The Sirius*.
30. See Cecil Woodham Smith, *The Great Hunger* (1962).
31. Charlotte G. O'Brien, *Light and Shade* (1878); *A Tale of Venice* (1880); *Dominic's Trials – An Irish Story* (1870).
32. See R. Welch, *A History of Verse Translation from the Irish 1789–1897* (1987).
33. See Sean O'Faolain, *The King of the Beggars* (1938); Oliver MacDonagh, *Daniel O'Connell* (2 vols) *The Hereditary Bondsman* (1988); *The Emancipist* (1991).

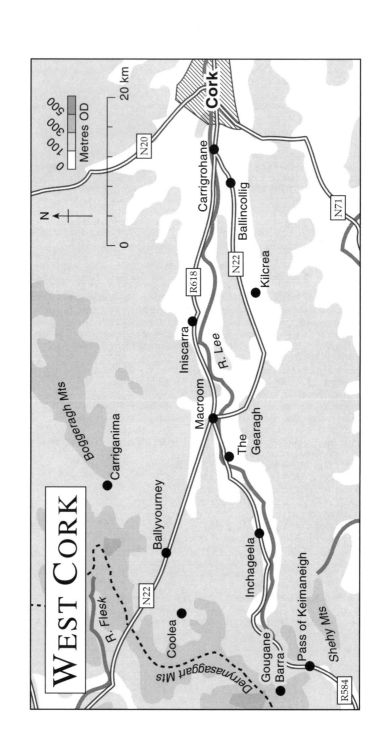

WEST CORK

Carrigrohane, Ballincollig, Iniscarra, The Gearagh, Macroom,
Carriganima, Ballyvourney, Coolea, Inchigeela, Gougane Barra,
Pass of Keimaneigh, Kilcrea

Missing from the map, the abandoned roads
Reach across the mountain, threading into
Clefts and valleys, shuffle between thick
Hedges of flowery thorn.
The grass flows into tracks of wheels,
Mowed evenly by the careful sheep;
Drenched, it guards the gaps of silence
Only trampled on the pattern day.

And if, an odd time, late
At night, a cart passes
Splashing in a burst stream, crunching bones,
The wavering candle hung by the shaft
Slaps light against a single gable
Catches a flat tombstone
Shaking a nervous beam in a white face

Their arthritic fingers
Their stiffening grasp cannot
Hold long on the hillside –
Slowly the old roads lose their grip. [1]

The barony of Muskerry is the country of old roads. The gaps of silence have not all been filled, as poet Eiléan Ní Chuilleanáin suggests in this evocation of a landscape no longer travelled. Yet the roads, the boreens and tracks leading into the hills, have their powerful singers. The mountainy townlands of West Cork have for centuries been rich in significance, sometimes as refuge, sometimes as inspiration.

The main road slicing through from Cork to Killarney only appears as a major route where it leaves the city behind and then at the other end as it enters the Kerry town of Killarney. Otherwise its twists and turns frustrate the motorist but satisfy the traveller eager to see beyond the hard margins and the traffic-calming measures.

It's important not to be too romantic about this most romantic of interiors. West Cork has its busy, modern, innovative towns. It has its large hotels as well as its small ones, its distinctive country homes as well as its cottages and cabins. The hydroelectric dam near Iniscarra may have produced a newly scenic route, but its main purpose is to provide power; the long lake and its drowned woods and farmhouses are incidental to that function. There may be small old farms in the rocky acres to the west, but most of the farming is thoroughly efficient and attuned to marketing and to Europe.

Yet – twilight on the road below this, the road through Aherla, the by-road to Kilcrea: the other world awaits the curious voyager. Along the Bride valley the shadows move and twist into the shapes of the past. At Coolea the hills hide a graveyard: I heard the keen there once while waiting for a funeral. It is an ancient sound. It drifted up through the trees as smoke drifts carrying alive the grief, it seemed, of ages.

Pattern days are still observed in this countryside: the shrines and holy wells are places of pilgrimage, the thorn bushes still flaunt the intercession-ary rags left behind by the faithful. In the heart of these heartlands the Cork writers set their stories, their plays, their verses. No one it seems can quite outgrow the mystic allure of the high valleys with tarns which turn blue under certain skies, black under others. The thick hedges of flowery thorn climb as far up the rock-face as they can, then collapse into a bouldered gush of water, cold as the caves. The rocks are clean and sheer, the fields are poor, stony, treacherous with bogs and banked with gorse, the grass-grown old roads disappearing into thickets of alder and hazel and sally bushes.

For years it seemed as if the desertion of West Cork, initiated by the Great Famine, would continue through this century too. Instead there has been a quiet revival with people finding reasons to stay here, to move here or at the very least to keep a foothold here, in small farms, craft-work, light industry. This may be a magical countryside of the past, but it is also rich with the excitements of the future.

Carrigrohane

He trod the dust in Cork and Poona as gaily as he polished stone till the dust reclaimed him. Lie gently, earth on one who was your own.

The inscription composed by the late Diarmuid Hurley of Cork was cut on this stone in the cemetery at Carrigrohane by Seamus Murphy (1907–75), author of *Stone Mad*.[2] The stone commemorates Isaac Forth, immortalised in that book as Danny Melt:

'Ah, well, there's a beginning and an end to all things', said the Gargoyle, on the way home one Friday. 'That's a nice thing happened this evening after all our time. The new broom made a good sweep. Athough, mind you, there are a few corners which seem to have escaped. He'll make a fortune out of the new lot of stonies he's going to bring in! 'Tis a hard thing, after all our time, to be told we are too old. An' Danny Melt supposed to be half-blind! Half-blind how are ye! He can nearly see round corners, but sure, they had to give some excuse. But I'm sorry for ye, Danny, after your thirty-three years.'

'I was that time there', said Danny. 'The same time Our Lord was on earth, in poverty an' suffering. And now I'm thrown on the rubbish heap. I wouldn't mind but I rocked that little caffler in his cradle, an' a cantankerous little divil he was. But sure, that's the way. 'Tis a long road that has no turning. But I'm as good a man as he has in the yard an' I'll have no trouble picking up a job.'

''Tis true,' said the Gargoyle. 'We may have had our little differences, but all the same, there isn't a man in the yard could turn a stone with you. We bankered some big stones in our day an' at a time when it had to be done with crowbars and planks ... But 'tis the gaffer I'm sorry for. He took it very badly, an' no wonder after his forty years' service. To be told after that time that you are no longer required is a blow. But I suppose it must come sooner or later. Anyway, the trade is nearly finished.'

'I told you that years ago,' said Danny. 'And you wouldn't believe me. The pre-cast concrete is going to wipe it out – door-blocks, window-heads, jambs – they can turn anything out in it, an' it does the job as well. People don't know the difference and, anyway, they haven't time to be thinking of that sort of thing. It's just slap it up and get it finished.'

'That may be,' said the Gargoyle, 'but 'tis a bad sign of the people ... We all know 'tis a question of money. Danny an' I were asked to come down in our wages, but we knew that was only the thin edge of the wedge. Some other excuse would have been found to gaff us off if that failed. But we're not done yet. If that gap is closed we'll open another.'

'Not a hope in hell,' said Danny Melt. 'Stone cutting is finished. 'Tis a back-number. But ye can talk about it till the cows come home, like ye always did.'

It is from those conversations till the cows came home that *Stone Mad* is composed, a threnody for the men of 'the dust', written at a time when their craft was about to disappear although their traces are left everywhere a stone has been raised above a grave, or a church, chapel or meeting-house built from quarried rock.

The book is an account of Murphy's apprenticeship. Born near Mallow but educated in Cork, he was influenced by Daniel Corkery and studied at the Crawford School of Art, winning the Gibson Bequest for a year's tuition in Paris and later developing his career as sculptor as well as stone-carver. His work will be found all over Ireland, and his many commissions included work for the Imperial War Graves Commission. His monumental busts and entablatures are in civic parks and offices of local and national governments, including the presidential residence at Áras an Uachtaráin in Dublin.

Describing him, the film-maker Louis Marcus writes:

... he was formed by an Ireland that is now as remote as only the recent past can be. It was the Ireland of an intellectual revival that promised a renaissance in life, art and thought ... As we know now, this broad ideal narrowed to a purely political aim and was lost altogether in the disenchantment of civil war. A frightened conservatism descended on Ireland for decades. Seamus was ever critical of this stagnation; as an artist, he felt its burden more than most. But he was never cynical. From some spring within himself he drew both the resilience to continue on his path and the optimism that marked his personality and his work.

His respect for 'that now-vanished fraternity of masons' recorded in *Stone Mad* was a response to

their reverence for the well-made thing, their insistence on the mastery of the hand before the mind and heart could properly speak. Seamus had to forge his own style just as much as those whose idiom was more ostentatiously 'original' ... his work preserves the things he stood for without flinching – the excellence that a few men once dreamt could be achieved for this island; and a synthesis of craft and art, of expression and feeling, towards which this uncertain age is still only groping. [3]

Stone Mad is a book which has many devotees; it is not presented as great literature yet it is considerably more than a memoir; it is not autobiograpy, although unconsciously it holds the essence of its author as well as of its subject. The stonies were craftsmen of a very particular kind; their methods, their attitudes, speech and histories, even their tools (the penny-faced hammer, for example) are recorded here with a simplicity which belies the philosophy of the book itself, and which captures the localised wit and comedy of craftsmen as confident of one another as the members of any bardic school.

View of Carrigrohane from *Lovely is the Lee* by Robert Gibbings

In a way to include Seamus Murphy in this chapter is to introduce him out of his place, which would be, perhaps, Wellington Road in Cork where he lived with his wife Maighréad, herself the daughter of the very fine sculptor Joseph Higgins of Youghal. Or Blackpool, where he had his studio and where he designed the Church of the Assumption and where *Stone Mad* is set. But Murphy keeps cropping up throughout the countryside – here in West Cork alone, for example, he is in Millstreet and Ballyvourney and Gougane Barra; his presence is unconfined.

Ballincollig

Carrigrohane leads into Ballincollig (the intervening traffic-island marked with the monumental sculpture by Michael Quain) which is now the largest town in the county, second in population only to the city itself. Lady

Catherine Tobin (1811–1903) was wife of Thomas Tobin of Ballincollig Powder Mills and lived at Oriel House. She published sketches and travel articles widely.

> *Flattery* I got for food
> In great Muscraídhe of Mac Diarmada,
> So that my chest dried up from thirst
> Until I reached Baile-an-Cholaig ...

The sarcastic poet from Kilcrohane, Aonghus Ruadh Ó Dálaigh, left the scorn of his tongue on the claims of the MacCarthys as noble overlords of Muskerry:

> The Clan MacCarthy are vain, but as deep as a churn;
> They grasp all you have, and give words in return.
> What good deeds you do them are written in water;
> But injure them once, and they doom you to slaughter.[4]

The libels of Ó Dálaigh – for which he was murdered – were believed to have been written at the commission of George Carew, lord president of Munster, victor of the Battle of Kinsale. Carew must have been particularly pleased at the slandering of the Clan MacCarthy; his pursuit and capture of the famed leader of this clan were crucial to the English defence of Munster which culminated at Kinsale.

Iniscarra

At the western end of Ballincollig town the road divides: straight on it leads directly to Macroom and then to Killarney; the right hand turn goes a little further inland to the village of Iniscarra. Caisleáin na hÍnshe (Castle Inch), the castle in the meadow by the river, is no longer visible; as the hydroelectric dam was built a few miles ahead the low-lying farmlands disappeared beneath the water, and with them went Castle Inch.

It was at Castle Inch that Florence MacCarthy (*c.* 1562–*c.* 1637) was confirmed as successor to his father Donogh MacCarthy Reagh, chief of Carbery – but as much more than that: he was acclaimed also as MacCarthy Mór, the Great MacCarthy, overlord of all the MacCarthy families. At this gathering his claim to be Lord of Muskerry was also conceded, so that in this one man was personified everything that could be claimed by the Clan MacCarthy.

In 1575 Sir Henry Sidney had gone on progress through Ireland, inviting the provincial magnates to meet him as his retinue moved from place to place, gathering them into his train as he went along. Those were the native chieftains into whose country neither the queen's writ nor the queen's deputy might venture, and Sidney's purpose was to meet them face to face so as to judge their character and loyalty and to impress them with the grandeur of her majesty's government.

> Two days before Christmas the stately train of the Deputy made its entry into the city of Cork. By this time it had collected every personage of note from the counties through which it had passed ... it thus chanced that, in addition to the rival houses of Ormond and Desmond, with the choicest gentlemen of their blood, this visit of the Deputy assembled within the city of Cork the three great chiefs of the Sept of the MacCarthys, with their wives and families. The Earl of Clancarty, by the Irish styled MacCarthy Mór, was accompanied by his countess, the sister of the Earl of Desmond, and his infant children ... No less than fourteen lords of counties, most of them his own race, attended him. The Lord of Muskerry, the wealthiest chieftain of the Sept, with a less attendance, and the Lord of the fertile lands of Carbery, Sir Donogh MacCarthy Reagh, both in especial favour with the Lord Deputy, were also there, the latter accompanied by his two sons, Florence and Dermod Moyle ...[5]

The reason the two chieftains were in special favour with Sidney was that they had pledged their allegiance to the crown. Three years later, when Florence was fifteen, his father died. It was vital to the English interests that he would continue what Donogh had begun in terms of that allegiance.

Much of Florence's life in Ireland was spent trying to regain, retain and regulate territories which were rightly his – but which had been appropriated by his enemies, some of them in his own family.

Florence might have slept more easily at Iniscarra if his restoration had come from the crown. Instead, his acclamation was being used by the Ulster Lords O'Neill, O'Donnell and Maguire as a statement in their march through Munster in preparation for their southern campaign against the English. Installed as head of his clan, Florence MacCarthy stood at the brink of disaster.

This MacCarthy lord, living for the moment within a few hour's walk of his clan's wealthiest family and strongest castle at Blarney, had spent his life trying to find a way of keeping a foot in three camps. He had to guard his own inheritance of Carbery to the south-west, he had to steer a path through the difficulties of his kinship with the Desmond interests, and he had to remain in contact with and on good terms with his most subtle and complex adversary, England's Queen Elizabeth and her representatives in Ireland.

At the time of his arrival at Iniscarra in 1600, these competing yet inter-linked loyalties were moving towards their military and historical climax late the following year at Kinsale.

Now thirty-seven, MacCarthy was already a veteran of war, diplomacy and survival. He had spent fourteen years in custody, most of them in the Tower of London. He was first cousin of the Earl of Desmond about whom rebellion was always a whisper and sometimes a roar. His father had been Sir Donogh MacCarthy Reagh of Carbery, his father-in-law was MacCarthy Mór, Earl of Clancarty, another kinsman had been Sir Cormac Mac Tieg of Muskerry.

Through these blood-lines Florence was in direct descent from Dermot, King of Desmond at the time of the Norman invasion in the twelfth century. That relationship was taken seriously by the English court (there is a geneal-ogy which shows that Elizabeth herself had MacCarthy blood: Dermot, King of Desmond, being an ancestor of Elizabeth, wife of Henry VII and mother of Henry VIII) and both the English and the native Irish recognised in him a vastly important element in their mutual struggle during the latter years of the Elizabethan conquest of Ireland.

Florence, according to his biographer, appeared before the world a linguist, a scholar, a subtle politician, a lawyer. He had been educated at home by the bards (in this case the Ó Dálaigh poets), professors and priests supported by his father, the other educational options of fosterage or tutors for the sons of Irish lords being unacceptable to Sir Donogh: '… the Irish chieftain well knew that in sending his son from him, he gave a hostage to his rulers, and that in domesticating a tutor within his family he maintained a spy.'[6]

Native succession to role and title followed through brothers and the sons of brothers. While Florence would eventually inherit his father's title it would not be until the last of his uncles died. But in his case even this claim had been complicated by Sir Donogh's decision to bring Florence, when lit-tle more than twelve, to serve in the English forces suppressing the Desmond rebellion. This pragmatic decision was tolerated but could not be approved by his people who would have been naturally sympathetic to the Desmond cause and aware, of course, that Florence was related to the Earl of Desmond.

Sir Donogh was succeeded by his brother Owen MacCarthy, although Flo-rence was bequeathed his father's great estates in Carbery. The destruction of the Desmonds in 1583 brought Florence to London, to court and to an annuity from the queen, and for a few years he moved easily between Ire-land and England.

But in the meantime MacCarthy Mór, the Earl of Clancarty, had no brothers. His son died while still a minor, and his heiress was Ellen, who had been with her father at that great gathering in Cork. Her sudden, secret mar-riage to Florence MacCarthy was not at all what the queen, determined to restrict the influence of the Irish lords, had planned as the future for Mac-

Carthy Mor's territories. The young couple were immediately imprisoned in Cork, Florence later being sent to the Tower of London.

Although Ellen escaped and was eventually to join Florence, he would remain in custody in London for the next eleven years. Then the queen sent MacCarthy home to rescue his barony from his inadequate uncle and predatory cousins; by reclaiming his people he would pacify them, and so, in a decision which later was to bewilder but not circumvent George Carew, lord president of Munster, Florence was freed from London and re-established in Munster.

By 1600 Carew's job was to anticipate and suppress the infiltration of Munster by the native lords of Ulster. The southward march of O'Neill and O'Donnell included this purposeful halt at Iniscarra; the restitution of Florence as clan leader by their approval was a deliberately political act and was recognised as such by Carew, who, notwithstanding the fact that Florence had a safe-conduct from the queen herself, invited him into the city of Cork where he was arrested and sent back to the Tower of London.

Although he lived to his mid-seventies Florence never saw Ireland again. In all he spent nearly fifty years in captivity of one kind or another, moving from the Tower to various other prisons around London, then to private but restricted houses and later again to a kind of liberty within the city itself. The letters collected by his biographer Daniel MacCarthy include his own statements, pleas and explanations; he comes alive too in the reports of Carew, of Cecil and Sidney and Norrys. In all these accounts from friends and enemies (and a surprising number of his enemies had some sympathy for him) – the man emerges: tenacious, subtle, cultured, cautious and brave. Iniscarra, which should have seen his victory, was his nemesis.

At Iniscarra the widening river makes an island of the little cemetery near the village.

> ... And June toppled backwards into Winter,
> The orchard became a white graveyard by a river,
> In the midst of the dumb whiteness all around me,
> The dark hole screamed loudly in the snow ...
>
> My mind was screwing itself endeavouring
> To comprehend the interment to the full
> When through the white tranquility gently flew
> A robin, unconfused and unafraid ...[7]

Seán Ó Riordáin (1916–77) was born in Ballyvourney where the Irish language, although fading as the common tongue of the community, had survived as the literary heritage of the area; it was his grandmother's everyday speech. After the death of his father the family moved to Iniscarra from where Seán, then fifteen, attended classes conducted in Irish at the North Monastery in Cork.

'Of our poets', writes Seán Ó Tuama,

> Seán Ó Riordáin seems to be more in the main classic European tradition than most others who have written verse in Ireland in the last fifty years. He stamps his own individual Irish personality on a western European mood and metaphysic which has been making itself felt since the time of Baudelaire ... That he is a 'modern' poet is due in the main to his own psyche, his special sensibility and the circumstances of his life.[8]

Those circumstances included the linguistic journey from his parents' home in Ballyvourney to that of his Irish-speaking grandmother, a journey as if from one world to another. They included also his employment in the offices of local government in Cork, his devotion to his mother and his chronic ill-health.

According to Ó Tuama, Ó Riordáin agonised endlessly in his work about his own personal dilemmas of faith and conscience, security and insecurity:

> This gives his poetry an overwhelming sense of search: at times a restless and agonised search, sometimes a witty intellectual search. His most memorable work is a handful of beautifully crafted lyrics, full of unique imagery, where his deep sense of terror and isolation is recorded.

Noting that his work has not yet been adequately translated, Ó Tuama believes that Ó Riordáin integrated in a new way fundamental aspects of European Catholic or post-Catholic sensibility with Irish tradition, bringing (with Ó Tuama's quotation marks) 'modern' literature in Irish into the mainstream 'modern' European tradition.

> Of his verse, one can say that the level and magnitude of Ó Riordáin's poetic achievement in general is remarkable, especially when one considers that the language he is using might have been given up for dead fifty years before he began to write. Few, if any other Irish poets since Yeats have composed so many lyrics bearing, as Ó Riordáin's best work does, the marks of high creative genius ... Unique also, within the Irish tradition he inherited, is the unflinching manner in which he makes his personal anguish and frustration the central matter of his poetic opus.

Thus 'Adhlacadh mo Mháthar' surprised and astonished those whose reading in Irish had taken in only traditional literature in that language:

On a frosty morning I went out
And a handkerchief faced me on a bush.
I reach to put it in my pocket
But it slid from me for it was frozen
No living cloth jumped from my grasp
But a thing that died last night on a bush,
And I went searching in my mind
Till I found its real equivalent:
The day I kissed a woman of my kindred
And she in the coffin, frozen, stretched. [9]

'There was also', wrote Seán Dunne (1956–95)

the poet Seán Ó Riordáin, *l'homme seul*. He was a shy figure in a rain-coat, his head bowed as he searched for his glasses before reading his poems to university audiences which always seemed to include a good many nuns. Isolated and ill, he became, more by reputation than acquaintance, a kind of exemplar: separate, sharp-eyed, odd, bothered, cantankerous, humorous. I went to his office in the Irish Department in UCC but could not muster the courage to knock. Had he answered, I would probably have had nothing to say. His presence was a stimulus in itself. [10]

Between Iniscarra and Macroom both banks of the Lee roll back into gentle pastoral landscape, the chosen subject of Alfred Allen (1925–) whose home at Ovens is passed as the main road sweeps westward. *Clashenure Skyline* (1970) and *Shades of a Rural Past* (1978) are among his collections of poetry, work which is distinguished by a style in which apparently simple technique is married to questioning insights; the landscape is carried in the verse according to a tradition of rural self-confidence.

The Gearagh

The flooded valley is exposed the closer the traveller gets to Macroom. The turn to the left just outside the town on the south bank of the river indicates the road to Bantry – a route which allows several options. Before any such decisions have to be made the first few miles of this route skirt the Gearagh, a man-made reservoir covering the remains of a post-glacial, alluvial oakwood.

To the unaccustomed eye the Gearagh, spreading from a defile with wooded banks, can look bleak even on the brightest day, yet it is in fact a lesson in recovery: 'It is hard to imagine what the area looked like before being flooded' writes Kevin Corcoran, a vast inland delta of inter-connecting, many-branched streams that encircled a maze of small and inaccessible islands, covered in oak forest …

Because the Gearagh was left to nature after being flooded, and not further tampered with, many of the plant species that had formerly occupied the ancient forest began to re-emerge from seed, re-colonising the marshy tracts and severed islands. Newly formed lagoons became sanctuaries for rare aquatic species that were being destroyed elsewhere, while the broad sheets of shallow water became a haven for migrant fowl, whose natural habitats are being vandalised by modern agriculture, industrial waste and ignorant developments. Defiantly, the trees too have begun to re-colonise the islands at the top of the reservoir, to form a water-locked, swampy woodland.[11]

Corcoran recalls the anguish of the people of this place when they had to leave it, and writes of one old man who refused to be driven from his farm but stayed on resolute and alone, marooned on his little island where one building remained. On a night of a great flood he was drowned as he tried to get back to his home by boat.

In the long grass of the Gearagh
You stretch and sleep
Your head at an angle to my head

A moth flits
And hovers above you
Makes a light brooch in your hair

Cows mooch in damp fields
Lazy heads lifted
When we pass on thin paths

Stumps of trees around us
A drowned forest and a drowned
Village called Annahala

Lichen on trees, moss on stones,
Sparrows – nifty commas –
Dart on the sky's wide page

I tell you of the man who rowed
Across the waters to his house

And drowned on his way home

Afternoon of perfume
Flowers crushed beneath feet
Scents yielded like secrets

Bog-cotton in a meadow
Lighter than your hair
Your fingers lighter than leaves

Your face smooth against mine
A slim wind between us
The ghost of an old argument

Scanning the lake for otters
We settle for paired swans
White porcelain among reeds

Islands stud the waters
Legions of the drowned
Raising their torn heads

Meadows shimmer with water
Tortoise-shell and meadow-brown
Butterflies in a haze of heat

I stroke your closed eyes
And kiss the lids, I nudge
The tip of each light lash.

Oak stumps everywhere
Suppurating wounds
The black days we have known

A heron stands
Sentry over water
Curled initial on vellum

As we cross old quarry roads
Hands linked like branches
Of rose-trees in a ballad [12]

The poet Seán Dunne was born in Waterford but having studied at University College Cork remained to live and work in the city. His poetry is collected in three publications: *Against the Storm* (1985), *The Sheltered Nest* (1992) and the posthumous *Time and the Island* (1996). An engaged and questioning personality, he became a journalist with *The Examiner* newspaper and also worked with the Triskel Arts Centre; his commitment to poetry was scrupulous but not austere and his work in other areas of literature (*The Cork Anthology* 1993, or the memoir *In My Father's House* 1991) was both adventurous and accommodating.

Macroom

Macroom is the geographical gatepost to West Cork. It grew where the Sullane river joins the Lee and stands on a plateau above the ten-arched bridge; all around it are the rocky foothills of what will become the Derrynasaggart Mountains, with the Shehy ranges to the south and the Boggeraghs to the north. The topographical change here is not dramatic: the town has a quiet civility and if there is a little more colour than might have been suggested in the more easterly towns, or if the street market has a certain natural gaiety, or the speech has a stronger, sharper edge to it, these are the only indications of a shift not merely of landscape but of mind.

Out of sheer politeness, for example, the town's American connections are extolled for the visitor: the thirteenth-century castle (its gateway remains showing signs of every architectural period since then, including this one) was taken by the MacCarthys a hundred years or so later and after the Cromwellian wars was given to Admiral Sir William Penn. His son, also William, lived here for some time as a boy and heard here the opinions of the Quaker Thomas Loe. Later, in Cork, to the outrage of his father, family and friends, Penn declared himself a Quaker, was imprisoned, grew understandably disenchanted with Ireland and with the main family home and obligations in England, and departed for America to become the founding father of Pennsylvania.[13]

When W.B. Yeats, as a director of the Abbey Theatre in Dublin, spoke somewhat ruefully about what he called 'the Cork realists' he was including the playwright T.C. Murray (1873–1959), who was born over a shop in Macroom's main street. Trained in Dublin as a teacher, he returned to work in Cork and in 1909 his first play *Wheel of Fortune* was presented at the Cork Little Theatre, which he had founded with Daniel Corkery. His play *Birthright* was produced at the Abbey in 1910; when this was taken on tour to America by the Abbey Players it was admired by Eugene O'Neill, whose influence may have helped Murray persist in his unsentimental attitude to Irish life. Certainly he did not succumb to the Yeatsian coils of Celtic mysticism, staunchly adhering instead to issues of land, family and religion as experienced and expressed especially by the rural communities he understood so well.

From 1915 to 1932 he worked as a headmaster in Dublin; his most famous play is *Autumn Fire* (1925) about an old man's marriage to a young woman, and others include *Aftermath* (1922) and one-act pieces such as *The Briary Gap* (1917) and *Spring* (1918). Vice-president of the Irish Academy of Letters, Murray also wrote *Spring Horizon* (1937), a memoir of his youth in the days of the Land League in Cork.

At the western end of the town, just before the castle, stands the town council office, the successor of the market-house which was one of the most famous buildings in Irish literary history.

> Mo ghrá go daingean tu!
> Lá dá bhfaca thu
> ag ceann tí an mhargaidh,
> thug mo shúil aire dhuit,
> thug mo chroí taitneamh duit,
> d'éalaíos óm charaid leat
> i bhfad ó bhaile leat.
>
> Is domhsa nárbh aithreach.[14]

> *My love forever!*
> *The day I first saw you*
> *At the end of the market-house,*
> *My eye observed you,*
> *My heart approved you,*
> *I fled from my father with you,*
> *Far from my home with you.*
>
> *I never repented it.*[15]

Yet this long resounding poem is a paean of regret. It was composed by Eileen O'Leary (*c.* 1743–*c.* 1800) on the death of her husband, Arthur, in 1773. The circumstances of his murder are variously reported: the Penal Laws in operation at the time meant that no Catholic might own a horse valued at more than £5 and Art O'Leary, a soldier and landowner, had a particularly fine mare.

At a race organised by the Muskerry hunt it outran that of the former high sheriff of Cork, Abraham Morris, who determined to possess it and who, on Art O'Leary's refusal to hand it over, had him killed near Macroom. As with most versions of such an event there is some truth in this story, which has at least an economy of approach to recommend it. But to do justice to the poem it must be read and understood within the literary as well as historical context from which it springs.

The long tradition of the wake, with the keen or caoineadh as its central constituent, is not exclusive to Ireland, where it has lasted from prehistory. Several people are involved, usually but not exclusively women (Art's father as well as his sister speaks in this lament). 'In Ireland', writes Seán Ó Tuama,

> the keen was typically a series of incantatory extempore verses lamenting the dead person, chanted to a recitative type air, and punctuated at regular intervals by wailing cries. It was mostly sung/recited over the corpse at the wake; but keening might also be heard, for instance, on route to the burial or at the graveyard ... [16]

The keen listed the achievements, family connections, and personal attributes of the dead.

A Catholic, O'Leary was a member of the minor nobility in the Ive Leara district. Educated abroad, he served as an officer with the armies of Hungary, and was something of a law unto himself. That may have been part of his attraction for Eileen, whose obedient first marriage to a very elderly husband had ended in her husband's death shortly before that first meeting at the market-house in Macroom.

Art was home on leave at the ancestral O'Leary lands near Rathleigh, outside the town. Eileen was the daughter of the O'Connells of Derrynane (and an aunt of that Daniel O'Connell who was to become known as 'The Liberator', the architect of Catholic Emancipation in Ireland). Her title as the composer of the 'Caoineadh' is always given as Eibhlín Dhubh Ní Chonaill – Black-haired Eileen O'Connell.

Her family home in Derrynane in Co. Kerry was one of the very few mansions to survive the destruction of the native Irish aristocracy in the sixteenth and seventeenth centuries. The life of such a house was self-sufficient but also sophisticated, there was much social and economic trafficking with France and Spain, and Eileen's first marriage would have been arranged with as much care for the family fortunes and status as for Eileen's own well-being.

By no stretch of the imagination could a suitor such as Art O'Leary be considered a match for the daughter of such a house; he was impetuous, rebellious, proud and perhaps violent in temper, hardened in battle, with a reputation as a womaniser. He was also several years younger than Eileen. Yet as the poem makes clear, she left her father's house for him and never regretted doing so.

Not long after their marriage Art became involved in the feud with Abraham Morris. As a soldier Art had continued to wear his sword in public, an act forbidden to Catholics. To this offence was added the matter of the bay mare, Morris's attempt to appropriate it, a skirmish between the two men and the outlawing of O'Leary.

As the poem recounts, from then on his visits to Eileen and their two children at their home were fleeting and furtive. Until, on a morning in early May in 1773, he set out to resolve this dilemma by killing Morris. Warned in time to set an ambush for O'Leary, Morris escaped, but O'Leary was shot as he rode, on his mare, to what he thought was safety near the village of Carriganima, between Macroom and Millstreet.

'Some of these verses are still being recited in the Irish-speaking districts of Cork and Kerry ... In the two hundred years since their composition various verses must, of course, have been added to or altered.'[17] Ó Tuama explains that two extended versions of the lament were written down in manuscript in the nineteenth century from the recitations of a professional keening woman, Norry Singleton. She had lived to a great age and the recitations were separated by as many as seventy years or so, but Ó Tuama's dedicated research made him 'fairly confident' that Norry Singleton's first version, in particular, 'is a close approximation to Eileen Dubh's original lament ...'

> This kind of literature above all is a collaborative event; while I am personally confident that Norry Singleton has transmitted most of Eileen Dubh's lines to us (if she herself has added a little creatively to them, that, for me, is not a critical issue). The only critical issue, I would submit for anybody who values literature in itself, is that the best version of the poem as a poem (within its own tradition) be provided ... 'The Lament for Art O'Leary' emerges finally not alone as a powerful dramatic lyric, but also as an absorbing documentary of a tragic happening.[18]

Certainly, the many translations of this long poem coincide as if it were composed by a single voice; it is too long to give in full in a volume such as this, and readers will find other versions in English or the original in Irish elsewhere. But for its evocation of this townland, of the people of the times, of the life lived and the enemies made by the O'Learys, of the passionate relationship between Eileen and her husband, and for its unwavering emotional authority, the following excerpts reward attention. (The numerals indicate the sequence of the extracted verses):

III

My friend forever!
My mind remembers
That fine spring day

How well your hat suited you,
Bright gold banded,
Sword silver-hilted –
Right hand steady –
Threatening aspect –
Trembling terror
On treacherous enemy –
You poised for a canter
On your slender bay horse.
The Saxons bowed to you,
Down to the ground to you,
Not for love of you
But for deadly fear of you,
Though you lost your life to them
Oh my soul's darling.

V

My friend you were forever!
When they will come home to me,
Gentle little Conor
And Farr O'Leary, the baby,
They will question me so quickly,
Where did I leave their father.
I'll answer in my anguish
That I left him in Killnamartyr.
They will call out to their father;
And he won't be there to answer.

VII

My friend you were forever!
I knew nothing of your murder
Till your horse came to the stable
With the reins beneath her trailing,
And your heart's blood on her shoulders
Staining the tooled saddle
Where you used to sit and stand.
My first leap reached the threshold,
My second reached the gateway,
My third leap reached the saddle.

VIII

I struck my hands together
And I made the bay horse gallop
As fast as I was able,
Till I found you dead before me
Beside a little furze-bush.
Without Pope or bishop,
Without priest or cleric
To read the death-psalms for you,
But a spent old woman only
Who spread her cloak to shroud you –
Your heart's blood was still flowing:
I did not stay to wipe it
But filled my hands and drank it.

A passage introduces the voice of Art O'Leary's sister whose verses accuse
Eileen of sleeping through his wake; this is Eileen's response:

XI

My friend and my lamb;
You must never believe it,
Nor the whisper that reached you,
Nor the venomous stories
That said I was sleeping.
It was not sleep that was on me,
But your children were weeping,
And they needed me with them
To bring their sleep to them.

XIX

My friend and my pleasure!
When you went out through the gateway
You turned and came back quickly,
You kissed your two children,
You kissed me on the forehead,
You said 'Eileen, rise up quickly,
Put your affairs in order
With speed and with decision.
I am leaving home now

And there's no telling if I'll return'.
I mocked this way of talking,
He had said it to me so often.

XX

My friend and my dear!
Oh bright-sworded rider,
Rise up this moment,
Put on your fine suit
Of clean, noble cloth,
Put on your black beaver,
Pull on your gauntlets.
Up with your whip;
Outside your mare is waiting.
Take the narrow road east,
Where the trees thin before you,
Where men and women will bow before you,
If they keep their old manners –
But I fear they have lost them.

XXII

My friend and my lamb!
Arthur O'Leary,
Of Connor, of Keady,
Of Louis O'Leary,
From west in Geeragh,
And from east in Caolchnoc,
Where berries grow freely
And gold nuts on branches
and great floods of apples
All in their seasons.
Would it be a wonder
If Ive Leary were blazing
Besides Ballingeary
And Gougan of the saint
For the firm-handed rider
That hunted the stag down,
All out from Grenagh
When slim hounds fell behind?
And oh clear-sighted rider,

What happened last night?
For I thought to myself
That nothing could kill you
Though I bought your habit.

XXXI

My love and my darling!
If my cry were heard westwards
To great Derrynane
And to gold-appled Capling,
Many swift, hearty riders
And white-kerchiefed women
Would be coming here quickly
To weep at your waking,
Beloved Art O'Leary.

XXXV

My love and my dear!
Your stooks are standing,
Your yellow cows milking;
On my heart is such sorrow
That all Munster could not cure it,
Nor the wisdom of the sages.
Till Art O'Leary returns
There will be no end to the grief
That presses down on my heart
Closed up tight and firm
Like a trunk that is locked
And the key is mislaid.

XXXVI

All women out there weeping,
Wait a little longer;
We'll drink to Art son of Connor
And the souls of all the dead,
Before he enters the school –
Not learning wisdom or music
But weighted down by earth and stones.[19]

The places invoked in this lament are still accessible to the traveller; the Gearagh has already been described, and on the road between Macroom and Millstreet to the north-west lies Carriganima, with Kilnamartra to the south-west of Macroom.

Carriganima

Carriganima was the childhood home of Fr Peadar Ó Laoghaire (1839–1920), author of the novel *Séadna* which was widely recognised at the time of its publication in 1904 as the first example of modern literature in the Irish language.

Ó Laoghaire's home was surrounded by the remnants of the Gaeltacht area which was also significant in the life and work of Seán Ó Riordáin, except that in the priest's boyhood the decline, while noticeable, would not have seemed terminal. The novel first appeared in the pages of *The Gaelic Journal* (an influential publication appearing from 1882), and in book form in 1904. Ó Laoghaire's story concerns a country shoe-maker who is forced by a series of unfortunate circumstances to sell his soul to the devil. This is of course the stuff of folk-tale and to a degree the novel maintains the style of the lore heard around the firesides of country homes. None of Ó Laoghaire's later novels achieved the same success as *Séadna* but he continued to write versions of Irish folk and fairytales as well as social and religious observations (including memoirs of the Great Famine). Above all, his work guided the attention of both writers and readers to the Irish language as a medium for fiction; he is still regarded as crucial to the development of what has become an energetic force in modern literature in Ireland.

Ballyvourney

In recent years the town of Millstreet has emerged from its former sleepy ambience to accommodate the extremely popular international equestrian events held there annually. Surrounded by hills and on the high road to Killarney the town is no longer somewhere simply to be passed through. At the Macroom side, a narrow road cuts through the Derrynasaggart mountains to Ballymakeera, and a little beyond is the village of Ballyvourney.

Julia Georgina Mary Kirchhoffer (1855–78) was a daughter of the glebe in Ballyvourney and was a writer of poems and essays published in *Lyra Hibernica Sacra* (with an introduction by M. Havergal) in 1885. Donncadh Ó Laoghaire (1877–1966) Gaelic scholar, poet, teacher and musician was a native of Ballyvourney, and so was the Irish-language poet Séamus Ó Céileachair (1916–).

The patron saint of this area, close to the mountainy borders with Kerry, is Gobnait, whose shrine here includes the site of her sixth-century nunnery, still a place of pilgrimage. The cemetery on the hillside now includes the graves of the poets Seán Ó Riordáin and Seán Dunne.

Coolea

Also buried here are composer Seán Ó Riada and his wife Ruth, who came to live in the village of Cúil Aodha (Coolea), on the high road from Ballyvourney to Kilgarvan in Co. Kerry. In this little hamlet where the Barr dínse and Ínse Mhor rivers meet the Sullane the ancient Dámhscoil Mhuscraí, the Muskerry bardic school, is still honoured each year. Part of that tradition was writer Donncha Ó Céileachair (1918–60), who was involved with the production of Tomás de Bhaldraithe's important Irish-English dictionary (1959). It was his father Domhnall Bán Ó Céileachair who had dictated the autobiography *Scéal mo Bheatha* (1940).[20]

Seán Ó Riada (1931–71) was born in Cork because his mother, a Creedon from Kilnamartra near Macroom, had already suffered several miscarriages and travelled from her home in Co. Clare to Cork city in a bid to ensure a safe delivery. The Macroom connection encouraged Seán when he was appointed to the music department at University College Cork, to search for a house in what remains of the West Cork Gaeltacht – the Irish-speaking district which has survived to this day.[21]

It is difficult to describe briefly the impact on the Irish public of the film scores written by Ó Riada which he based on traditional Irish airs and songs; these in themselves were familiar to many people, but their heroic potential was unimagined until his orchestral arrangements transformed them. At the same time Ó Riada was central to the popular revival of Irish traditional music, until then confined either to the village-hall conventions of the *ceilidhe* band or to the more remote and specialised usages of the *sean-nós* (old style) singers.

In Dublin he had formed the group Ceoltóirí Chualann which won both national and international acclaim; also a composer within the classical European tradition and an important figure in national musical circles Ó Riada bridged the gap between the small, Irish-speaking community and the cosmopolitan life and society of the capital without apparent difficulty.

This was a time of unforgettable cultural excitement; group after group of young men and women were singing Irish ballads and playing Irish airs with an unusual respect for authenticity. It was a time of discovery; the skills were always there, but now the atmosphere was one of intellectual sharing, of competitive provenance. From those times came groups such as The Chieftains and De Danann; Ireland rediscovered at least some of its heart-music and made it famous in a way which was utterly contradictory to the style of, for example, Moore's Melodies. These new music-makers exposed the spine of history running through the country's musical heritage; even local history took on a new edge.

Ó Riada was not a man of one school or fashion, and his original compositions moved with authority between conventions. But at Cúil Aodha he wrote two masses which incorporated the songs of the district and which also resurrected ancient prayers and by putting them to music ensured their survival. Parts of the Ó Riada masses are now sung in schools all over Ireland.

Ó Riada's choir, Cór Chúil Aodha, can still be heard in the local church; sometimes this choir, now led by his son Peadar Ó Riada, gives concert performances in Ireland and abroad. Its style is ornamented only by timbre; the words and music have a relationship which is as soul-shivering as Palestrina but which is authentic to the locale, to the devotional tradition of the people and to their language.

Seán Lucy (1931–) was professor of modern English at UCC until he left to teach in America. His 'Unfinished Sequence for Seán Ó Riada' is one of the national outpouring of literary compositions resulting from the early death of an artist whose impact on the country was immense during his lifetime and which, assessed and re-assessed in the years since then, still seems to resound from this small village set in the upland valley in the Derrynasaggart mountains.

VII Homo Ludens

And he told this story
of the old singer and the tape recorder:
of how the old man listened to his own voice
while fierce anxiety turned down his mouth
until he heard his strengthening voice
move into life again
Then sat with concentration till the song was over,
flung his cap on the floor between his boots
crying,
'I'll never die!'

Another night Seán sat down at the piano
when we were drinking poitín and pints of stout
and played that tune to me for the first time,
that air of pride and loss,
of the sharp love that has accepted loss.
And in his hands our deadly lasting sadness
became acceptable
so I was moved to tears;
not drunk but steady,

I cried
and when he finished cursed him saying, 'You bastard,
you took me by surprise.'

He stood up with his fingers round my arm
smiling and laughing:
pleased with my understanding,
more pleased by his power,
most deeply pleased by music
by the thing itself.

One afternoon he said,
A man should dance on his own floor.

And he danced. [22]

Inchigeela

The closer hinterland of Macroom includes the villages of Ballingeary and
Inchigeela, of Reenanaree and Toons Bridge:

Less than two hours later I got off my bicycle on the hillock outside
Inchageelah, always afterwards to be my mark of arrival in the true
West. Beyond the first foothills, across the loose stone walls of the road,
the outcropping rock, the sparse, wind-torn trees, the first few tiny fields
excavated painfully by generations of cottiers out of a hard, infertile,
sweat-making land softened only by the reed-edged lake, I saw the
smoke-blue mountains now quite near. On their peaks white clouds,
larger far than themselves, rose into the blue sky. I heard over my head a
lark trilling invisibly. When I saw and felt all this, and knew that all
about me people spoke an ancient tongue, that I could as yet only partly
interpret, I experienced the final obliteration of time that turns a
moment into eternity ... I passed through my mirror into reality. I ped-
alled on past the village, on beside its lake, now appearing, now
disappearing, past small white cottages, through the village of Beal-atha-
'n-Ghaorthaidh, after which I came on the Lee again, now a mere rocky
stream, until I came to the farm and farmhouse, called Tuirin Dubh,
where I was to stay ... [23]

Remembering Inchigeelagh and Ballingeary, Sean O'Faolain in *Vive Moi!*
notes that he is cycling not only towards a language but towards his love:
'... I heard a girl's laugh from behind the fuchsias, and looking through it I

saw Eileen's brown eyes laughing at me between its scarlet bells … she looked at me as I did at her, quizzically and affectionately, our barrier and our bond.'

The rapture of this experience however, yielding though it does the hill-top climbs at Gougane Barra, the change of his name from Whelan to O'Faolain, the days in the village studying the language, the nights on the lake if the moon was up – that rapture was not enough to revive the 'ancient tongue': 'So the old life dies, the old symbols wither away, and I and my like who warmed our hands at the fires of the past are torn in two as we stand on the side of the bridge and look back in anguish at the doomed Ireland beyond it.'

In the townland of Garrynapeaka, in the district of Inchigeelagh, in the parish of Iveleary, in the barony of West Muskerry, in the county of Cork, in the province of Munster – as he magniloquently styles his address, lives the Tailor.

His small whitewashed cottage, with its acre of ground, stands at the brow of a hill, at the side of a road which winds and climbs into a deep glen of the mountains bordering Cork and Kerry. [24]

The Tailor – who indeed had been a tailor, once upon a time – was Tadhg Ó Buachalla, and with his wife Ansty was the subject of *The Tailor and Ansty*, written by Eric Cross and published, to the consternation of the district and the outrage of the government, in 1942.

The day was ended. All the labours of the day were done. The shutters were drawn across and the door was closed against the night. The lamp on the wall was lit. The sign of all these things was that Ansty was at last still, and was sitting by the fire gazing into the heart of it.

'People do often say that a man who is smart is as wise as King Solomon, and I have always heard tell that King Solomon was the wisest man that ever lived. But I have always had my doubts about that too,' mused the Tailor.

'You see he had ten thousand wives, and I can't put the two things together rightly in my mind, so that they make sense.'

'Ten thousand wives! Glory be!' echoes Ansty, automatically.

Then she repeats it. 'Ten thousand wives!' A note of interest has come into her voice, and she wakes up from her fire-gazing. Slowly she reckons up on her finger-tips, ignoring the thousands, for thousands are in the domain of heaven and hell and London and America. They are merely words. They do not exist. She counts back the ten again and springs into activity.

'Ten thousand wives! Hould, you ould divil! It's your beads you ought to be telling instead of your jokes.'

'I've reckoned it up, and no matter how frolicksome a man might be it would take him nearly on thirty years of nights, without having any holiday at all, to get his conjugal rights from the lot of them.'

'Thirty years of nights? Without a holiday? Glory be!' Ansty ponders, bewildered by the powers of reckoning. 'Thirty years of nights, and he a king? ... King!' she spits with contempt. 'King, am bostha! That wasn't a king. He must have been an ould tomcat ... Thirty years of nights! The Lord save us ...'

'Of course, being a king he could get what help he liked, but what the hell was the use of that? That only makes matters worse and makes him out to be a bigger class of a fool still. What sense is there in a man getting married if he is going to let someone else have all the fun? So I have never been able to make out rightly if he was the wisest man or the biggest damn fool the world has ever known.'

'Thirty years of nights!' still echoes and swirls around in Ansty's mind. She chuckles to herself and repeats the phrase again and again. 'Thirty years of nights! Ring a dora!'

'Then he must have been pretty busy besides, for kings were no fun in those days. They had a lot to do.'

'No fun in those days? Gon rahid! Have you taken leave of your senses entirely? Thirty years of nights. Ten thousand wives. And he says they had no fun in those days! That for the senseless talk by him who thinks he's the whole push. No fun in those days, indeed!' Ansty is almost paralysed with contempt, but the Tailor pays no attention at all to her. The conversation is on a plane far above her level ...

'Marriage is a strange thing when you come to look at it rightly. First of all a man is clean mad to get married, and when he is married he wonders what the hell happened to him.'

'How well you got married yourself', asserts Ansty.

At last the Tailor pays attention to her.

'Thon amon dieul! was there ever a day since that I didn't regret it?' he asks, as though the question was barely worth asking. 'Anyway,' he adds after a pause, 'I was only "alludin".'

From this allusion the Tailor goes on to give an account of how marriages were made in that time, in that countryside. And although the Tailor was a story-teller, with occasional wild fancies to colour his anecdotes, and as firm a grasp on the likelihood of supernatural happenings as on the regular arrival of his government pension, his presentation of the facts of rural life as he and Ansty knew them was accurate and valuable. It was this lode of country wisdom, laced with the conclusions of his own life's encounters, which drew people to him from several cities. With them came others, some to be friends for life, and among them came Newry-born Eric Cross (1905–80), the Boswell to the Tailor's Johnson.

The group of friends included Seamus Murphy the sculptor, Nancy Mac-Carthy the chemist, Fr Traynor, known as 'the Saint', from Dublin, and Frank O'Connor; when Cross's book appeared they were all delighted and Nancy MacCarthy went out to the cottage to read them the enthusiastic reviews.

Frank O'Connor explains what happened next:

> But we were all too innocent to anticipate the effect the book would have on Mr de Valera's well-educated government. It was banned as being 'in its general tendency indecent'. I didn't mind their saying that about my own work. After all, you don't take up a dangerous trade like literature in Ireland without developing the hide of a rhinoceros and renting a house in a strategic spot with direct access to the sea. What alarmed me was that the Tailor and Ansty lived in a mountain townland where people still believed in the fairies. It wasn't only an unpleasant situation, it could be a dangerous one …
>
> The man [who defended the book] was a Protestant landlord, Sir John Keane, who tabled a motion in the Senate condemning the Censorship Board. Everyone interested either in censorship or in Irish public life would do well to get hold of the four day debate in the Senate Proceedings for 1943. Reading it is like a long slow swim through a sewage bed.
>
> Keane insisted on reading from the book over the impassioned protests of the other senators who dreaded – it is on the record – that pornographers would buy the proceedings of the Irish Senate as an anthology of evil literature, and that prize collection of half-wits ordered the quotations to be struck from the record … [25]

The chief government spokesman was Professor William Magennis of the National University of Ireland; when the government had proposed him as a member of the Board of the Abbey Theatre, W.B. Yeats said he would rather close the theatre altogether than accept him. Instead Magennis was appointed to the Censorship Board.

In Ansty he saw 'what in the language of American psychology is called a moron – '; in the book itself he recognised 'a campaign going on in England to undermine Christianity. It is financed by American money. The society that is the main agent in the endeavour to put in paganism instead of the Christian creed and practice includes Professor Joad and George Bernard Shaw.'

Hilarious as this may seem now, it reflects an almost hysterical conviction among some Irish legislators of the time that freedom from English domination of Ireland could never end until Ireland's literature was purged of that country's religious and cultural influence.

For instance, the *Catholic Bulletin* in 1935 carried an article by Conor Malone which declared that

> English literature in the mass, even as done in our schools and colleges today, is a poisonous substance, nationally and religiously considered. Its whole line of writers from Bacon to Macaulay and from Spenser to Wordsworth, Tennyson, Masefield, drips at every pore with intellectual and moral poison.

Fr T. Corcoran, a member of the Dáil Commission on Education and Jesuit professor of education at the National University in Dublin believed that the aim of English studies in Ireland should be merely functional; modern English literature, he said, was rarely of structural merit, and its prose, in particular, was amorphous in form and indeterminate in outline. To eliminate any possibility of contamination by the Protestant ethos which was carried in such writing he made a case for the teaching of English in Irish schools through the translations of classics of European literature, thus emptied of English ideas, in no way penetrated by English thought.[26]

View of Inchigeela from *Lovely is the Lee* by Robert Gibbings

At the same time the determination of the Fianna Fail government to restore Irish as the spoken language of the entire population aggravated distrust of English against which, as a Minister for Education said in 1941, 'a most intense war' would have to be carried out if Irish was to replace it. It was the cultural paranoia of convictions such as these which influenced the Irish Censorship Board and even the Irish government in 1943.

Ironically enough both spoke Irish as natives, the Tailor especially having a rich vocabulary and a fine store of inherited folklore, the very material the government was trying to enshrine. Parliamentary proceedings were published in the newspapers and were read by the neighbours of the Tailor and Ansty.

But the Tailor and Ansty had to live through it all. To all intents and purposes they were boycotted. Each week, Guard Hoare, an old friend of theirs, cycled out to see them from Ballingeary – a warning to hooligans. One afternoon three priests appeared and forced the old man on to his knees at his own hearth and made him burn his copy of the book – 'eight and sixpence worth' as Ansty said to me. To her, eight and sixpence was an awful lot of money ... Traynor and I motored down to see them, and when we were leaving we found the front door jammed. Some hooligans had jammed the branch of a tree between the latch and the wall, and Jackie, their son, had to climb through the little window to release us. Ansty was hysterical, and the Tailor patted her gently. 'Easy, girl, easy!' he whispered. 'At our age there is little the world can do to us.'[27]

Gougane Barra

Both Tim Buckley and his wife Anastasia lived close to Gougane Barra and are now buried there, under a headstone which shames the prudes and puritans. Designed and cut by Seamus Murphy, it gives their names with the simple added inscription: 'A star danced, and under that I was born'.[28]

Also buried at Gougane is their friend Fr Tim Traynor, whose grave is on the green island from which, so many hundred years ago, St Finbarr is said to have left his monastery to follow the rising river as far as its meeting with the sea at Cork.

Five miles above Ballingeary Gougane (pronounced Googawn) is reached. Gougane Barra, a valley withdrawn, a garden enclosed, the holiest place I know. Here, by this quiet pool, where, for a thousand years, tired souls have prayed, there is the peace that passes all understanding. Mountains on all sides rise twelve hundred feet above the lake, forming a vast amphitheatre whose floor is silver. Small emerald fields dot the margin of the lake. Above them gigantic boulders split from the purple hills pile high.

Day after day I climb the hills. Heather and heath, heath and heather, cotton-grass, loosestrife, and myrtle. Lichens on the rocks, exquisite minute chalices dusted with silver, and miniature ivory antlers crested with crimson, springing through the stellate moss. Stars of the butterwort and clusters of London pride in the crannies. Dark pools whose lights shine blue. Bogs deep with sphagnum moss, peat-forming pockets in the groins of the hills. With each step upward a wider horizon. So it should be with life; our outlook ever widening towards the infinite rather than narrowing to the vanishing point of our own identities.

And from the summit, vistas of sea and land, of infinite cloud-spread sky. Here one may walk and hear a voice that tells of order in a seeming chaos. [29]

Of Robert Gibbings' several books two are about Cork – *Lovely is the Lee* (1945) and *Sweet Cork of Thee* (1952). Soldier, artist and writer, Gibbings (1889–1958) was reared at Carrigrohane near Cork city where his father was rector. His novel *John Graham, Convict* (1937) is said to have inspired Patrick White's novel *A Fringe of Leaves*. A great traveller, he is best known as the author of accounts of journeys made along rivers: *Sweet Thames Run Softly* or *Coming Down the Wye*, for example. Like these, his books on Cork and the Lee are illustrated by his distinctive engravings. He is buried beside the Thames in the churchyard at Long Wittenham, Oxford.

His epithalamion for Cork, for the west of the county and especially for Gougane Barra, introduces the reader to a steep-sided glen set deep in the heart of the mountains south-west of Macroom. A rough triangle could be drawn from Ballyvourney to Inchigeela, with Gougane Barra as its apex and Ballingeary on a twist in the river before it swells into the lake.

The trouble in Ireland is not the getting to a place but the getting from it. It would seem that all roads lead to your destination. Can you tell me where this road takes me? asked a friend of mine in County Clare. 'Begor, ma'am, it will take you to anywhere in the world you want to go,' was the reply. The trouble lies in getting away after you have arrived. I once dropped in on a stranger for a cup of tea and I stayed with him for a fortnight. In 1944 I went to Gougane Barra for a fort-night and I stayed there seven months. Five years later I went there in the spring for another fortnight and stayed there most of the summer. What with the lake and the island and the mountains and the Cronins I seemed to get anchored. [30]

The spring which floods the lake at Gougane Barra is the source of the river Lee; the reputation of the island depends on Finbarr, patron saint and possible founder of Cork city. The little hermitage is a seventeenth-century relic of the seventh-century monastery, preserved by The Revd Denis O'Mahony (d. 1700) who also rebuilt the courtyard with its adjacent cells, living in one of them until his death, after which he was buried here.

View of Gougane Barra from *Lovely is the Lee* by Robert Gibbings

For those who knew Gougane, or Valley Desmond, before the Forestry Commission moved in during the last half of this century, the dramatic glacial valley has been improved at the cost of much of its intimidating grandeur. Now a National Park, its heights have been made more accessible to walkers with a road (pot-holed here and there) taking cars into the heart of the massif.

The levels are provided with picnic tables, a thatched hut in the idiom of the African kraal provides toilet facilities (along with other shelters in the forest), and coniferous afforestation has softened the outlines and imposed monotony where wilderness had triumphed. Here and there the tall stands of pine impose a tenebrous atmosphere, but elsewhere the timber is either withering or felled; on the road approaching Gougane from Ballingeary the effects of cropping the conifers are sadly obvious. Around the lake the laurels, hollies, and silver birches surge from the mossed earth, grazed by impassive sheep.

The source of the Lee is well labelled here, but the cataracts which fling themselves into the tarn seem less impetuous, thin shadows now of J.J. Callanan's verses:

> There is a green island in lone Gouganebarra,
> Where Allua of song rushes forth as an arrow;
> In deep-valleyed Desmond a thousand wild fountains
> Come down to that lake from their home in the mountains …

Callanan too is buried on the island, where a modern extension to a well-made pastiche Hiberno-Romanesque church is an unfortunate intrusion. Roads and car-parks and other amenities may be necessary, but the romantic loneliness of the valley has been replaced by a prettiness which is almost disappointing. Still, for the walkers at least, there are heathery upland routes which, with persistence, yield wonderful views over the peninsulas to the south, as well as opportunities to see unusual plants, with great drifts of bog-myrtle and the remnants of the birch and hazel woods clinging to the escarpments. Oaks once grew here in the valley; the new forests have banished light from the undergrowth but a grove of deciduous larch has allowed the regrowth of native woodland plants.[31]

Perhaps in a way it is appropriate enough that this ancient site has lost its mystical isolation now that the saint's presence here has been proved to be something of a fantasy. Cork's St Finbarr emerged as a scholarly personality during a political crisis in ecclestiastic affairs involving England, Ireland and Rome during the very late eleventh century when sees were properties of immense importance.

At that time the shrines of particular saints implied a kind of ownership, and even wealth, as shrines invited pilgrims and patrons. Well endowed with friaries, monasteries and hospitals, Cork already had a devotional cult of St Finbarr, but the accretion of character, provenance and creativity which developed around him was more the result of stage-management than native faith.

There was a real Finbarr, but he had nothing to do with Cork and certainly not with the foundation of the city. He was from the Ards peninsula in the North of Ireland and his followers established a series of penitential monasteries, of which Gougane Barra is believed to have been one. His life was written by Irish scholars in Cork at the end of the twelfth century, which made him available to the local prelates as an important argument for the integrity of their authority. This whole fascinating process is explored by Pádraig Ó Ríain in his *Beatha Bharra: St Finbarr of Cork, the Complete Life* (1994).[32]

We loved this valley, lake, ruined chapel and rude cloister because of their enclosure, their memories, and their silence. Many times then and in after years we entered the silent dead-end coom to climb the mountain beyond. Once we got lost there in a summer fog, aiming for the minute loch up there called the Lake of the Speckled Trout, dark as ink and cold as ice water, visited otherwise only by mountain sheep. When we reached the top of the coom after some tough climbing, the fog lifted and we came on another valley, and a vast view westward across other mountaintips far over the sunset sea. On those fortresses what could touch us? We enjoyed among them what I may well call a juvenile fantasy of grown desire, planning tiny cottages on either side of this lost valley or that, facing one another, so that by day we would descend to the lake and be together there and by night see, each, the other's beckoning light across the darkness of the glen.[33]

Sean O'Faolain describes Gougane Barra as he remembers making that cultural pilgrimage for the sake of the Irish language; he uses the location also, and very significantly, in several short stories, most notably in 'The Silence of the Valley'.[34]

The fastness in which the east-flowing river Lee has its source is also the bedrock of the Ouvane river which runs southward from these mountains. The road which tracks its course goes on to Kealkill and thence to Ballylicky with a choice of Bantry or Glengarriff after the junction with the main highway on the coast. That choice to be made at the edge of the sea feels as if a new country has been reached, so absolute seems the interior through which the journey has just been made.

For if the decision is to turn southwards to the sea then the sharp angles of the road lose their margins, the grass disappearing into rock, the rock soaring to looming heights as if to meet like stone trees overhead, so narrow is the defile. This is the Pass of Keimaneigh (Céim an Fhia, the leap of the deer):

This pass runs through a wild and magnificent gap in the Shehy Mountains and is one of the finest and most savage things of its kind in the whole of Ireland. It is almost a mile long and is bounded on each side by precipitous walls of rock, with massive boulders, some as big as a small house, lying tumbled together in the greatest confusion and displaying in their every rift and crevice an astonishing abundance of ferns, heaths and wild flowers that are all part of the extraordinary flora of West Cork, Clare and Kerry. Prominent among these plants was that saxifrage, lovingly known in the Irish countryside as St Patrick's Cabbage ... [35]

Richard Hayward, and his illustrator Raymond Piper, were searching for standing stones and stone circles and found them, in this case, by taking a turn to the right at Kealkill village; later they found the Kilnaraune Pillar Stone near Bantry – carved indeed but not a pillar stone as it is clearly the shaft of a broken cross. Hayward's engaging book is a useful companion for anyone keen on discovering ancient church sites, graveyards and pre-Christian archaeology throughout Munster – west and south-west Cork being a particularly rewarding terrain.

But Keimaneigh has its Irish singers too, chief amongst them being the poet Máire Bhuidhe Ní Laoghaire (1774?–1849) who was born near Inchigeelagh. After her marriage to Seamus de Burca of Skibbereen the couple settled on a farm at Keimaneigh where Máire had nine children. Although she was illiterate she was reared in that oral tradition of a community which handed on songs and poems through the generations; to this she added her own compositions – love-songs and hymns and at least one excercise in the political format of 'aisling' or dream-figure representing the victimised Ireland.

Her resounding piece is the lament 'Cath Céim an Fhiaidh', an account of a battle which took place in the glen in 1822 between the secretive White Boys and the local yeomanry: like much of her poetry it is rich with the imagery of the place itself and for those who know the song it is impossible now to wander through the defile without remembering:

Cois abhann Ghleanna an Chéama i nUíbh Laoghaire 'seadh bhím-se
Mar a dtéigheann an fiadh san oiche chun síor-chodhladh sóghail,
Ag machtnamh seal liom féinig ag déanamh mo smaointe
Ag éisteacht i gcoilltibh le binn-ghuth na n-éan ... [36]

The main road from Gougane Barra back to Macroom links Ballingeary with Inchigeela on the north bank of the river. It is worth finding the little road that winds along the southern bank, for here the lakes with their densely reeded fringes and their tiny outcrops of islands make delightful stopping-places. Officially this is Lough Allua (and there is a pretty parking place on the other bank) but it seems more like several lakes than one, so winding and so hidden is the conformation, from rocky shores to the sudden glades of ash and birch and alder along the banks.

Nowhere here is far from Macroom (birth-place of Padraig Ó Cruadhlaoigh (?–1930), first principal of the Dámhscoil Mhuscraí in its revised form) but the river's course has cut a valley between the Shehy and the Derrynasaggart Mountains and when the road emerges at last above the Gearagh the atmosphere changes. From here the river fills its banks and the fields are healthy and wide, the floor of the valley visible for miles. Behind have been left the fortesses of rock, the icy rushing streams brown from the peat-bogs, the terrain in which the remnants of an entire culture can still be read.

It is too soon to leave it. There is another way back to Cork: after Macroom, facing east, head off to Crookstown and from there go through the Bride valley towards Aherla. This road is almost parallel with the main road and is linked with it like a grid with several small but well-maintained lanes (everything in this fertile valley is in good order).

Over here, near the lovely long fields of Ryecourt, stands Kilcrea Castle, an early seat of the MacCarthys of Muskerry and Earls of Clancarty; it was built initially by Cormac Laidir MacCarthy, the fifteenth-century builder of Blarney. He was killed in 1495 by his brother and his nephew at Carrignamuck Castle in Dripsey, near Macroom.

Kilcrea

A few fields away and closer to Ballincollig a small sign indicates Kilcrea Friary. Originally a sixth-century cell of St Cera, the friary was established for the Franciscans by Cormac Laidir who is buried here; among the priests of its later history were the historian Philip O'Sullivan whose history of Catholic Ireland was published in 1616.

> There is something very awful and solemn when one enters these reverend piles, once erected for the uses of religion. Long sounding aisles intermingled with graves and human bones, the twilight vaults, and caverns piled with skulls, and the gloomy darkness occasioned by the height of the walls over-grown with shrubs and ivy, so sadden all the scene, that he must be a person who never reflects at all, if he thinks not of futurity, on entering ...
>
> From the gateway of this abbey to the road, there are high banks on either side formed entirely of human bones and skulls, cemented together with moss; and besides great numbers thrown about, there are several thousands piled up in the arches, windows, (etc.) &, which shew this place formerly to have been a very great cemetery. At the end of a lane leading to this ruin stands a large wooden cross since the time of the demolition of the abbey, and this entrance is by an avenue of venerable oaks. The river Bride winds sweetly away through the vale below this ruin ... [37]

When Eibhlín Dhubh Ní Chonaill spoke of her husband Art Ó Laoghaire entering 'the school', this is where she meant. His burial in the family graveyard had been forbidden on the grounds that Ó Laoghaire was an outlaw. He was buried in a field and later taken here to the ruined monastery, or 'school', not to learn wisdom or music but to prop earth and stone, with Eibhlín's own words as his epitaph:

Lo! Arthur Leary, generous, handsome, brave,
Slain in his bloom, lies in this humble grave.

The tomb is directly eastward of the map showing the different areas of the monastery; it has a table-top and is surrounded by a rusting rail. The inscription is difficult to read and there is nothing either on the map or the tomb itself to indicate its significance.

The aisles have been cleared of bones and the windows and arches of skulls; the venerable oaks also have been removed although the path into the abbey is still edged with rounded swards. In a corner near the east window a plaque marks the tomb of Cormac Laidir MacCarthy, and Art O Leary lies here still, surrounded by all the nobility of Muskerry.

Notes to West Cork

1. Eiléan Ní Chuilleanáin, 'Old Roads'.
2. Seamus Murphy, *Stone Mad* (1950 with illustrations by Fergus O'Ryan; 1966 with illustrations by William Harrington, 1997).
3. Louis Marcus, *The Seamus Murphy Catalogue,* The Blackstaff Press (1982).
4. O'Donovan (ed.), *The Tribes of Ireland* (1852).
5. Daniel MacCarthy *The Life and Letters of Florence MacCarthy Mor* (1867 and 1975). Sir Henry Sidney (1529–86) was three times Lord Deputy of Ireland. He was the father of Sir Philip Sidney, the famed soldier-poet, for whom Spenser, a close friend, wrote the elegy 'Astrophel'.
6. MacCarthy, op. cit.
7. Seán Ó Ríordáin, 'Adhlacadh mo Mháthar' (1945) (tr. Valentine Iremonger).
8. Seán Ó Tuama, *Repossessions* (1995).
9. Seán Ó Ríordáin, 'Reo' (Frozen) tr. V. Iremonger; O Riordáin's poetry is collected in *Eireaball Spideoige* (1952) and *Brosna* (1964) and the posthumous publication *Tar Éis mo Bháis* (1979); see also Seán Ó Coileain, *Seán Ó Riordáin, Beatha agus Saothar* (1982).
10. Seán Dunne (ed.), *The Cork Anthology* (1993).
11. Kevin Corcoran, *West Cork Walks* (1991).
12. Sean Dunne, 'One Sunday in the Gearagh' from *Time and the Island* (1996).
13. William Penn, *My Irish Journal 1669–1670* (ed. Isobel Grubb, 1952).
14. Eibhlín Dhubh Ní Chonaill, 'Caoineadh Airt Uí Laoghaire' (*An Duanaire*, 1981).
15. Eilís Dillon, tr. 1971.
16. Seán Ó Tuama, 'The Lament for Art O'Leary' in *Repossessions* (1995).
17. Ó Tuama, op. cit.
18. Ó Tuama, op. cit.
19. Eilís Dillon, translation (1971) in Ó Tuama, *Repossessions.*
20. Padraigín Riggs, 'Donncha Ó Céileachair' (1978); another storyteller from Cúil Aodha was Amhlaoibh Ó Loinsigh (1872–1924), for whom see 'Scéalaíocht Amhlaoibh Í Loinsigh' (ed. Donncha Ó Croinin, 1971).
21. Tomás Ó Canainn and Gearóid Mac an Bhua, *Seán Ó Riada, A Shaol agus a Shaothar* (1993); this examines both the life and the music of Seán Ó Riada;

Ó Riada's music programmes for RTE were edited by Thomas Kinsella and Tomás Ó Canainn as *Our Musical Heritage* (1982).

22. Sean Lucy, *Unfinished Sequence and Other Poems* (1979).

23. Sean O'Faolain, *Vive Moi!* (1993).

24. Eric Cross, *The Tailor and Ansty* (1942).

25. Frank O'Connor, introduction to *The Tailor and Anstey* (1964).

26. Further information on this subject can be obtained from John Coolahan, 'The Secondary School Curriculum Experiment 1924–42, The Case of English' in Greaney and Molloy (eds) *Dimensions of Reading* (1986).

27. Frank O'Connor, op. cit.

28. James Cahalan's 'Tailor Tim Buckley, Folklore, Literature and Seanchas an Tailliúra', *Eire-Ireland* (Summer 1979) offers material and insights to the history of the Tailor and story-telling in Irish life. Aindrias Ó Muimhneacháin (b. 1905) has recorded in Irish the anecdotes of Timothy Buckley in *Seanchas an Tailliúra* (1978).

29. Robert Gibbings, *Lovely is the Lee* (1945).

30. Robert Gibbings, *Sweet Cork of Thee* (1952).

31. Fuller enjoyment of Gougane Barra is available to those who follow it through the pages of *West Cork Walks* by Kevin Corcoran (1991).

32. See also Ó Riain, 'The Making of a Saint: St Finbarr of Cork 600–1200' (Irish Texts Society 1997).

33. O'Faolain, op. cit.

34. In *Midsummer Night Madness and other stories* (1932) and *The Man Who Invented Sin and other stories* (1949).

35. Richard Hayward, *Munster and the City of Cork* (1964).

36. See Donncha Ó Donnchu (ed.), *Filíocht Máire Bui Ní Laoghaire* (1931).

37. Smith, *History of Cork* (1774).

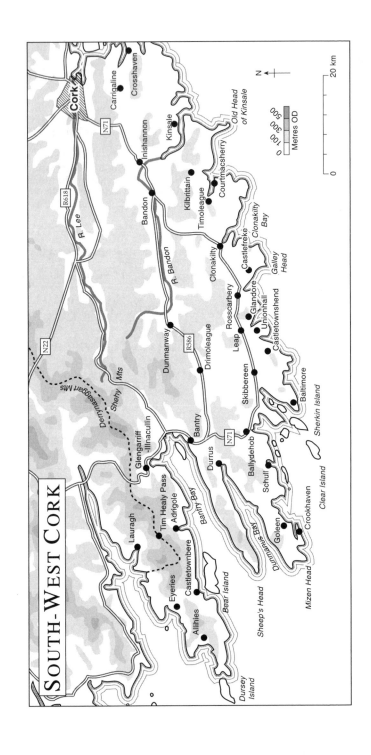

SOUTH-WEST CORK

N

20 km

Metres OD
0 100 300 500

Cork
Carrigaline
Crosshaven
N71
Inishannon
Kinsale
Old Head of Kinsale
Bandon
Kilbrittain
Courtmacsherry
Timoleague
R. Lee
R618
R. Bandon
Clonakilty
Castlefreke
Clonakilty Bay
Galley Head
Glandore
Rosscarbery
Unionhall
Leap
Castletownshend
Dunmanway
R586
Drimoleague
Skibbereen
N22
Derrynasaggart Mts
Shehy Mts
Bantry
N71
Baltimore
Sherkin Island
Glengarriff
Ilnacullin
Durrus
Ballydehob
Schull
Tim Healy Pass
Adrigole
Bantry Bay
Goleen
Clear Island
Lauragh
Crookhaven
Dunmanus Bay
Everies
Castletownbere
Bear Island
Sheep's Head
Mizen Head
Allihies
Dursey Island

SOUTH-WEST CORK

Carrigaline, Crosshaven, Kinsale, Inishannon, Bandon:

(a) Timoleague, Kilbrittain, Clonakilty (Castlefreke), Rosscarbery, Leap, Glandore, Union Hall, Castletownshend, Skibbereen, Baltimore, Ballydehob, Goleen, Crookhaven, Durrus, Bantry

(b) Dunmanway, Drimoleague, Bantry, Glengarriff, Castletownbere, Eyeries, Allihies, Dursey Island, Tim Healy Pass, Adrigole, Bantry

*... I seem best to remember those magical evenings when two or three boat-loads
of us would row 'up the river', which is no river, but a narrow and winding sea-
creek, of, as we hold, unparalleled beauty, between high hills, with trees on both
its sides, drooping low over the water, and seaweed, instead of ivy, hanging from
their branches. Nothing more enchanting than resting on one's oars in the heart
of that dark mirror, with no sound but the sleepy chuckle of the herons in the tall
trees on the hill-side, or the gurgle of the tide against the bows, until someone,
perhaps, would start one of the glees that were being practised for the then
concert – there was always one in the offing – and the Echo, that dwells opposite
Roger's Island, would wake from its sleep and join in, not more than half a
minute behind the beat.*

*Or out at the mouth of the harbour, the boats rocking a little in the wide
golden fields of moonlight, golden as sunlight, almost, in those August nights,
and the lazy oars, paddling in what seemed a sea of opal oil, would drip with the
pale flames of the phosphorus that seethed and whispered at their touch ...*[1]

> Floodtide!
> Flood or ebb upon the strand!
> What the floodtide brings to you
> Ebbtide carries from my hand.
>
> Floodtide!
> Ebbtide with the hurrying fall!
> All have reached me, ebb and flow,
> Ay, and now I know them all.
>
> Floodtide!
> Cannot reach me where I call;
> None in darkness seeks my side,
> Cold the hand that lies on all.
>
> Happy island of the main
> To you the tide will come again,
> But to me it comes no more
> Over the blank, deserted shore ...[2]

*T*wo voices cross the promontories of the Atlantic edge of Europe;
geography separates them by fewer than fifty miles, the time between
them is reckoned in aeons. Edith Somerville remembers, as she mourns the
loss of Violet Martin, the days of captured Ascendancy ease at Castletownshend, days of tennis parties and glees and sketching picnics.

From her rock on a neighbouring headland the Hag of Beara, an Cailleach Bhéarra, mourns the loss of the pagan dominance she represented, or embodied, through ages before a Christian foot touched Ireland.

The deeply indented coast from the western edge of Cork harbour to the southernmost tip of the county represents in geography fractured holdings whose earliest placenames still have meaning today. The hills are rich in pickings for the archaeologist – cairns and dolmens and wedge tombs, early Christian ecclesiastical sites, standing stones, ring forts and promontory forts – while the lower levels provide stone circles and other indications of neolithic settlements as proof that from Ireland's earliest history the economic and defensive advantages of these headlands were recognised and exploited. The river-spliced mountainous hinterland, often of bog and moor, can still appear inhospitable, daunting to those who travel in comfort, although ideal for tourism's journeymen and foot-soldiers.

The sea around these harbours offered rich fishing grounds; the bogs behind them offered fuel. The mountains provided protection, the valleys, sheltered by woods and watered by the many small rivers, provided pasture and game. Those who settled here left their traces, and while to the visitor their voices may be as extinct as the oaks which once thickened the valleys and sloping hills, the subterranean echoes have been heard by more recent interpreters and colour, even today, the legends and literature of Carbery and Beara.

It may seem an audacious connection, yet there is a link through history and literature between the mythological but powerful imagery of the Cailleach Bhéarra and Hilaire Belloc. The link is only place, but it is powerful.

These southern fastnesses gave security for centuries to the native landowners and lords; their wars were with one another, and even then accommodations were worked out to mutual advantage. With the greater colonisation which followed the Battle of Kinsale the south-west, for all its roughness, attracted the attention of those incomers who could not find a foothold in the already over-populated territories closer to Dublin and other cities. The condition of the Irish ancestral families deteriorated dramatically from the middle of the seventeenth century; few opportunities of resistance were available, none of honourable change. Instead they sought service in foreign armies; James Swanton of Beara joined Berwick's Irish Regiment in France as a young man – later he would be known as the great-grandfather of Hilaire Belloc.

Most of this territory was originally Corca Luighe, a pre-Christian settlement spreading along the south-western littoral. As the early kingship of the Desmonds consolidated throughout Munster the local families affiliated where they were not extinguished; with the eventual domination of the MacCarthy clans in these districts the rule of the Lords of Carbery was almost sovereign in itself, especially when the Desmond power waxed and waned through the sixteenth century. This was that family of MacCarthys who created their strongholds north, south and west of Cork city and who enforced the allegiances of the ancient but by then vulnerable families, the O'Mahonys, O'Dalys, O'Driscolls and O'Sullivans among them – relatively modern names in terms of the history of these peninsulas.

The O'Mahonys had moved as far south as Mizen; the ruins of their many castles still cling to the countryside, one of the more dramatic being Dun Locha (built 1207) at Three Castle Head near Mizen, although the main fortress was Ardinentant. The O'Mahonys were cultured, travelled and sophisticated, but suffered for their involvement in the Desmond Rebellions of 1569–83 and at the defeat of the Irish cause in the Battle of Kinsale in 1601. Ruin came by 1641, with the O'Mahony chieftain 'Lord of the Western Lands' and his adherents stripped of their holdings and reduced to exile or beggary.

The O'Mahonys had achieved an accord with the MacCarthy overlords, whose advances through Carbery and Beara copied the success of other branches of that family elsewhere in Munster. The O'Driscolls dominated the peninsula to the west, the harbours and coves of Sherkin Island, of Baltimore, Cape Clear and Castlehaven; the O'Sullivans were concentrated in Beara by the end of the sixteenth century.

The most notorious of the O'Dalys was Angus (Aonghus Ó Dálaigh, d. 1617): a member of a learned family whose bardic school was at Farranamanagh near Kilcrohane. Ó Dálaigh was a satirist of substance. After the Battle of Kinsale he was reputed to have been commissioned by Sir George Carew, victorious president of Munster, to discredit the remaining Irish nobility; he was murdered by a man whose family he had slandered in those verses.[3]

A route from Kinsale to Bantry, roughly the loop thrown in this chapter around south-west Cork, embraces the barony of Carbery, although digressions are inevitable in so spectacular a landscape.

The literary heritage of this countryside mirrors the fortunes of its people, only a few of whom contributed to it but then, at least, memorably. The predictable names are those of Somerville and Ross; less obvious perhaps are George Bernard Shaw, or Dean Swift, or J.G. Farrell or Mary Norton. More obscure to the visitor are the poets of these places from Timoleague to Baltimore.

The amateur historian and genealogist exploring this landscape may find some difficulty in that academic studies adhere to ancient place and family names without always giving the modern counterpart. At the same time there are many colourful, but possibly inaccurate or at best generalised, local histories available. Although it is a hefty book, *The Castles of County Cork* by

James N. Healy (1988) gives an almost stone by stone account of the comings and goings – as well as the buildings – of septs, tribes, families, lords and kings which is both interesting and useful, but not indisputable. On a much smaller scale walkers especially will value the *Guide to the Sheep's Head Way* (1996) which maps the peninsula of Muintir Bhaire between Dunmanus Bay and Bantry Bay.

The growth in tourism in South West Cork has had one very pleasant effect on the area – a number of excellent restaurants, small hotels and guest houses of the highest standard are now available to visitors, and in unexpected places: Durrus, for example, or Goleen, or Ballydehob or Baltimore. Some may be seasonal; others, in Kinsale, Skibbereen, Bantry or Schull remain open all year but perhaps with amended times. There are gardens (Creagh, Liss Ard, Durrus, Bantry, Goleen) and there are festivals such as the already internationally renowned Chamber Music Festival at Bantry.

Carrigaline

South of Cork city the town of Carrigaline spans the Owenboy river, the road eastwards to Crosshaven edged with the disused railway line forming a margin where the river broadens between two bends. This wooded lake-like stretch is called Drake's Pool: Sir Francis Drake, or one of the ships under his command, is said to have sailed in here in search of escaping Spanish vessels after the Armada. At the far side of the river stands Coolmore, a late eighteenth-century house of classical austerity built by the Newenham family as if to downface its more ancient neighbours, the castles of Carrigaline on one side and that of Aghamarta on the other. At Coolmore lived Thomas Newenham, (1762–1831) Member of Parliament and author of essays, commentaries and journals, and Molly Keane (1904–96) visited the house to watch the BBC filming her novel *Good Behaviour*, [4] when Coolmore's facade, avenues, fields and foreshore were used for the exterior sequences.

The road skirts the river until the myriad masts of Crosshaven's Royal Cork Yacht Club – reputedly the oldest in the world and transplanted here from its origins in Cobh – come into view where the river flows into Cork harbour. Crosshaven has for many generations been a seaside resort, linking with the bays of Myrtleville and Fountainstown; it stands at the entrance to the harbour, with Cobh dominating the northern shore, and with the coast-guard cottages and lighthouse of Roches Point the landmark to the east:

Rocks jagged in morning mist.
At intervals, the foghorn sounds
From the white lighthouse rock
Lonely as a cow mourning her calf,
Groaning, belly deep, desperate.

I assisted at such a failure once;
A night-long fight to save a calf
Born finally, with broken neck.
It flailed briefly on the straw,
A wide-eyed mother straddling it.

Listen carefully. This is different;
It sounds to guide, not lament.
When the defining light is powerless,
Ships hesitating down the strait
Hear its harsh voice as friendliness.

Upstairs my wife & daughter sleep.
Our two lives have separated now
But I would send my voice to yours
Cutting through the shrouding mist
Like some friendly signal in distress.

The fog is lifting, slowly.
Flag high, a new ship is entering.
The opposite shore unveils itself,
Bright in detail as a painting,
Alone, but equal to the morning.[5]

Poet John Montague (1929–) was born in New York and reared in Northern Ireland, but after an academic career in France and America had come to teach at University College Cork where his influence was crucial to several students who were later to develop their own strong poetic skills. His many collections include *The Rough Field* (1972), *The Great Cloak* (1978), *The Dead Kingdom* (1984) and *Mount Eagle* (1988) as well as later work which has also been much anthologised and his *Collected Poems* (1998). His collection of short stories *Death of a Chieftain* (1964) has recently been re-issued.

Now a teacher at the State University of New York at Albany, he is the first incumbent of the chair of Irish poetry, an appointment established by Trinity College Dublin and Queen's University Belfast, and to which he was welcomed by Nobel Laureate Seamus Heaney as 'the ideal holder of this uniquely important office'. His poems, said Heaney, have become part of the memory of who and where we have been: 'he is one of those through whom succession passes.'[6]

'The Point' recalls Montague's tenancy of a coastguard cottage here; despite its rural evocations, the imagery recalls to Cork readers the shrouding sea-mists, the foghorn, the white beacon and its slicing light, and, on some summer evenings, the entrancing sight of a great liner anchored in the roads, its terraced windows gleaming in the coral-tinted dusk.

A native of this village of Crosshaven was John Bernard McCarthy (1888–1979), playwright and short story writer, one of the group characterised by W.B. Yeats as 'the Cork Realists'; his plays were produced by the Abbey Theatre in Dublin and dealt with contemporary rural and maritime issues. Although his later drama was performed mostly by amateur groups while his short stories were published by the Catholic Truth Society of Ireland, his novels (*Covert* [1925]; *Possessions* [1926], *Exiles* and *Bread* [1927]) were published by Hutchinson of London. He also produced poems, while working for most of his life as the local postman.

The attractive coast road swings across the headland to Myrtleville, a tiny but much-favoured beach now surrounded by little villas. Among the older houses is the former Mirmar, built by Sir John Trant and originally known as the 'Cottage on the Rocks'. As a member of the diplomatic corps Sir John travelled widely, accompanied by his daughter Clarissa whose *Journal of Clarissa Trant* recounts her various experiences as well as giving a glimpse of life in this small and once relatively isolated cove.

Legend of such substance that it was included in the brochure of sale for the house (now the Bunnyconnellen Hotel) insists that Victor Hugo was a guest at the cottage – but this is debatable; Clarissa (who was not in love with Ireland) confines her local commentary to personal observations and to visits with the Newenhams of Coolmore and the Hodders of nearby Hoddersfield.

The sea-scapes expand from the cliff road to Fountainstown, birthplace of Liam de Róiste (1882–1959), nationalist MP for Cork city and a member of the first Dail in 1919. Disillusioned and despairing after the Civil War he retired from politics and concentrated instead on working for the revival of the Irish language, writing many poems as well as two short plays.

From here towards Carrigaline (the childhood home of the poet M.J. Barry, a contemporary of Thomas Moore and contributor to *The Nation*) the way lies behind the main road to Crosshaven, high enough to give views over fertile acres with Cobh's cathedral a pinnacle in the distance as the sea drops behind. To the south the coastal plain is fissured by inlets: Ringabella, Roberts' Cove, Nohoval, and a scattering of villages. By Tracton and Ballyfeard the route to Kinsale joins the main Cork road, skirting Oysterhaven Creek near Belgooly before slanting towards the harbour guarded by its twin forts and the town nestled in the angle between sea and land.

Kinsale

It was on the northern flank of the Bandon river, which enters the sea at Kinsale, that one of the most resounding battles of Irish history took place. Fought in a few hours on Christmas Eve of 1601, it was not the last but was almost the last, and certainly the most determinant, engagement of a war which had lasted for almost the final decade of the reign of Elizabeth I.

The efficiency and scope of the Elizabethan plantations of Ireland had subdued Munster, Leinster and Connacht, three of the four provinces of Ireland, during the latter half of the sixteenth century. Only Ulster remained unharnessed to the new English determination to make shires of the provinces; its native chieftains realised that their cherished independence was doomed unless they resisted.

Led by Hugh Maguire (who was to die in a skirmish outside Cork city when he was attacked by Sir Warham St Leger – himself fatally wounded by

Maguire), Red Hugh O'Donnell and his father-in-law Hugh O'Neill, Earl of Tyrone, the lords of Ulster gathered in revolt. Their success against the crown's forces in 1597 encouraged similar actions through the south of the country. It also encouraged O'Neill – who was a sophisticated, English-educated courtier as well as a well-trained and experienced soldier – to move towards Munster where he expected not only local support but also the arrival of a Spanish expedition for which he had been negotiating for several years. It was during this movement southwards that O'Neill got the better of the Earl of Essex who returned in disgrace to London and a traitor's death.

In September of 1601 the Spaniards landed at Kinsale, too far south, and too few in number, for O'Neill's comfort, which was also disturbed by the strengthening of the English forces under Lord Deputy Mountjoy and Sir George Carew, lord president of Munster. Commanded by Don Juan de Aguila, the Spanish troops were made welcome in Kinsale and lodged in the castles which have since been replaced by James' Fort (1602) and Charles' Fort (1677).

Mountjoy struck at Kinsale in October, landing from Oysterhaven Creek and trapping the Spanish in their castles outside the town; this forced O'Neill and O'Donnell into a march from the north to the south of the country, gathering some native support on the way from O'Sullivan Beare and the O'Driscolls from the Cork/Kerry borderlands and James the Earl of Desmond.

The English, in their now-customary device of divide and conquer, had the assistance of the Earl of Thomond and the Earl of Clanricarde. The 3,000 besieged Spaniards were powerless to help their Irish allies in the battle which followed; although a second group of 200 under Alonzo del Campo had arrived to swell the 6,000-strong Irish force. Spies and bad weather damaged the plans of the Irish, to which Mountjoy was already alert. From their base at Coolcarron – the hilly ridge can still be seen from Kinsale – the Irish marched to meet the English just north of the town, but were forced back towards Millwater where they stood their ground. Within a few hours they were routed by Mountjoy's cavalry; the retreat was the beginning of O'Neill's final journey in Ireland.

With O'Donnell, O'Neill escaped capture and he and his diminishing band of followers reached Ulster where with the remaining northern chieftains he witnessed, after submitting to and being pardoned by Mountjoy, the gradual dissolution of all his rights, status and claims.

In fact O'Neill had been relatively well treated by Mountjoy when they met for the Treaty of Mellifont in 1603; until his death in 1606 Mountjoy defended O'Neill at court – but he had also ceremonially shattered the ancient crowning-stone of the O'Neills, symbolising, accurately enough, the utter extinction of the old order.

Yachts off Cork Harbour, Irish School, 18th Century

Historian Roy Foster's unsentimental assessment of Kinsale and its significance (not least in terms of the relationship between England and Spain) admits the decisive local importance of 'events at that obscure Cork fishing-town';[7] for once, he writes, the archaic language of the biographer of Red Hugh O'Donnell found its appropriate pitch:

> Though there fell in that defeat at Kinsale so few of the Irish that they would not miss them after a while, and indeed did not miss them even then, yet there was not lost in any defeat in recent times in Ireland so much as was lost there ...
>
> There were lost there all who escaped of the noble freeborn sons of Mil, valiant, impetuous chiefs, lords of territories and tribes, chieftains of districts and cantreds; for it is full certain that there will never be in Erin at any time together people better or more famous than the nobles who were there, and who died afterwards in other countries one after another, after being robbed of their patrimony and of their noble land which they left to their enemies in that defeat. There were lost besides nobility and honour, generosity and great deeds, hospitality and kindliness, courtesy and noble birth, culture and activity, strength and courage, valour and steadfastness, the authority and sovereignty of the Gaels of Ireland to the end of time.[8]

O'Donnell, still trying to get Spanish assistance, died, possibly poisoned at Carew's instigation, in Simancas in 1602; he is buried in Valladolid. His successor was his brother Rory; after Kinsale Rory too submitted to Mountjoy but continued to negotiate with the Spanish from his home in Ulster. Inevitably O'Neill, now fifty-seven, was suspected of complicity in O'Donnell's activities; as the English pursued Rory a disheartened and isolated O'Neill joined his escaping vessel and in 1607 sailed with O'Donnell from Lough Foyle, intending to reach Spain but going instead to Rome, where he died in 1616.

Describing this departure as 'an ill-considered and completely unexpected action', Foster comments that it provided a great historical set piece which was interpreted symbolically by both sides:

> The English argument held that the Ulster lords had formally identified themselves as fugitives and outlaws; the Irish, that English rapacity had forced them out. O'Donnell emphasised, in addition, religious persecution. O'Neill, characteristically, did not. His fight was not a defeatist recognition of political impotence; he had adapted with striking effectiveness, blocking the Dublin government's plans and ruthlessly using his English contacts, until compromised by O'Donnell. But what mat-

tered was the symbolic image of the last great Gaelic chieftain joining the world of the Irish exiles.[9]

For the sake of romantic symmetry O'Neill's departure has been described as The Flight of the Earls, although in fact the disapora had begun after 1601, with Red Hugh O'Donnell dead in Spain only a year later, and Rory O'Donnell dead by 1608. Yet there is no doubt that the Battle of Kinsale was the last gamble of a Gaelic system, riven within and disparaged without, in the game of sovereignty in Ireland. Nor is there any doubt that O'Neill and O'Donnell and their fellow lords knew that this was the one last desperate chance, the opportunity which had to be grasped whatever the odds. With their defeat and departure ended the world and the culture mourned in the poetry which was to survive both, if only for a while.

After the battle the besieged Spanish came to terms and were sent home by Mountjoy. O'Sullivan Beare retreated with his supporters to his fortress at Dunboy. His progress westward was charted by the Earl of Thomond, acting as Carew's spy; in May of 1602 Carew marched his army along the Sheep's Head peninsula, crossing to Beara by boat and, by the middle of June, shattering the castle with cannonades. After a terrible struggle the defenders, who had no escape route, surrendered. There were, at the end, no more than eighty men; all were hanged in the marketplace of Castletownbere.

They did not include Donal Cam, O'Sullivan Beare. Again he had evaded capture, but the scorched earth policy of Thomond and the horror of the deaths in the marketplace had left him few places in which to hide. As the winter closed in he led 1,000 companions, less than half of whom were soldiers, from Glengarriff to a refuge in Leitrim.

This is the second legendary march associated with the Battle of Kinsale. Friendless, without resources and in the dead of winter the company trekked through mountains and bogs, crossed the Shannon, keeping away always from traitorous towns, suffering from snow and skirmishes alike. They reached O'Rourke of Breffni early in 1603 – all thirty-five survivors.

Donal Cam tried to reach Hugh O'Neill, only to learn of his submission to Mountjoy. Instead O'Sullivan went to Spain where he was assassinated in Madrid in 1618. The Earl of Desmond was betrayed to Carew and died in the Tower of London in 1608.

Kinsale, formerly a de Courcy holding, knew prosperity after those terrible times. Its harbour was once of premier importance in the land, ships for the navies of England being built here and the sheltered harbour being used as a naval base during the seventeenth and eighteenth centuries. Streets twist through the town which is built at the foot of a hill; the names retain their old usages – Rampart, Compass, the Mall, the Quay – and many of the buildings indicate the influence of the traders and merchants who visited and settled through the years. Kinsale functions now not only as a town with its own local government structures, trade and shipping and with a remarkable reputation for world-class cuisine in its many restaurants, but also as a glamorous suburb of Cork city, its golf clubs, marina and generally attractive architecture conferring a new distinction which almost rivals the old.

Among its ancient buildings is that of St Multose Church, the oldest parish church still in use in Ireland. Officially dating – with amendments – from 1190, there are earlier traces on this site, and it is certain that Christian worship has been continuous here for 1,400 years.

Within its walls is contained much of the history of Kinsale, from important medieval monuments to modern dedications; one of these is for floodlighting, a gift commemmorated by the exquisite calligraphy of Elizabeth Friedlander (1903–84) designer of endpapers and jackets for the first series of Penguin Classics, who lived in Kinsale for twenty years.

In the hall near the West Door of the church is the large timber tablet carrying the Chudleigh memorial, translated Latin verses celebrating the skills, and misfortunes, of shipwrights Thomas Chudleigh and his son: the elder had produced a flat-bottomed boat which Cromwellian forces wheeled to Killarney and used to attack the Royalist Ross Castle from its own lake. The younger, buried with his father in a vault near the gallery stairs, designed the Royal Navy frigate *H.M.S. Kinsale* (*c.* 1700).

> Others may place their hope in Saints and Angels Jesus
> Behold the venerable name which has delivered us.
> Together with his father lies Thomas surnamed Chudleigh,
> Both built ships for the Kings of the English.
> The skill of the father was conspicuous; alas! alas! his age was short,
> He caused a ship to be sailed on land.
> A ship to be sailed on land. Kerry knows it well.
> The capture of Ross Castle, with difficulty, proves it.
> Proceed, O Muse, I pray; endeavour to sing of the son.
> He was most talented, endowed with equal art.
> He built a ship for the King, to which Kinsale gives its name.
> But great was the praise given to another.
> He built it, I say, reader, another bore off the treasure.
> Thus for another, not for itself, the vine has sweets;
> Thus for another, not for itself, the horse carries burdens;
> Thus for another, not for itself, the dog courses the plains;
> Thus for another, not for itself, the very ship sails.

A less anonymous poet is quoted in the large stained-glass window in the Southwell Chapel; commemorating the Dorman family – which included the playwright Lennox Robinson – artist Kate O'Brien of An Tur Gloinne portrays sunset and evening star, twilight and evening bell from Tennyson's 'Crossing the Bar'.

The much-travelled novelist Aidan Higgins (1927–) lives in the town; his book *Langrishe Go Down* (1966) was an important literary event in Ireland and his subsequent writing, including *Bornholm Night Ferry* (1983) and a series of short stories, makes revelatory connections between his Irish and foreign experiences. The full fruit of these is attractively presented in *Flotsam and Jetsam* (1996), the memoir *Donkey's Years* (1997) and *Dog Days* (1998).

A life lived elsewhere also informs the work of poet Desmond O'Grady (1935–), another resident of Kinsale. In his search for Ezra Pound, he says (in the preface to *Trawling Tradition* 1994) 'getting at him I fell off Ireland's edge of Europe', but get at him he did, to such an extent that for a while he acted as Pound's secretary. Writing and teaching in America, Egypt, Iran and several European countries O'Grady also began to flourish his skills as a translator, beginning with poems in the Irish language.

Translation, he believes, keeps him active with the purpose of language, and wherever he has sailed he has cast his nets. *Trawling Tradition* ranges from classical Greek, Chinese and Arabic poetry to Anglo-Saxon, to Renaissance Irish lyrics, to the poets of the Baltic, of Croatia, of France and Germany, of Italy, Greece, Turkey, Spain and Russia. O'Grady's publishing career began in 1956; *The Dark Edge of Europe* (1967), *Alexandria Notebook* (1989) and *My Fields This Springtime* (1993) are among the collections of his original poetry which is in continuous publication – although there is also something of himself in all he translates.

The poet Derek Mahon (1941–) lived in Kinsale for some years; a poet of departures and returns and peregrine imagination, his characteristic scenery, according to critic Terence Brown, 'is one of seashore and island, of wave and sky'.[10] His collection *The Hunt by Night* (1982) is dedicated to the memory of the novelist J.G. Farrell (1935–79), author of *Troubles* (1970), the Booker Prize-winning *The Siege of Krishnapur* (1973) and of *The Singapore Grip* (1978). Farrell was drowned while fishing in stormy weather near his new home on Bantry Bay. Earlier one of Mahon's most famous poems 'A Disused Shed in Co. Wexford' (1975) was written for Farrell. Mahon has translated Philippe Jaccottet, Molière, Gerard de Nerval and Racine, co-edited with Peter Fallon the *Penguin Book of Contemporary Irish Poetry* (1990) and among his many poetry publications his *Selected Poems* appeared in 1990 and *The Hudson Letter* in 1995. *Journalism*, a collection of his essays and reviews for journals from *The New Statesman* to *Études* and *Vogue* magazine, was published in 1996.

Mahon was born in Belfast, and another Northern poet, Louis MacNeice (1907–63) is remembered here in Kinsale as the husband of singer

Hedli Anderson MacNeice. Living in a slate-fronted house in Scilly for nearly fifteen years and opening nearby her 'Spinnaker' restaurant she was an inspirational early force in the development of Kinsale's gastronomic reputation.

The novelist Margaret Barrington (1896–1982) lived for many years in West Cork; born in Co. Donegal she was married to the historian Edward Curtis of Trinity College, Dublin and later to the writer Liam O'Flaherty from whom she separated in 1932. During the Second World War she moved to Kilmacabe House in Leap, but later moved to Kinsale where she died. Her novel *My Cousin Justin* was published in 1939 and reissued by Blackstaff Press in 1990. Her first book was *David's Daughter, Tamar*, a collection of short stories re-issued by Wolfhound Press in 1982.

The novelist Alannah Hopkin (1949–) lives in Kinsale. Her novels *A Joke Goes a Long Way in the Country* (1982) and *The Outhaul* (1985) were followed by her study of Ireland's patron saint – *The Living Legend of St Patrick* (1989) – and by short stories, journalism and literary criticism.

Poet and novelist Jerome Kiely (1925–) was born here. He was ordained priest in 1950, and since then produced the novel *Seven Year Island* (1969), and several collections of poetry including *Yesterdays of the Heart* (1989).

For four years after his retirement from his position with the Customs and Excise Kinsale was the home of the poet Padraig Fallon (1905–74), described by Robert Welch as one of the few writers in English to engage seriously with the Gaelic literary tradition during the 1940s and 1950s[11]. Verse dramas on radio, as well as plays for the Abbey Theatre and Telefís Éireann added to a literary reputation which grew despite Fallon's reluctance to publish. That repute was more than justified on the posthumous publication of his *Poems* (1974) and *Collected Poems* (1990) with an introduction by Seamus Heaney. Both Fallon and his wife Dorothy are buried in Kinsale.

There are many reasons to linger in Kinsale, to explore the headland forts or the beaches to the south, and to enjoy the town itself which, although suffering from some crass planning decisions, still maintains a rare and compelling architectural integrity.

Inishannon

Travelling inland, the curve of the inner harbour follows the estuary of the Bandon river, and the road lying alongside, passing the battlefield on its way to Inishannon, climbs through steep and wooded shelves above the river which is crowded with reeds; the margin has been tamed in one stretch into a woodland walk. A ruined castle adds to the atmosphere which has an almost medieval texture as hills collapse into marshes and the river's golden edges merge with water-meadows and low-lying farms.

Inishannon is the home of Alice Taylor (1938–) who has achieved international popularity with the unaffected and heartwarming nostalgia of her memoirs of life and people in the countryside of her youth. *To School Through the Fields* (1988 and 1999) was the first of these, and was followed by such titles as *Quench the Lamp* (1990), *The Village* (1992) and *The Woman of the House* (1997) with several other publications including poetry.

East of Inishannon is Ballinhassig, birthplace of Jeremiah J. Callanan (1795–1829); born into a medical family he first attempted to study for the priesthood at Maynooth but then entered Trinity College Dublin intending to carry on the family profession. Poor health and an increasing devotion to poetry ended this period, and his writing was encouraged by Maginn in whose father's school in Cork he was taught for a while by Thomas Crofton Croker and the historian John Windele.

His work appeared in *Blackwood's Magazine* but incipient tuberculosis, an ardent, restless personality and unsettled life (complicated by a love-affair with a non-Catholic) led him eventually to take a position as tutor to a Cork family in Lisbon. He translated some poetry from the Irish, the best known of which is the Jacobite song 'An Droimeann Donn Dílis', while the most famous of his poems is probably 'The Outlaw of Loch Lene', published in *Blackwood's* in 1828 and acclaimed for its wistful imagery: '... I think as at eve she wanders its mazes along/The birds go to sleep by the sweet wild twist of her song.'[12]

In Cork Callanan is best remembered for his verses celebrating the beauties of Gougane Barra but he was never to return to his native county. Although on board ship and ready to go home, Callanan became so ill with a throat infection that he was immediately returned to shore, where he died.

Bandon

From Inishannon the Bandon river leads on to the town of Bandon, formerly known as Bandon Bridge and largely the foundation of the first Earl of Cork, Richard Boyle. An acquisition from the immense appropriations (over half a million acres of the province of Munster) which followed the quelling of the Desmond rebellions from 1569 to 1583, Bandon was offered to a colony of settlers from Bristol, the Earl confiding that 'no popish recusant, or unconforming novelist being admitted to live in all the town.'[13]

Bandon was for four years the home of the infant William Hazlitt (1778–1830), whose father was the Dissenting Minister for the town; it was also the home of Nicholas Brady (1659–1726), a clergyman who worked in Cork, London and Stratford-on-Avon; he is best known for his metrical version, with Nahum Tate, of the *Psalms of David* (1696), for his verse translation of *The Aeneids* of Virgil (1716) and his verse tragedy 'The Rape' (1692).

Born in Bandon, Sir Richard Cox (1650–1733) was a barrister who returned to Ireland after working for some years at Grays Inn, London. His Irish career was fractured by English politics which made him at one time the recorder of Kinsale, at another governor of Cork, at yet another lord chancellor of Ireland and later again saw him called before the Irish parliament to defend himself (successfully) against charges levelled by his peers. He was at the Battle of the Boyne with Prince William of Orange whose claim to the throne of England he supported vigorously, and while temporarily displaced by changes in government wrote his *History of Ireland* (published in two volumes in 1689 and 1690). An earnest evangelist, he wrote essays and addresses on religious allegiances as well as publishing, in 1711, *An Inquiry into Religion, and the use of Reason in reference to it.* He is now best remembered as the father of Michael Cox, Archbishop of Cashel and builder of one of the most beautiful houses in all of Ireland, Castletown Cox in Co. Kilkenny, said to be the masterpiece of architect Davis Duckart.

Margaret Wolfe Hungerford (1855–97) was the wife of Henry Hungerford of Bandon; the daughter of a canon of Ross Cathedral (she was born in Rosscarbery) she produced in her relatively short life a succession (more than thirty) of romantic novels and short stories. She also produced three children in her first marriage to Dublin solicitor Edward Argles, and three more in the five years of her marriage to Hungerford. She died of typhoid fever – which must surely have had something to do with exhaustion – in Bandon.

Even more prolific – of books if not of children – was Elizabeth Thomasina Meade (1854–1914), daughter of The Revd R.T. Meade and wife of Toulmin Smith with whom she moved to London; there she edited the *Atalanta* magazine for girls, with H. Rider Haggard and R.L. Stevenson among the contributors. Most of her nearly 300 books were for young women; she made the genre of the girls' school story popular and professionally rewarding. Barrister and journalist George Bennet (1824–1900) was born here; when settled in America he established the town of Bandon in Oregon. Also a native of Bandon is Risteard Ó Glaisne (1927–) an Irish-language journalist who has also published short stories and essays.

At Bandon the road divides: at the main bridge there is the opportunity to turn right and travel inland to Dunmanway and Bantry, or by turning left to go more sharply south towards the peninsular bays. Taking this option, there is another diversion just outside the town, where a fork to the left off the high road to Clonakilty leads to the harbour villages of Kilbrittain and Courtmacsherry.

This delightful route rises above the valley of the Arigideen (or little silver river) which flows into Courtmacsherry Bay. A detour leads to Coolmain Harbour. In Rathclarin churchyard is the grave of the novelist Donn Byrne (1889–1928). Brian Oswald Donn-Byrne, although born in New York, was reared in the North of Ireland and studied the Irish language in University College Dublin. He had bought Coolmain Castle with £2,000 won at Cannes; for previous summers he had rented it, but had only been in residence as proprietor for three days when he drowned after his car swerved into the high tide in Courtmacsherry. His affection for Irish poetry and history led to his novel *Blind Raftery* (1924), and other titles include *Hangman's House* (1924) *Brother Saul* (1925) and *The Power of the Dog* (1929). His tombstone carries a refrain from an Irish song: 'Tá mé mo codhladh is ná dúisigh mé' – roughly translated as 'let me sleep, don't waken me'.

The ancient names of O'Mahony, O'Cowhig and MacCarthy cluster around such buildings as Kilbrittain Castle, with the relatively newer additions of de Cogan, de Courcy and Barry Roe adding to the historical complexities of ownership and allegiance, especially during the supremacy of the Desmonds as Lords of Munster. Kilbrittain was in the hands of the MacCarthy Reaghs of Carbery by the fourteenth century and again, after an interval of dispute, by 1500.

Finín MacCarthy Reagh (Finghín MacCarthaigh Ríabhach) died in 1505; the *Book of Lismore* was composed for him and his wife Caitlin by Aonghus Ó Callanáin and consists of 198 folios including poems, texts on religion, the lives of the saints, the voyage of Marco Polo, monastic rules, sagas and stories. It was seized with the capture of Kilbrittain Castle in 1642 by Lord Kinalmeaky; a son of the Earl of Cork, Kinalmeaky sent it home to his father at Lismore. It was discovered there by workmen in 1814, after which its various parts were distributed to scholars for copying with the eventual loss of about fifty folios. Reassembled as far as possible, it was sent to Chatsworth, the seat of the Dukes of Devonshire, inheritors through marriage of the Earl of Cork's Irish estates. The ironies of history seem to be condensed in the image of this great book of the MacCarthys being known to history and international scholarship through the initially casual protection of their conquerors.[14]

Timoleague

The coast road to Timoleague fringes the harbour with the wooded village of Courtmacsherry across the water. In the spring the woods covering the furthest headland are brilliant with bluebells, and here the nightingale still sings. Formerly MacCarthy territories, these districts of Ibane and Barryroe later came into the hands of the Earls of Barrymore (who sold them off again in the eighteenth century). The village of Timoleague is situated where the Arigideen is forded for a causeway leading towards Courtmacsherry, and at the brink of the estuary stand the ruins of the Franciscan friary founded by Donal Glas MacCarthy in 1312.

Dedicated to St Molaga and therefore the house (*tig*) of Molaga, this foundation gives the village its name, although an earlier Moril castle is believed to have been on the site. In this abbey, in 1629, the scribe Micheál Ó Cléirigh copied pages from the great MacCarthy book.

Ó Cléirigh (?1590–1643) was one of the scribes responsible for the *Annals of the Four Masters*. These make up a monumental record of Irish history from the earliest times to 1616, and were written with the scholars Cúchoigríche Ó Cleirigh, Fearfeasa Ó Maoilchonaire and Cúchoigríche Ó Duibhgeannáin. A native of Co. Donegal and a member of a learned family, Micheál Ó Cléirigh was ordained as a Franciscan lay-brother in Louvain and travelled throughout Ireland to study and copy manuscript material, working with contemporary Irish scholars in Ireland and abroad. At Louvain Ó Cleirigh published his Irish lexicon, *Focloir no Sanasan Nua* (a new vocabulary or glossary) in 1643.

Timoleague Abbey was destroyed with the dissolution of the monasteries in the sixteenth century; in 1604 the returning monks restored it only to see it finally ruined in 1642 when Kinalmeaky's troops laid waste to the town during the Confederate Wars. Its gaunt, lonely profile at the edge of the river, and the desolation implied in its destruction, provoked the poem 'Machtnamh an Duine Dhoillíosaigh' by the West Carbery poet Seán Ó Coileáin (?1754–1817).

'Oiche dom go doiligh dubhach ...' is the opening line of the poem which is known to many Irish schoolchildren; its atmospheric incantations suggest the anguish of the scribe for a civilisation which has been obliterated. The abbey was for centuries the burial-place of the noble families of the area and the MacCarthy Reagh tombs are here along with those of the O'Donovans and de Courcys; they include that of Edmund de Courcy, bishop of Ross, who was buried here in 1518.

Ó Coileáin, once meant for the priesthood, would also have relished Timoleague's reputation as a storehouse for the best Spanish wines. When the estuary was navigable to the bridge, Timoleague, according to Smith, was 'much resorted to by the Spaniards, who imported large quantities of wine here; and it is said, there were formerly no less than 14 taverns that sold sack in the town ...'[15]

At the other side of the bridge to the abbey are the shortened remains of Timoleague Castle, which now stands in the gardens of Timoleague House (these are open to the public in summer). Also in the grounds is the little church of The Ascension, where the walls of the aisle and chancel are covered in exquisite and unexpected mosaic designs in commemoration of the Travers family of Timoleague House and of Surgeon-General Crofts of the Indian Medical Service.

Clonakilty

Clonakilty with its deep sea-inlet and wide beaches (especially at Inchydoney and Owenahincha) is a town which is now carefully managed, although its wild headlands and coves have been transformed into untidy suburbs through careless planning, and there is constant development pressure on its outlying marshes and sand-dunes. It was founded in 1605 in much the same way and by the same man – Richard Boyle – as was Bandon. George Bullen (1816–94) was born in Clonakilty and became keeper of printed books in the British Museum; the American newspaper editor David Goodman Croly (1829–86) was also a native of the town, and so was the poet Eugene Davis (1857–97) who was educated largely in France. A contributor to *The Nation*, he was also believed to have been involved in the exposure – and confession – of Richard Piggot as forger of letters implicating Charles Stewart Parnell with nationalist murders. While teaching in the town, Wexford novelist Eamon McGrath (1929–) published *Honour Thy Father* (1970), *The Charnel House* (1990) and *The Fish in the Stone* (1994).

From Clonakilty the road to Rosscarbery passes Sam's Cross, where a memorial by the Cork sculptor Séamus Murphy marks the birthplace, at nearby Woodfield, of Michael Collins (1890–1922), 'The Big Fellow' of now almost legendary status in the history of the Irish War of Independence. Closer to Bandon, near Crookstown, is Béal na Bláth where Collins was gunned down and killed during the Irish Civil War which followed Independence.[16]

The promontory edging Clonakilty Bay to the west ends in Galley Head, and close by are the ruins of Castlefreke, an old castle restored by the Freke family to designs by Sir Richard Morrison. Several fires followed by generations of neglect (the Earls of Carbery, who once owned more than 13,000 of these acres, ended in the renunciation of the title and the emigration to East Africa of the last lord) have now left the castle as a turreted but roofless shell, prominent as Camelot, staring out to sea as if awaiting the sails of its heraldic rescuers.

All day there raged a foaming green and purple storm, with snatches of sun through scudding rags of clouds. Now the wind has fallen and the sun is setting in a golden fume. A liner crosses the sun's disc, battling with the waves, making little headway. She keeps far out, knowing what befalls her if she comes too near: Dulig's sword; Galley's fierce snout; Kinsale's butting head.

My nightmare is that one evening an American liner will run ashore on the strand; hordes of ravenous passengers will stream up to the house. They will walk in without ringing the bell. They will demand drink and food and beds, and the Yankees will be contemptuous as there is no lift. A millionaire will sleep in my bed, while I, like a sparrow, roost upon the housetop.[17]

In her diary, Lady Mary Carbery of Castlefreke (1867–1949) writes with great love of the castle which she kept going after her early widowhood until it was taken over by her son John. She edited the diaries of an earlier chatelaine, Mrs Elizabeth Freke, which she had found in the house; using her special gift for absorbing the stories told by others, she based her highly successful book *The Farm by Lough Gur* (1937) on the tales of Mary Fogarty of Bruff, in Co. Limerick. Her second marriage was to Kit Sandford, founder of the Boar's Head Press and owner of the Golden Cockerel Press which published books on vellum and handmade paper, using antique typefaces and morocco or pigskin bindings. The Golden Cockerel Press was earlier owned by Robert Gibbings.

Rosscarbery

The beautifully situated town of Rosscarbery is reached by a causeway (recently contradicted by an incongruous modern hotel at one end) bridging a deep inlet from the bay. A sea-marsh on one side with the sea itself ringing beyond the dunes, a lake on the other with the town mounting the gentle slopes above, the little town was once a hamlet known as Ros Ailithir – the headland of pilgrims.

The ancient shrine there was that of St Colman, but the town itself grew around the sixth-century foundation of St Fachtna, one of the most famous of those monastic schools which, for a while, won Ireland its reputation as an island of saints and scholars. The foremost monastery of all of Corca Luighe this is said to have included St Brendan the Navigator among its pupils; a teacher, Airbertach mac Cosse, was ransomed by Brian Boru, High King of Ireland, from marauding Norsemen in 990. The invading Danes ruined the monastery in the tenth century, but a thirteenth-century Benedictine priory was a place of pilgrimage until the dissolution of the monasteries under Henry VIII. In the meantime the Synod of Kells in 1152 established Ross, or Ros Ailithir, as the see of the diocese of Ross, which it remained until it was absorbed (with Cloyne) by Cork in 1617.

When Patrick Pearse reminded a thronged funeral in Dublin that the English could not hope to quell Irish republican revolt so long as they had 'left us our Fenian dead!' he was speaking at the grave of Rosscarbery's most famous son, Jeremiah O'Donovan Rossa (1831–1915). Born in a modest house on the town's main street and later a shopkeeper in Skibbereen, O'Donovan Rossa founded the Phoenix Literary and Debating Society as a way of airing political and economic issues; this later became part of the Fenian organisation. O'Donovan was married to Mary Irwin, a well-known poet of her times.

For activities associated with Irish Republican Brotherhood Rossa was imprisoned for six years; released on condition of exile he went to work in America from where he edited *The United Irishman*, becoming the American figurehead of the Fenian movement while amassing fighting funds for the republican activists in Ireland. His autobiography is in two volumes: *O'Donovan Rossa's Prison Life* (1874) and *Rossa's Recollections* (1898). He is buried in Glasnevin, where Pearse delivered the funeral oration.

The hilly fields and headlands which surround Rosscarbery and which change only in height and hollows as the road sweeps on southwards are thick with mottes, circles, and wedge-tombs. Ruined houses are much in evidence, such as the Jacobean Coppinger's Court near Glandore, or Benduff Castle, a holding of MacCarthy Reagh until the Cromwell era and later the home of the Quaker William Morris who was several times visited at Benduff by his friend William Penn prior to Penn's voyage to America.

Another ruin is that of Derry, built by Horatio Townsend, author of the *Statistical Survey of the County of Cork* (1810). In this substantial Georgian house was born Charlotte Payne Townsend (1857–1943) who was to marry George Bernard Shaw in London in 1898. At Derry, for the three summer months of 1905, Shaw worked on *Major Barbara*; a later visit included work on *St Joan* in Glengarriff.

Charlotte, as Shaw wrote to Ellen Terry, was 'a restful person, plain, green-eyed, very lady-like, completely demoralised by contact with my ideas, forty, with nice rooms on a solid basis of £4,000 a year, independent and unencumbered, and not so plain either when you are in her confidence.'[18]

Charlotte did not wait for contact with Shaw to be demoralised. Caught between a socially ambitious and disappointed mother and a docile, country-loving father, her childhood was unhappy and unsettled. A good, if home-based education (neighbouring Big Houses used a system of sharing visiting tutors for specialist subjects such as foreign languages, grammar, science or music) enriched her life at Derry. She shared her father's interest in the tenants, in matters of the parish and locality, in riding to hounds and above all in his library.

All these, despite her frequent visits to the country houses of friends (including the Kingstons of Mitchelstown) were left behind when she went to live in London, where her friendship with Beatrice and Sidney Webb brought her into contact with Shaw for whom, for a while, she worked as a typist.

Although they later moved to a country house of their own, the Shaw's social life remained closely tied to London and their friends in the city. It was of these she wrote to T.E. Lawrence after attending the cremation of Jane, wife of H.G. Wells, in 1927.

> It was dreadful – dreadful – dreadful ... the organ began a terrible dirge. We all stood up – and stood for what seemed hours and hours and hours, while that organ played on our nerves and senses and knocked them to pieces. H.G. began to cry like a child ... Then there came a place where the address said 'she never resented a slight; she never gave voice to a harsh judgement.' At that point the audience, all more or less acquainted with many details of H.G.'s private life, thrilled, like corn under a wet north wind – and H.G. – H.G. positively howled. You are no doubt aware that he was not a conventionally perfect husband – and the slights Jane did not resent – O it was hideous – terrible and frightful.[19]

In 1928 Lawrence in Karachi sent Charlotte *The Mint* in manuscript: 'It is a splendid thing,' she wrote back, 'Heart searching in its depth and force ...' Their letters indicate a strong mutual affection – 'I've had an Ayot feeling over me lately', he wrote on receipt of her praise for *The Mint*, referring to the Shaws' home at Ayot St Lawrence.

Another letter from Charlotte to Lawrence was a description by her of a new novel based on the life – and loves – of Michael Collins. This was *Jane Carroll* (1927), by Ernest Temple Thurston, husband of the Cork writer Katherine Cecil Thurston (née Madden (1875–1911)). The Thurstons married in 1901 and separated in 1907, but Katherine retained her married name as an author.

Her first important novel was *John Chilcote, M.P.* (1904), which was adapted as a stage play by Ernest Thurston. Other titles include *The Gambler* and *The Mystics*, but her most successful book was *The Fly on the Wheel* (1908/1987), a study of an Irish town (Waterford city) in which religious divisions prevent the happy resolution of a love-affair, with the heroine committing suicide as a consequence. Perhaps it was this outcome to the novel which prompted the belief that Katherine Thurston herself had committed suicide when she was found dead in her room in Moore's Hotel in Cork three years later – a few weeks before the date of her second marriage. According to the coroner's report, the cause of death was asphyxiation.

Charlotte Shaw's letter to T.E. Lawrence concerned Ernest Temple Thurston's treatment of an unnamed woman friend of Charlotte's whom Charlotte assumed (and who seemed to assume herself) to be the eponymous Jane Carroll: '*Her* name I somehow don't feel inclined to write', she told Lawrence, but the veil is very thin: I don't think you can help knowing who she is ... About this book, for instance, I think she is proud of it, & glad it has been written ... I have never asked her if any of the incidents ever took place, but she told me once, 'I *was* in an ambush with him' – which makes me think that none of the other things happened as they are described ...

Charlotte was writing as someone who knew Michael Collins. She was in Dublin at the time of his death in 1922. She states as a fact what seems to have been the central theme of the novel:

Michael and a number of the others had made a vow to keep chaste & sober for 3 years at the time they had declared the Republic, & (one can never *know*). I am almost certain in my own mind Michael did not break that vow. If he had I think it not improbable one of the others would have killed him, as it describes in this book ...

She goes on to remark that the author had caught her friend's 'little clever way of talking – her wit & readiness, & her — diplomatic ability ... She is beautiful, even still, & has a charm far more rare than her beauty.' [20]

While it may be accepted that a vein of austere self-denying nationalism united some of the Republican leaders of the War of Independence, there seems to be little agreement as to whether or not Collins himself would have subscribed to such a puritanical vow – despite the evidence of his letters which are full of mass-going and invocations.

Leap

The main road from Rosscarbery to Skibbereen passes Leap; at the right hand side a pretty white house in the Queen Anne style stands with its back to a slate quarry, trees softening the surrounding rocks. Mary Norton lived here from 1972 until shortly before her death in 1992, and it was here that her mysterious and beautiful book *Are All the Giants Dead?* (1975) was written.

The success of *Bedknobs and Broomsticks*, a story for children, encouraged Mary Norton in the use of her unique imaginative gift, which led to the publication of *The Borrowers* (which won the Carnegie Medal) in 1952. The complete, and completely detailed, lives of her tiny characters who live by 'borrowing' what larger humans discard remain among the most enchanting creations in children's literature: she once confided that her sense of scale was due to having exceptionally short sight.

Never a writer of saccharine reassurances, Mary Norton, having sent the borrowers Afield, Afloat and Aloft to the delight of children (and lately cinema-goers) throughout the world, produced, in *Are All the Giants Dead?* a novel which explores the ever-after conclusion of most fairy-tales. There is a look to the house at Leap that makes quite likely the peopling of wonderland with an ageing Jack and his beanstalk and a lonely bejewelled toad and a Sleeping Beauty whose favourite card-game is Patience.

Glandore

At Leap there is a choice of direction: either straight on to Skibbereen or a left-hand fork to Glandore, a small village at the edge of the sea where the native community expands dramatically in summertime as the stately homes and villas around it fill up for the season. New plans suggest there are going to be many more of these in the coming years.

Carhoogariff is close to Glandore, and there William Thompson, born the son of a wealthy and charitable merchant in Cork city, inherited 14,000 acres on which he spent his life attempting to establish practical examples of his philosophical convictions.

> When William Thompson surveyed his lands in Carhoogariff, West Cork, he saw beauties of the rich green countryside but also saw the depths of human poverty and frustration among the poor farmers and peasants. Increasingly, he grew uncomfortable with his ascendancy class and propertied existence – a class position completely unearned by himself.

Thus Dolores Dooley begins *Equality in Community* (1996), her comprehensive study of the life and work of William Thompson (1775–1833), and Anna Doyle Wheeler (1785–1850?).

Although much of what he achieved among his tenants died out as his own immediate presence was removed, Thompson was a profoundly compassionate socialist, a radical and independent thinker influenced both by the Irish abuses of absentee landlordism and by the theories of English and Continental economic reformers and philosophers. He committed himself to a solitary life in Glandore, where he had a tower erected from which to observe the passage along the horizon of his merchant ships and where he gradually adopted a life of abstention from alcohol and meat. From here he wrote treatises on the principles of the distribution of wealth, on the establishment of co-operative communities, on equal pay for equal work, on education and on women's rights.

The most significant of these was probably his *Inquiry into the Principles of the Distribution of Wealth* (1824), and – despite its snappy title – the work on which he co-operated with Tipperary-born Anna Doyle Wheeler Thompson, *Appeal of One Half the Human Race, Women Against the Pretensions of the Other Half, Men, to Retain them in Political and Thence in Civil and Domestic Slavery* (1825).

Although living a life of considerable self-abnegation Thompson was deeply committed to ideas of human happiness, enrichment and empowerment. As an atheist in a small community he was isolated from his peers; there was confusion about his funeral (he was given a church ceremony before his will, expressly forbidding any such thing, was read, and his body had to be disinterred so that it could be given to science) and his fortune, which he bequeathed to the co-operative movement, was disputed to such an extent that most of the money was used up in litigation.

At much the same time as Thompson, James Redmond Barry of Barryroe, near Timoleague, was engaged in the promotion of similar ideas. A member of a land-owning family of Norman descent, his strong humanitarian principles encouraged him to initiate a series of improvements among his tenants. He also worked among the fishing communities of the south-west, not least Glandore, where he revived the village's fishing industry and where he provided free schools for the children of the parish as well as a School of Industry, model farm and carpentry workshop. [21]

On his estates Barry laid out farms whose acreage was decided by the size of the tenant family and for which he provided fruit trees, livestock, beehives and outbuildings. He lost his public status, however, when he declared his support for an anti-tithe agitation organised by the people of nearby Myross and also, perhaps, when he made his opposition to absentee landlords and the activities of agents and bailiffs too obvious.

Glandore is a harbour, and in Irish literary tradition one of the three great waves of Ireland was Tonn Cliodhna, the wave of Cliona, Queen of the Gaelic underworld, in Glandore Harbour (the other two are in Dundrum Bay, Co. Down, and at the mouth of the river Bann). A fourth ominous wave is Tonn Toime, in Castlemaine Harbour in Kerry.

The moaning of these waves was held to be a portent of great change or disaster. The Kerry poet Aodhagán Ó Rathaille (?1670–1729), who must have known this district of West Cork from his time spent travelling around Bantry, based his great lament for the vanished native nobility on hearing the waves crashing on his sleepless ear one night in Castlemaine. An old man living in poverty and unable to provide for his family or to achieve the status to which he is entitled as a poet of the aristocracy, he links the destruction of his MacCarthy patrons with his own condition and that of his country.

In his English version the poet James Stephens (1880–1950) chose to make the sounding wave that of Tonn Cliona in Glandore. Here the translation is by Thomas Kinsella (1928–):

Is fada liom oiche fhírfhliuch gan suan, gan srann,
gan ceathra, gan maoin caoire ná buaibh na mbeann;

anfa ar toinn taoibh liom do bhuair mo cheann,
's nár chleachtas im naíon fiogaigh ná ruacain abhann ...

A thonnsa thíos is airde géim go hard,
meabhair mo chinnse cloíte ód bhéiceach tá;
cabhair dá dtíodh arís ar Éirinn bhán,
do ghlam nach binn do dhingfinn féin id bhráid.

The drenching night drags on; no sleep or snore,
no stock, no wealth of sheep, no horned cows.
This storm on the waves nearby has harrowed my head
– I who ate no winkles or dogfish in my youth! ...

Great Carthy, fierce and fine, who loathed deceit;
with Carthy of the Laoi, in yoke unyielding, faint;
and Carthy King of Ceann Toirc with his children, buried;
it is bitterness through my heart they have left no trace ...

You wave down there, lifting your loudest roar,
the wits in my head are worsted by your wails.
If help ever came to lovely Ireland again
I'd wedge your ugly howling down your throat! [22]

Another observer of the howling waves of Glandore was Dean Jonathan Swift (1667–1745) of St Patrick's Cathedral, Dublin, author of *Gulliver's Travels* (1726). And of much else besides, from political treatises and economic proposals to poetry, satire and parody – his *Drapier's Letters* (1724), which won him the Freedom of the City of Dublin, were pamphlets written in response to a proposal for a separate halfpenny coinage for Ireland.

But it was an unusual tangle of love and money which in 1723 drove Swift to the parish of Myross (where the Irish poet Seán Ó Coileáin ran a hedge school), near Glandore. His relationship with Esther Van Homrigh ('Vanessa', 1688–1723) had deteriorated to the point of extinction.

She was a young woman fond of literature, whom Decanus, the Dean, called Cadenus by transposition of the letters, took pleasure in directing and instructing; till, from being proud of his praise, she grew fond of his person. Swift was then about forty-seven, at an age when vanity is strongly excited by the amorous attention of a young woman. [23]

Esther, who returned from London to her father's estates in Co. Kildare in order to be near Swift, knew about and was jealous of the Dean's affection for 'Stella' (Esther Johnson, 1681–1728 who also moved to Dublin from her home in England for the Dean's sake). Already fatally ill with consumption (tuberculosis) Vanessa confronted Swift in a fierce row which proved to be their last meeting. It is accepted that he had already planned to leave Dublin, but her sudden death precipitated what to many commentators looked like flight.

Swift rode southwards and spent four to six months in Carbery, mostly with friends in Myross but also with The Revd William Somerville at Glenbarrahane in Castletownshend; the Somerville family called the house 'Laputa' in honour of the Dean's visit, and a tower in the village is still called 'Swift's Tower'.

Here, or at Rock Cottage in Union Hall or at Myross Wood just outside Leap – both places at the edge of Glandore Harbour – the Dean received news of Vanessa's will. It was not good news. Made a few weeks after their parting and only a month before her death Vanessa left the bulk of her fortune to the philosopher The Revd George Berkeley with whom she was only recently acquainted. She also left instructions for the publication both of her correspondence with the Dean, and for the publication of Swift's poem 'Cadenus and Vanessa', which he wrote while still fond of her.

In Myross, therefore, the beleaguered, disappointed and possibly guilt-stricken Dean heard the thundering waves of Glandore and Castlehaven as bruiting personal misfortune or at least offering nature's perspective on the little tragedies of mankind. He wrote in Latin the verses 'Carberiae Rupes', which were translated by The Revd Dr William Dunkin and quoted in Smith's *History of Cork*:

> Lo! from the top of yonder cliff, that shrouds
> Its airy head amidst the azure clouds,
> Hangs a huge fragment ...

Serene as things may appear, the scene alters dramatically with winter, when goats cropping the turf on the headlands are swept to death in the sea and 'the frighted fisher with desponding eyes / Tho' safe yet trembling in the harbour lyes ...'

Nothing is what it seems, everything is capable of violent or sudden change. Cork was to prove this again to the Dean when in 1736 Cork Corporation agreed to award him the Freedom of the City in recognition of *Drapier's Letters*. The Dean was not without enemies in Cork and the corporation's belated bestowal of the Freedom in an un-inscribed silver box (when gold was used for others) and the manner of its presentation to the Dean led to the direction, in his will, that the box be given to a friend to 'keep the tobacco he usually cheweth, called Pigtail in it.'[24]

Union Hall

Across the harbour from Glandore is Union Hall, and here lived Colonel Hall, who was responsible for the development of the copper mines whose now disused shafts litter parts of West Cork. At Allihies the mine was taken over by the Puxley family, whose fortunes became the subject of the novel *Hungry Hill* (1943) by Daphne du Maurier (1907–89).

Cornish miners were imported to work the lodes, and the ruins of their little village lie between the two main shafts at Allihies. Hall, by re-awakening and re-working the ancient mines and opening new ones ensured nearly a hundred years of employment in these places.

Colonel Hall was the father of the journalist Samuel Carter Hall (1800–89), who with his wife Anna Maria Fielding (1800–81) wrote *Ireland, its Scenery, Character, Etc.* (1842). The Dublin-born Anna Maria was a hardworking and successful novelist and writer of short stories, comic plays, poetry and magazine articles but she also wrote many studies and sketches of Irish life and customs. She and her husband commissioned the memorial to Thomas Moore at his burial place in England.

Castletownshend

The land of south-west Cork is latticed with tiny roads which all lead somewhere and, eventually even to the desired destination. But our road turns back towards the highway for Skibbereen, and along it after a few miles a small junction on the left leads to Castletownshend.

For one of the most famous villages in Ireland, Castletownshend remains the quiet enclave it was in the days of its renowned inhabitants, Somerville and Ross. Somewhat blighted by the introduction of PVC windows, the houses still follow the slope of the precipitous main street where the cleft tree marks the junction of The Mall and the quay in front of the castle marks the limit of the village.

Marking Glen Barrahane parish, the lovely church of St Barrahane stands on the hill above the 'new' castle and close to the ruins of the old one. Castletownshend is on the very edge of the harbour of Castlehaven, and is still alive to the names of the interlinked families – Coghills, Somervilles, Townshends and Chevasses – which are evoked in any reading of the lives of Edith Oenone Somerville (1858–1949) of Drishane House and her cousin Violet Florence Martin (1862–1915) of Ross House in Co. Galway.

The relationship they formed as adult companions – still tirelessly exhumed in search of latent lesbianisn – was based on difference rather than on likenesses. Edith was the eldest of eight children with an exacting mother whose tongue (as a character in *The Irish RM* remarks) 'would clip a hedge'; her efforts to support herself by her drawings were not only a way of relieving the family finances but also of reducing her mother's dependence on her for constant company. Violet, already a journalist, was facing the task of restoring the huge, decrepit family home abandoned on the death of her father who had been almost beggared by his relief efforts during the Great Famine. She found in Edith a witty, energetic and resourceful ally; Edith found in Violet an admiring and warm-hearted friend. Their collaboration is one of the most remarkable in the history of literature; their friendship was one of soul as well as heart, of mind as well as manners. Their needs spoke to one another, and met.

Exclusivity in anything was difficult for young women of their background in those days. Violet became a friend of all the family, where Edith was also particularly close to her sister Hildegarde with whom, years later, she ran the first pedigree herd of Friesian cattle in Cork. It was Hildegarde too who later established a successful farm for cultivated violets, of which, on the day before Christmas Eve 1915, Edith was to create Martin's funeral wreath.

> The doctrine that sincere friendship is only possible between men dies hard ... The outstanding fact, as it seems to me, among women who live by their brains, is friendship. A profound friendship that extends through every phase and aspect of life, intellectual, social, pecuniary. Anyone who has experience of the life of independent and artistic women knows this; and it is noteworthy that these friendships of women will stand even the strain of matrimony for one or both of the friends. I gravely doubt that David saw much of Jonathan after the death of Uriah ...[25]

Edith Somerville said that her meeting with Violet Martin was 'the hinge of my life'. The junketings of their Irish RM stories suggest gaiety, gallantry and constant fair weather, but in fact heartbreak, financial anxiety and family disputes wreaked havoc from time to time. Edith, whose first – and favoured – suitor was dismissed because of inadequate means and whose second preferred her as a literary dilettante, never underestimated the fatal power of family obligations.

> To attempt anything serious or demanding steady work is just simply impossible here, and I feel sickened of even trying ... whatever is done must be done by everyone in the whole place and as the majority prefer wasting their time that is the prevalant amusement.[26]

The cousins' literary successes were taken relatively lightly at home; they were expected to leave off work for boating and tennis, fancy-dress and country visiting (which included visits to Charlotte Payne Townsend – Edith's cousin 'Lottie' – and her husband, regarded by Edith as 'her cad – for cad he is, despite his talent'[27]). Throughout her life Edith, also a good singer, played the organ in St Barrahane's church; in this churchyard she now lies next to Martin. But she and Martin left off work voluntarily for only two good reasons: to make tours about which they could write and therefore earn some money and to hunt.

In fact for years Edith made more money buying and selling horses than with her books. She was a superb horsewoman and kept the hounds for the West Carbery Hunt with which she and Martin rode; their formal photographic portraits in full riding kit show all the dignity of Edith's role as Master. Although Martin did hunt again after a shattering fall in 1898 (she was extremely short-sighted and gamely faced into any obstacle that came her way), it was believed that the fall, in which the horse rolled on her, contributed to her death in 1915.

The charm of *Some Experiences of an Irish RM* (1899 and subsequent volumes) is the collection of characters amongst whom the reader lives for the duration of the stories: dogs, people, horses, even the fields, rivers, villages and barns are all drawn with skilful appreciation. But although the Irish RM (Resident Magistrate) is the creation by which Somerville and Ross are best known, it was not the first, or the best, of their work.

> Miss Mullen's heaving shoulders and extended jaw spoke of nothing but her determination to outscream everyone else. Miss Hope-Drummond and the curate ... were singing primly out of the same hymn-book, the curate obviously frightened. The Misses Beattie were furtively eyeing Miss Hope-Drummond's costume; Miss Kathleen Baker was openly eyeing the curate.[28]

In *The Real Charlotte* the organist's view of the congregation is a hint of the tensions within a small, closed community in Ireland. This is not 'safe' humour, although it distracts the reader's attention, for a while, from what is really going on. As Declan Kiberd has observed in his study of the book, 'Like other novels of manners, this is designed not just to be read but to be re-read, and its art is a strategy of preparations.'[29]

The Real Charlotte (1894) which succeeded the mild success of *An Irish Cousin* (1889) (disparaged by its authors as 'the shocker' as a way of averting family sarcasm) and of *Naboth's Vineyard* (1891) – this is recognised as their masterpiece. An important and influential study of the various forces afflicting the history of the Big House in Ireland, it is set against the domestic intrigues for land and for love.

Travel books, more RM stories, more novels and articles followed in shared lives in which two subtle minds brought out the best of one another. This should have ended with Martin's death of a brain tumour in 1915, but Edith was convinced that the strength of their communion survived death itself and she continued to publish her books under the signature of Somerville and Ross. The best of these was *The Big House of Inver* (1925), but there were many others, all worth reading, including *Mount Music* (1919), which is set among landlords and tenants affected by the Irish Land Acts at the end of the nineteenth century.

The later Somerville and Ross books do have a trace of sentimentality; it is as if the absence of the business-like Martin released Edith's feeling for colour, sometimes of a purplish tinge. *Irish Memories* written in 1919 gives a foretaste of the soft-focus approach the grieving Edith used when writing of Violet Martin, and this tone lingers in some of the subsequent novels.

> I will say nothing now of the time that we spent in Kerry; a happy time, in lovely weather, in a lovely place. It was the last of many such times, and it is too near, now, to be written of. I will try no more. Withered leaves, blowing in through the open window before a September gale, are falling on the page. Our summers are ended ... But there is a thing that an old widow woman said, long ago, that remains in my mind. Her husband – she spoke of him as her 'kind companion' – had died, and she said to me, patiently, and without tears,
> 'Death makes people lonesome, my dear.'[30]

Castlehaven, before the Somervilles and Townshends, had seen rampant death in its own slice of history when, just before the Battle of Kinsale, a small Spanish fleet was sheltered there and welcomed to the castle by its proprietors, the O'Driscolls. There are several versions of the naval engagement which followed the arrival of the English defenders early in December 1601 with both sides claiming victory; the battle itself however was only a footnote to the Battle of Kinsale which followed within weeks, but it was from Castlehaven that Red Hugh O'Donnell sailed for Spain and his death in Simancas.

The dispossessed O'Driscolls were replaced by Bechers from Bandon and Cork who settled in Castlehaven. Later colonists were the Somervilles and Townshends who have given the village its name and the district – still wild in many ways, still beautiful – its fame.

Skibbereen

Skibbereen, on the Illen river, is a thriving market town which in summer takes on a cosmopolitan glamour due to being a conduit to the fashionable coves and villages further south. Its own personality survives this invasion, for despite being of relatively recent foundation it is a fusion of two much older settlements. Skibbereen, in fact, could survive anything, having recovered from the frightful effects on the town and its vicinity of the Great Famine (1846–48).

'Are we living in a portion of the United Kingdom?' asked the outraged Revd Francis Webb, rector of Caheragh, south-west of Skibbereen, who knew that the incredible answer was 'yes':

> I saw the bodies of Kate Barry and her two children very lightly covered with earth ... the flesh completely eaten by dogs ... two most wretched looking old houses with two dead bodies in each, Norry Regan, Tom Barry, Nelly Barry (a little girl) and Charles MacCarthy (a little boy) all dead about a fortnight and not yet interred. [31]

By virtue of its size and location Skibbereen was the focus of much of the attention given to the famine, although the reports concentrating there were drawn on the events in the districts all around it from Baltimore to Ballydehob and Schull and Durrus. The *Southern Reporter*, for example, declaimed in 1847 that 'Every civilised nation, aye, savage nation on earth is familiar with Skull, the place of the Skulls'; as Patrick Hickey points out in his story of the famine. [32]

Schull and Skibbereen had become synonyms for famine – partly as a result of the illustrations by James Mahoney for the *Illustrated London News* in 1847. One of the tragic ironies of these places was that the abundant use of seaweed as manure had increased the fertility of the potato-growing acres and therefore the dependence of the cottiers on the potato as a staple food. Thus when the blight struck the disaster was immediate and terrible.

While local relief began quickly throughout the country it became obvious that the scale of the famine was beyond individual efforts. Gradually government action supplied replacement foreign grain and helped provide soup-kitchens but the stern insistence on self-help rather than charity (so that the soup had to be paid for by men earning a shilling a week on 'relief' roadworks) meant that often the neediest were denied any help other than the workhouse.

Land-owners provided as much work as they could finance (many of the fine demesne walls throughout Ireland were built in the famine) but they too discovered how finite their resources were under such an onslaught –

and with clergymen (and the clergy wives) and doctors they too suffered, if not from starvation, from disease and death from the associated fever, heartbreak and the strenuous social work they undertook. As many as 123 doctors died of fever during the famine year of 1847 alone; forty Church of Ireland clergymen, including R.B. Townsend, rector of Abbeystrewery at Skibbereen, died of famine-related diseases.

In his play *Souper Sullivan* the writer and broadcaster Eoghan Harris (1943–) takes as his theme the complex, divisive and often mis-represented motives of those trying by their own means and usually out of their own incomes to succour their tenants and neighbours. This is not yet a comfortable subject for Irish audiences – the soup-kitchens were sometimes used by misguided evangelists as a means of winning the native, Catholic population over to Protestantism; to be a 'souper' is the reverberating insult of those times. The play, produced at the Abbey Theatre in 1985, was a stunning success.

The Skibbereen soup-kitchen was funded by people who bought supplies of tickets for distribution to the poor. The workhouse was thronged by emaciated and destitute people who made their despairing way there only as the very last resort and for whom, in the end, it had nothing to offer. Run by usually officious and fatally parsimonious Poor Law guardians, these institutions were almost under siege; a particularly ill-judged attempt to control access through insisting that no one owning more than a quarter-acre of land was eligible for entry did, for a while, reduce applications.

This extraordinarily cruel clause (introduced by the Dublin MP William Gregory) meant that men in possession of that small plot of land on which they grew the food by which they lived could only be taken in to the workhouse or given any kind of relief if they surrendered their holding. Instead, they abandoned their families. Land offered some hope for the future, even if for the present nothing could be grown, and the idea of parting even with their tiny patches was anathema. They sent their wives and children to the workhouses as widows and orphans; were the ruse discovered, these innocent victims were ejected, but the practice became so widespread and the obligation to refuse food or shelter to starving children became so onerous that the rules were either relaxed or left to the dubious discretion of the guardians.

At Skibbereen the grossly overcrowded workhouse, described as 'a magnate for misery', closed to new inmates in January of 1847; it had been built for 800 people and by December of 1848 housed 2,800. In Bantry the inmates were fed only once a day and very badly at that – in fact the institution ran out of food entirely by the end of May in 1847.

The thousands of deaths in these districts were not all caused by hunger: fever, dysentery and scurvy were among the most frequent killers. From a population of 43,266, more than 7,000 died and nearly 1,000 emigrated.

The light on the Fastnet Rock, visible from the coasts of all these rocky villages around Skibbereen, became for most of that multitude disappearing westwards the last beacon of Ireland: 'deor Eireann', it was called – Ireland's tear-drop.

Peadar Ó hAnnracháin (1873–1965) of Skibbereen was a poet who became editor of *The Southern Star* newspaper for a year while also keeping a farm and acting as registrar for the county council. An organiser for the Gaelic League, he joined the Irish Volunteers in 1913, as a result of which he was imprisoned several times between 1916 and 1921. His poetry is collected in *An Chaise Garbh* (1918) and *An Chaise Riabhach* (1937); his play *Stiana* was performed at the Abbey Theatre in Dublin in 1944.

Sisters Mary Ellen (1840–1906) and Agnes Mary (1842–1907) Clerke were born in Skibbereen, later moving to Dublin and later again to Cobh. They travelled widely and translated from the Italian, German and Arabic, with Mary Ellen's poetry being published, with considerable success, as *The Flying Dutchman and Other Poems* (1881). Agnes Mary, on the other hand, was a scientist, and her outstanding work was *A Popular History of Astronomy During the Nineteenth Century* which became a standard textbook.

Young Irelander Joseph Brenan (1828–57) was born in nearby Clonakilty but spent much of his childhood in Skibbereen; he was a close friend of James Clarence Mangan (1803–49) and a contributor to *The Nation* newspaper, through which he developed his friendship with Ellen Mary Downing, known as 'Mary of The Nation'.

The daughter of the resident medical officer at the Cork Fever Hospital Ellen Mary was said to be of delicate disposition; the suppression of *The Nation* in 1848 and the disappointment of Brenan's departure for America in 1849 encouraged her to enter the South Presentation Convent in Cork that same year. Ill-health, amounting to paralysis, made this an unsuitable vocation and she returned to civilian life for a while, deciding later to keep her religious name and vows and to live as a member of the Third Order of St Dominic.

She wrote devotional poetry for children but was considered for a time to be one of the foremost women poets of *The Nation,* although later she wrote only for *The United Irishman*.[33] Brenan made his way to America where he worked as a journalist and where he died, almost completely blind, in New Orleans.

Editor and amateur historian J.M. Burke (1873–1936) was born in Skibbereen and educated at the then Queen's College, Cork. A barrister, TD and local councillor he was also editor of *The Southern Star*, formerly known as *The Skibbereen Eagle*. This was the newspaper which won international distinction when in September 1898 it warned its readers that it was keeping its eye on the Czar of Russia.

From Skibereen the road towards Rath and the islands leads along the estuary of the Illen river towards Baltimore. From any height here the view is of Roaring Water Bay and the archipelago formed by Carbery's hundred isles. The heights themselves sweep back from the road towards Mount Gabriel but the tussocky landscape is marshy, thick with heathers, merging unexpectedly into bog and cut by roads thin as threads. One of these leads down to Lough Hyne, the land-locked sea-inlet surrounded by wooded hills:

> I love to sit here for hours on end watching the river flow seaward out through the rapids. Then quite amazingly before your eyes, as the tide turns, the powerful bosom of the ocean forces its way back up the river channel to meet the out-coming river-rage. Ultimately the two forces equate and lock! For a brief moment, the entire river is held in an eerie and stifled silence.
>
> Finally the ocean wins, forcing the river to retreat, reversing it back up into its imprisoning mountain tomb. Gracefully, as if in an underwater ballet the swards of giant *kelp* that pointed seaward now begin to stand up vertically, arching their fronds over the silent waters. [34]

This inland sea-lake is below sea-level at high tide, which causes the phenomenon described above by Kevin Corcoran – the river flowing backwards towards its source. The sea enters through a narrow creek; its tidal action has created a remarkable marine aquarium here, a delight for the visitor because of its setting and strangeness, but also a natural laboratory used by University College Cork for the study of coastal marine biology.

Another little road off the main road from Skibbereen to Ballydehob swerves down to Rosbrin Harbour, passing one of the many O'Mahony castles which stud these peninsulas; Rosbrin was the home of McTeig O'Mahony who soldiered with O'Neill at Kinsale.

Much earlier it was also the home of Finin O'Mahony, a scholar mentioned in the *Annals of Loch Cé* who died at the O'Mahony castle of Ardintenant nearby in 1495.

Contemporary writers such as Victoria Glendinning and Tomi Ungerer live either permanently or in holiday homes throughout West Cork. The Danish writer, Erik Haugaard, has made his home at Ballydehob, from where he has continued to publish his novels and stories for young readers. He is recognised as the definitive translator into English of Hans Christian Andersen; he has written many novels including *Hakon of Rogen's Saga* (1963), *The Little Fishes* (1968) and *Under the Black Flag* (1993). Prizes and awards include the Boston Globe-Horn Book Award (1967), the Children's Literature Association Phoenix Award (1981) and the Japan Foundation Fellowship (1981).

He settled in Ballydehob about twenty-five years ago with his first wife, poet Myrna Seld (d. 1981).[35]

Skirting the bay and running between the sea and the foothills of Mount Gabriel, the road spills down into Schull, a popular resort from which seasonal ferries ply to the island of Cape Clear. While pressure to suburbanise the village is growing, there are still splendid vistas to be gained from the hilly paths around it, not least the mountain road weaving around Knocknageeha and Mount Corin on the way to Durrus.

Popular legend has it that the old rectory at the end of the village was used as a base by Sir John Moore when his ships were blown off their course for the Peninsular Wars, where he was to die at Corunna.

There are old mine shafts throughout these hills, linked with the very early discovery of copper and the construction here of neolithic ring-forts revealed by the gradual erosion of the boggy terraces of the mountains. Despite the build-up around Schull it is easy still to find wild, windswept valleys, with the last ruined cabins the only reminders now of the ravages of the famine years; near the summit of Mount Gabriel is a little lake, said to be the hole left when the devil tore out the rock which became the Fastnet.

Creeks, inlets and castles are the features of the lower landscape; the peninsula divides and sub-divides, the sea glittering between headland and island and making it impossible often to tell one from the other at a distance. Cape Clear remains one of the few inhabited and prosperous islands in Ireland; its identity as an Irish-speaking community brings it students and scholars every summer.

Toormore, Goleen, Crookhaven are villages set on the very edge of the coves south of Schull – Crookhaven, with its restored coastguard cottages, on an isthmus which makes a bay of the water between itself and Goleen. The white towns against the blue sea take on an Aegean intensity of colour when seen from the hills; in summer and autumn the fuchsia fringes the roads with crimson hedges, and the layers of fern and heather stretching away from the paths are broken here and there with the green of tiny meadows, unexpected pastures ripening towards autumn and splashing the brown and purple slopes with gold.

Hidden from the visiting eye are the little cemeteries, each called a 'cillín': they can be identified usually in triangular patches of ground near or outside regular church-yards or at a cross-roads. Protected by banks or ditches and marked, if at all, by flat white stones, uneven in shape and irregular in placement, they contain the graves of babies buried before baptism. According to the old religious teaching unbaptised infants, still marked by the stain of original sin, could not see the heaven reserved for luckier children. Limbo was their theological destination; their families left them symbolically outside the fold.

These small sites are not unique to Cork, but their clusters in these districts are more numerous than usual – possibly, again, as a result of the Great Famine.[36]

The spectacular strands of Barley Cove and the coastal indentations of many mountain streams rushing to the sea capture the eye as the road leads to the Mizen Head. At Toormore a sign says 'Altar', indicating the site of the church built by the evangelical William Fisher as part of a scheme of famine relief (the name Altar indicates the wedge-tomb nearby).

At Crookhaven Marconi erected his radio mast before moving to a signalling station at Brow Head; the Fastnet Rock has its white tower signalling its warning to shipping, and on the edge of Mizen Head, the most southerly point in Ireland, the Fog Signalling Station has been closed down for its original function but opened up as a tourist attraction.

It combines that useful mission now with its other role as location of the Differential Globe Positioning Satellite; the station houses are museums of the quiet lives endured here since 1909. To reach them the visitor must climb the rocky but well-marked path across the cliff and then cross the short suspension bridge over the chasm which separates the Mizen from the mainland. The Fastnet light splits the horizon on the one hand, on the other the headlands unfurl from the mountainous hinterland with the Miskish and Caha ranges blurring the outlines of Beara and the higher Kerry hills beyond, the prong of Sheeps' Head introduced by the jagged profile of Three Castle Head over Dunlough Bay. Dunmanus Bay opens out with Durrus a smoky cluster at its inland extremity; behind is Roaring Water Bay.

The path foams with sea-thrift, campion and wild thyme; autumn gorse surges up through the turf; lark, wheatear and stonechat flicker after the insects feeding on the vetches and heathers. Around the cliffs scream the gulls, guillemots, kittiwakes and fulmars, sometimes puffins. Seals, dolphins, even whales drowse in the calmer lagoon beyond the fissure in the red sandstone cliff.

The caravan parks disappear in the rise of the ground towards Knocknamadree. At Dunmanus the tiny islands hint at refuge from the storming of the castle, many times; a ring fort behind the castle suggests aeons of siege. Wild as it seems at these cliff-tops, the sea around this coast gave many villages employment in fishing and fisheries.

Baltimore

One of the most successful fishing towns was Baltimore, formerly Dunashead, reached easily from Skibbereen and with its open harbour shielded only by the long hump of Sherkin island.

The O'Driscolls controlled the wealth of these townlands, levying the visiting smacks which came after rich crops of pilchard and mackerel. This was also an ideal coastline for smuggling, in which lord and tenant, friend and foe alike engaged through the centuries. It was an hospitable coast too for raiding parties from other lands – Vikings after plunder, the French after fish. And profitable for pirates. As early as the fourteenth century the O'Driscoll hold on the fishing grounds had aroused the enmity of Waterford, where fishing was also a crucial means of livelihood, and through several centuries a feud developed and was inflamed time after time between the two ports.

Piracy was a risk for all who travelled by sea in the sixteenth and seventeenth century – and even for those who stayed at home, when their homes were along the Atlantic coast, as was the town of Baltimore.

In 1631, Algerian pirates looking for easy pickings but unable to make their way into Kinsale went westwards instead, picking up two Waterford vessels on the way. The captain of one of these was Thomas Hackett of Dungarvan, Co. Waterford; he agreed to guide the Algerians into Baltimore.

'On the 20th of June 1631', writes Smith,

> a most terrible disaster happened this colony. In the dead of night two Algerine rovers landed their men, and having plundered the place, they made a great number of the inhabitants prisoners, with above 100 English, and carried them all to Algiers. Among others, William Gunter, a person of some credit, had his wife and seven sons carried away ... Those Algerines were piloted into Baltimore by a Dungarvan fisherman, one Hacket, whom they took at sea for the purpose, and who for this fact was afterwards condemned and executed. Two ships of war called the Lyons Whelps stationed at Kingsale received timely notice of this intended descent, but they did not stir to intercept them. [37]

The summer sun is falling soft o'er Carbery's hundred isles,
The summer sun is gleaming still through Gabriel's rough defiles,
Old Inisherkin's crumbling fane looks like a moulting bird,
And in a calm and sleepy swell the ocean tide is heard ...

A deeper rest, a starry trance, has come with midnight there;
No sound, except that throbbing wave, in earth, or sea, or air.
The massive capes and ruined towers seem conscious of the calm;
The fibrous sod and stunted trees are breathing heavy balm ...

All, all asleep within each roof along that rocky street,
And these must be the lover's friends with gently gliding feet –
A stifled gasp! a dreamy noise! 'The roof is in a flame!'
From out their beds, and to their doors, rush maid, and sire, and dame,
And meet upon the threshold stone the gleaming sabre's fall,
And o'er each black and bearded face the white or crimson shawl;

The yell of 'Allah' breaks above the prayer, and shriek, and roar –
Oh, blessed God! The Algerine is lord of Baltimore ...

Mid-summer morn, in woodland nigh, the birds began to sing:
They see not now the milking-maids – deserted is the spring!
Mid-summer day – this gallant rides from distant Bandon's town;
These hookers crossed from stormy Skull, that skiff from Affadown.
They only found the smoking walls, with neighbour's blood besprent,
And on the strewed and trampled beach awhile they wildly went;
Then dashed to sea, and passed Cape Cleire, and saw five leagues before
The pirate galleys vanishing that ravished Baltimore.

Oh! some must tug the galley's oar, and some must tend the steed;
This boy will bear a Scheik's chibouk, and that a Bey's jerreed.
Oh! some are in the arsenals, by beauteous Dardanelles;
And some are in the caravan to Mecca's sandy dells.
The maid that Bandon gallant sought is chosen for the Dey:
She's safe – he's dead – she stabbed him in the midst of his serai;
And when, to die a death of fire, that noble maid they bore,
She only smiled – O'Driscoll's child – she thought of Baltimore ...[38]

Most of the hostages taken were not the native population but a small group of English people brought in by Sir Thomas Crooke (whose name is given to Crookhaven) who was trying to establish his rights to the forfeited lands of Finin O'Driscoll. Beacons were set up around the coast but many people left the area, some following Finin himself who went to live at Lough Hyne. Yet it was the absence of fish rather than insecurity which forced people away from Baltimore, the pilchards disappearing in the eighteenth century, gradually being replaced by mackerel and herring.

Baltimore today is a busy town, especially in summer. Boat-building and repair services have revived, cottage industry has been sustained and in at least one case has flowered into a factory. The village has become a much-favoured summer sailing retreat for people from all over Ireland and abroad, with new recruits learning their skills at three different sailing schools and clubs.

The islands which crowd the estuary of the Ilen as far as Skibbereen are also popular – one can be reached by a causeway, another is famous for its restaurant which attracts boat-loads of clients on summer evenings.

The ruined friary on Sherkin Island where Maurice O'Fehily was a scholar is marked by its few, recently refurbished, walls; it was founded in 1460 by Florence O'Driscoll for the Franciscans but burned down, in 1537, by a invading party from Waterford which also fired the O'Driscoll castle of

Dunalong. Looking eastwards from the friary the white warning beacon above Baltimore can be seen across the harbour.

Sherkin, where an independent marine reseach centre was established several years ago, is one of the rare islands on which the population has remained constant and may even have increased in the last twenty years; it boasts immaculate beaches of white sand and clean clear green water. With only a little motorised traffic and a frequent ferry service to the mainland, it is noteworthy even on this coast.

Sherkin is not the only island off this peninsula: its old name was Inis Kieran, after St Kieran who was born on Cape Clear island to the south. Clear is separated from Sherkin by a narrow channel and a regular ferry goes out from Baltimore.

> The inhabitants here are generally a very simple honest people, thieving being a vice little known among them. If a person be found guilty of a crime, he is directly banished to the continent, which is the greatest punishment they can inflict on the criminal, who endeavours all he can to remain on the island ... Most of the inhabitants are strong and healthy, and are seldom invaded with disorders, dying generally of old age, chiefly owing to their temperate living, hard labour, and clearness of the air ... They are kind to each other, courteous to strangers who very rarely are seen on the island, and are excellent pilots, being all fishermen.[39]

The continent was the mainland: the people of the Cape refer to it as Ireland, so independent is the tradition of this community. It is one of the very few Irish-speaking districts left in the country, and this has helped it survive as every summer brings pupils from the mainland to study in its Irish college, supported by government grants. Of its two harbours, the one to the south was used during the American Civil War for a telegraph system with a submarine cable linking the island to Baltimore and thence to Dublin and Europe; the American news arrived by ship and was then transmitted by cable.

Now it is the sheltered north harbour which is used for traffic, and close to it a bird sanctuary has been established so that professional and amateur ornithologists can study migrating flocks. Through the centuries fishing and farming have been the way of life on the island; to these, and its repute as a place of pilgrimage and its educational importance, is now added its recreational attractions for the many summer sailors who set out from Schull and Baltimore.

The poet Orla Murphy (1948–) lives near Baltimore, which was also the childhood home of Michael Fitz-James (de Courcy) O'Brien (1828–62). During the Great Famine he began to write for *The Nation*, but briefly enriched by a legacy, he went to London where he spent the lot. From England he travelled to America and for a while earned his living by writing stories, plays and verses of Gothic fantasy. He then enlisted in the Union Army and died from wounds received during the Civil War. His collected works were published in 1881.[40]

Durrus

At Toormore, west of Schull, the traveller can take the road north-west along the edge of Dunmanus Bay towards Durrus as an alternative to the mountain road from Schull. This will pass Dunmanus Castle and the stone circle at Drumbeg, and from the village of Durrus (where the novelist J.G. Farrell is buried) will lead either to the main Bantry road or else to the next peninsula, Muintir Bhaire, or the Sheep's Head peninsula.

This is a wonderland for the naturalist and archaeologist, and its wonders have been made accessible by a local group, led by the late Tom Whitty, which with the co-operation of local farmers has mapped a walk covering the entire length of the peninsula with many intermediate or alternative routes for the less athletic. Holy wells, stone circles, promontory forts dot the headland; the O'Mahony bardic school is found at Farranamanagh near Kilcrohane where Aonghus Ruadh Ó Dálaigh composed his satirical verses – his house can be seen at Cora, about two miles away. At Ahakista stands Cork sculptor Ken Thompson's poignant memorial to the victims of the Air India crash of 1985.

The late novelist and screen-writer Wolf Mankowitz (d. 1998) lived at Ahakista where the road winds under the slope of Roskerrig. His novels, stories and plays include *The Bespoke Overcoat*, the collection *Samson Riddles* (1972) and the short stories *Days of Women and Nights of Men*. A native of the Jewish community of London's East End, Mankowitz also wrote film scripts *The Millionairess* (1960) and the James Bond film *Casino Royale* (1967); *A Kid for Two Farthings* was adapted for a film by Carol Reed, and he worked with Orson Welles on an adaptation of *Treasure Island*; while producing novels, plays and short stories he was also an expert on antiques and wrote studies of both Charles Dickens and Edgar Allan Poe. [41]

The road rises with Seefin mountain, the view eastwards is towards the Mizen peak, Three Castle Head and Mount Gabriel. The shore at the western edge of Seefin is washed by Bantry Bay; from here the Beara Peninsula stretches from Dursey island to Glengarriff, the dark mass of the Miskish and Caha mountains folding over one another in a prelude to the Kerry peaks.

Bantry

The industrialisation of Bantry Bay with the introduction of the Gulf Oil terminal on Whiddy Island has left lasting intrusions on the landscape here, to which have been added (as interminably elsewhere around the west coast of Ireland) the grilles of fish-farming businesses. Modernisation of the town has continued through the last twenty years, and it has now long outpaced its first important economy based on sea-fishing. Tourists visiting the town are drawn to the park, gardens and rooms of Bantry House, set on a terraced location above the bay and the centre, each summer, of the West Cork Festival of Chamber Music which attracts musicians from all over the world.

The stable-yard here has been restored to house the Armada Museum, referring not to the Spanish Armada but to the French fleet which arrived in 1796 in an attempt to bring Wolfe Tone back to Ireland to lead the United Irishmen in revolt against the English government. The ships, weathering the December storms, were seen early in the bay and the alarm raised; but it was the weather which scattered the fleet and separated its most important ships so that the French retreated after a few days. Tone was to try again and in 1798 was captured at Lough Swilly. Defended by John Philpot Curran he was sentenced to death; he tried to cut his own throat and although this was a failure he he died from the effects of the wound.[42]

The learned bardic family of Ó Dalaigh which was well known after the twelfth century is linked to Dunamask, near Bantry town.

The enormous Bantry House archive has now been lodged with the Boole Library at University College Cork; among its family items are some letters of Olive, Lady Ardilaun (d. 1925), daughter of the third Earl of Bantry and wife of Sir Arthur Edward Guinness, Lord Ardilaun. She collected family papers, especially those relating to Richard White, the first Earl of Bantry.

Novelist Gaye Shortland (c. 1950–)[43] is from Bantry, a town which also produced the Sullivan brothers: Timothy Daniel (1827–1914), journalist, poet and politician, nationalist MP and Mayor of Dublin (1886–87), whose published work includes *Lays of the Land League* and *Prison Songs* as well as *Dunboy* (1861); owner of *The Nation*, his most enduring song is 'God Save Ireland'.

His brother Alexander Martin Sullivan (1830–84), a journalist, barrister and historian, was involved in the formation of the Home Rule Party, edited *The Nation* and became a Member of Parliament. His memoirs are published as *Old Ireland* (1927) and *The Last Sergeant* (1952).

From Bantry to Glengarriff the main road hugs the bay along a route which introduces the visitor to the effects of the Gulf Stream on the south coast of Ireland: although later in Kerry the impact is more noticeable, here a certain luxuriance in the roadside gardens emerges, unexpected trees appear, the hills are hidden with shrubbery and cloaked even to the summits with greenery.

Glengarriff

At Ballylickey (where the river Ouvane leads back towards Kealkil and the Shehy Mountains and Gougane Barra) is the former home of botanist Major P.P. Graves (1876–1953) who was for forty years a foreign correspondent for *The Times* of London. Ruins here indicate the sway of the ancient O'Sullivan family of Beara, former owners of Bantry and Whiddy and builders of Carriganass Castle and Reenadisert House.

Glengarriff lies ahead, situated under the crowding mountains and at the corner of a deep inlet studded with tree-covered islands. The village itself, despite the imposing hotel, is no longer distinguished, the long main street little more than an over-crowded marketplace battlemented by tour buses. But Glengarriff is a place of departure: there is the dramatic tunnelled road through the Caha mountains to Kenmare, and there are the boats to carry passengers across the bay to the island of Illnacullin where the Irish government has taken over the famous Garnish gardens established here by Annan Bryce in 1910.

The gardens were designed by architect Harold Pinto to complement a house, and later developed by Murdo MacKenzie. The house was never built but a casita of Bath stone and a loggia hung with wisteria and facing a classical pool encrusted with lilies are among the architectural elements of the plan.

A stunning composition links the formal borders to alleys of rhododendron and azalea, linking also the little temple at one end of the island to the Martello watch-tower at the other, and all in perfect visual amity with the natural backdrop of mountain and sea. The short boat-trip includes a diversion to watch the seals basking on the warm rocks in the bay. Even waiting for the boat at the little pier in a rocky cove is a pleasure.[44]

Stephen Gill, in his 1998 biography of William Wordsworth, quotes the poet's description of his visit to Glengarriff in 1829, where his party 'called on Mr White, Brother to Lord Bantry, at his beautiful cottage or castle upon Glengariffe bay, walked about his charming grounds, lunched with Mrs White and her two interesting daughters.'

Glengarriff is also the departure-point for the Beara Peninsula, the road again winding along the shore towards Adrigole, the mouth of the river flowing from the clefts of Hungry Hill. At Bank Harbour a French Huguenot settlement led by Jacques de la Fontaine attempted to establish a fishing colony at the end of the seventeenth century. Although this failed, de la Fontaine himself was rewarded for defending his colony against French marauders; he was later captured by the French, rescued by his wife, and retired with his family to Dublin.

Castletownbere

Fishing is the life of Castletownbere; its hospitable harbour, sheltered by Bere[45] Island, is home to one of the largest white fishing fleets in Ireland and a major port for the trawlers and factory ships of many nations. This industry has coloured the life of Castletownbere and it is a lively town despite its apparently remote location.

'I think it was his "History of Ireland, Heroic Period" that started us all', said W.B. Yeats of the work of Standish O'Grady of Castletownbere.[46]

Standish James O'Grady (1846–1928) was the son of a titled Protestant clergyman (he was born at the Glebe House) who sent him to Trinity College in Dublin where, instead of taking orders as had been expected, he decided to qualify as a barrister. Having absorbed the legends of his birthplace, he pursued this interest in Dublin, where through manuscript collections and histories he discovered a wealth of epic material and an Irish past of which he had been ignorant.

He became convinced that all that had once made Ireland great existed still; heroism, he was to insist later, was a prophecy rather than a tradition. It was his use of these ideas which, as Yeats said, began the Celtic literary revival of the turn of the century.

In fiction and in cultural essays O'Grady encouraged a greater awareness of the mythological heritage of Ireland; he encouraged the Anglo-Irish to take up opportunities for cultural and spritual leadership abandoned by the dispossessed native Irish. By popularising myths in novels such as *The Flight of the Eagle* (1897) or the trilogy on the Cuchulainn stories *In the Gates of the North* (1901), O'Grady made a national impact; in using his learning by publishing his own history of Ireland in two volumes – *History of Ireland; the Heroic Period* (1878) and *History of Ireland: Cuchulainn and his Contemporaries* (1880) – he produced the material which was to stimulate the writers of the Literary Revival.

O'Grady's thesis through everything was the ancient nobility of the Irish race and the entitlement of the Irish people to the knowledge and inspiration contained within the ancient cycles of stories. Unlike his Limerick-born cousin Standish Hayes O'Grady (1832–1915), he was not an Irish scholar, but in reviving interest in, for example, the scholar Eugene O'Curry (1794–1862), the self-taught son of a pedlar, or in the work of Sylvester O'Halloran (1728–1807) who wrote the *General History of Ireland* (1774), O'Grady led many others towards the wealth of mythological allegory and metaphor.

One of those who put this to good use was Yeats himself; his poetic image of Standish O'Grady, whose heroic concepts did not survive the events of 1916 (and who was to leave Ireland finally and to die in the Isle of Wight) is included in 'Beautiful Lofty Things': 'Standish O'Grady supporting himself between the tables/Speaking to a drunken audience high nonsensical words ...', but there, at least, O'Grady is included among 'All the Olympians; a thing never known again.'

The O'Sullivans of Beara made their fortress in Dunboy Castle, at the edge of the sound between the mainland and Bere Island, and from there for several centuries they, like the O'Driscolls at Baltimore, controlled the fishing, native and foreign.

Following the Battle of Kinsale Donal Cam O'Sullivan, known as O'Sullivan Beare, retreated to this stronghold at Dunboy. He was pursued by George Carew, president of Munster, with 4,000 soldiers. The castle was surrounded, offers of surrender were refused and the cannons shattered the walls. Everyone within was killed either in the battle or later in the town square; refugees from Castletownbere who had fled to Dursey Island were also massacred. O'Sullivan escaped by virtue of having left the castle a few days before the siege in order to meet a Spanish ship at Ardea on the other side of the peninsula; it was after this that he undertook the march to Ulster with his few remaining followers.

Dunboy itself was ruined, but its site was used for the building of a house for the Puxley family, the mine-owners of Hungry Hill. It was destroyed by the IRA in 1921. It is a ruin upon a ruin. The Puxleys and their mine were the subject of Daphne du Maurier's novel; the Puxleys and the O'Sullivans, the people they displaced, were the subject of *The Two Chiefs of Dunboy*, written by J.A. Froude.

Co. Cork ends at Ardgroom harbour; just over the border, near Lauragh on Kilmacillogue Bay, is Dereen, where the fifth Marquis of Lansdowne created a sub-tropical garden around the family's summer house. To this delightful retreat (it is open to the public) summer after summer came James Anthony Froude (1818–94) described by A.L. Rowse as, after Macaulay, 'the most brilliant writer of all the English historians of the nineteenth century'.[47]

A contentious and controversial historian with a habit of telling the truth as he saw it (with almost calamitous consequences when he wrote a biography of his friend Thomas Carlyle), Froude made no friends in Ireland with *The English in Ireland in the Eighteenth Century* (1872–74); Rowse makes the case that the novel arose from the fusion of two episodes described in that history:

The story, that of two chiefs, the Catholic Irishman and the Protestant Englishman, Morty O'Sullivan and Colonel Goring – the expropriated chieftain and the colonizing intruder in occupation of Sullivan's ancestral lands – is in its main outlines a true story of the 1750's. Colonel Goring was, in fact, an upright revenue-officer, John Puxley, bent on doing his duty with little aid or encouragement from the government in Dublin, who was waylaid at a forge on his way to church at Glengariff and murdered by Morty O'Sullivan and his companions. The murder was then revenged by Puxley's nephews, who ran Sullivan down to his lair and burned it over his head ...

Shorn by Rowse of the 'historical disquisitions' which Froude could not bear to omit, *The Two Chiefs of Dunboy* is a terrific story; its background is the smuggling which was rife among these bays and creeks, its context is the very real struggle between the upright colonist who discovers, in Ireland, that he is iniquitous to the native, and the ancestral chief or his heirs who cannot make peace with their usurpers.

The murder of Puxley by Morty Og had more to do with O'Sullivan's trade in human cargo than in wine: his boats ferried young Irishmen to France where they enrolled in the Irish Brigades. O'Sullivan was a veteran of Fontenoy, had fought in the war of the Austrian Succession and had fought for 'Bonnie' Prince Charles at Culloden. After Puxley's murder he retreated to France but returned to visit his family at home. He was betrayed, ambushed, and killed; buried immediately in Dunboyne, his body was dug up and taken to Cork where it was ceremonially beheaded.

A nephew of the famous Donal Cam O'Sullivan, historian Philip O'Sullivan Beare (?1590–1634) was born on Dursey Island, Beara's furthest point south. One of four surviving children in a family of seventeen, he was sent to Spain after the Battle of Kinsale. Educated in Compostella, he wrote an Irish version of the Elizabethan wars: *Historiae Catholicae Hiberniae Compendium* (1621); among other works was *Zoilomastix*, a refutation of the Norman or English versions of Irish history. Written in 1626 it was discovered at the University of Uppsala in Sweden and published in 1960 edited by Thomas O'Donnell.

Allihies

Climbing over the hill to to Allihies and the remains of the copper mines discovered by Hall and worked by Puxleys, the narrowing road goes through Eyeries, birthplace of the Irish language writer Diarmuid Ó Súilleabháin (1932–85). Working as a teacher in Wexford Ó Súilleabháin centred his novels in Beara. An innovative and adventurous writer determined to address issues of nationalist politics and social change, Ó Súilleabháin's published works include *An Uain Bheo* (1972), and *Ciontach* (1983) and emphasise in their vigour and originality the degree to which Irish as a medium has been revived by Irish writers.

The coast after Eyeries swings in a loop around Coulagh Bay to Kilcatherine Point. Árd na Cailleach is the height of the Cailleach, the Hag of Beara. Here she stands, Beara's ancient goddess, the Hag on her lonely outcrop. It is no surprise that legends should have accumulated around this rocky tusk; Beara is laden with Bronze Age relics. It is believed that it was at Allihies that the Milesians, Ireland's first invaders, came ashore. Of all the pagan reminders none has proved more durable than this Hag: '[her] reputation as a figure of significance would, then, appear to span the worlds of Celtic mythology, Gaelic medieval literature and modern Irish and Scottish folklore with, in each case, a possible Norse connection', writes Gearóid Ó Crualaoich.[48]

The figure has been closely studied by Irish and foreign scholars, not so much for its relatively unassuming if stark formation but for the wealth of reference and association which has gathered around it, or her, through the years.

> One of the chief ways known to us in which Cailleach Bhearra is established in medieval tradition in the ranks of the sovereignty queens is the use of her name to identify the subject of the celebrated old Irish 'Lament of the Old Woman of Beare'. In the second quatrain of this poem the line *Is mé Caillech Bérri Buí* occurs and it is a line rich in ideological import with its overtones of Christian religion, Celtic mythology and localized political topography. Buí was claimed as a divine ancestress by the Corca Loigde – a leading tribe of the Erainn of West Munster – whose territory once included the whole of the Beara peninsula and the chief residence of whose over-king was at Dun Boy (Dun Buithe).[49]

'And long since the foaming steed, And the chariot with its speed, And the charioteer went by – God be with them all say I ...'[50]

From here the Kenmare river narrows back towards that distant town; it was from Ardea on this shore that the O'Sullivans left for Spain. From Ardgroom to Lauragh the road crosses the border into Kerry. Froude's Dereen was part of the Kerry estates granted to William Petty (1623–87), physician-general to Cromwell's army in Ireland and founder of the Dublin Philosophical Society. His family prospered and were raised to the nobility as Shelbournes and Lansdownes; a cartographer as well as a colonist his most famous work is *The Political Anatomy of Ireland* (1691); his *Down Survey* (1684) was the forerunner of the Ordnance Survey maps.

Tim Healy Pass

Near Lauragh there is a turning up into the hills; the signs say the 'Tim Healy Pass'. This wonderful, swooping road is cut on a ledge of the Caha Mountains; the local people warn drivers to keep their eyes on the road – 'if you go over there you'll be rolling for a week!' – but this is increasingly difficult as the vista of the Kenmare River drops behind and Bantry Bay opens up before.

Below is the dark green lake of Glanmore amidst its dark green fields;

beyond is the Atlantic. Born in Bantry town, Timothy Michael Healy (1855–1931) was parliamentary correspondent of *The Nation* in 1878 and then became secretary to Charles Stewart Parnell (1846–91); MP for Cork city, leader of the Irish Parliamentary Party and at one time 'the uncrowned king of Ireland', Parnell was finally driven out of politics when his party split on the revelations of his adulterous affair with Mrs Katherine O'Shea. Healy, always independent, broke with Parnell and became his bitterest accuser and enemy after Mrs O'Shea's divorce, and crowned his own political career by his appointment as first governor-general of the Irish Free State in 1922.

This route across the peninsula ends in Adrigole, from where it is an easy run along the shore of Bantry Bay to the town of Bantry. It would, of course, have been easier, if Bantry were the desired destination in the first place, to go straight to Bantry by turning right at the bridge in Bandon.

That route follows the north bank of the Bandon river to Dunmanway. Between Ballineen and Dunmanway is Manch, where Somerville and Ross located the 'Manch Run' in *The Silver Fox* (1897). At Fanlobbus near Dunmanway is Togher Castle, home of the MacCarthy Donn (or Downey) and of that Tadhg an Duna who is celebrated in Aogán Ó Rathaille's poem – 'I Walked All Over Munster Mild': the poet, visiting the castle, thought that 'the vanished dead returned to life/young men revelling, meat and wine,/punch being drunk, and brandy ...'[51]

He was mistaken; despite 'people leaving, people arriving/people pleasantly chatting with us,/people praying on the cool flags/meekly melting the heavens', this was now the house of an English lord – but at least one who was not mean to the wanderer.

Notes to South-west Cork

1. E. Œ Somerville and Martin Ross, *Irish Memories* (1917).
2. 'The Old Woman of Beare', tr. Frank O'Connor in *Kings, Lords and Commons* (1959).
3. John O'Donovan (ed.), *The Tribes of Ireland* (1852).
4. Molly Keane used the pseudonym M.J. Farrell for her early novels and plays; other later titles include *Time After Time* (1983) and *Loving and Giving* (1988); her anthology *Ireland* was compiled with her daughter Sally Phibbs in 1993.
5. John Montague, 'The Point', from *The Great Cloak* (1978).
6. Tribute by Seamus Heaney, *Magill Magazine* (February 1999).
7. Roy Foster, *Modern Ireland 1600–1972* (1988).
8. The Revd Paul Walsh (ed.), *The Life of Red Hugh O'Donnell* (Beatha Aodha Ruaidh Ui Dhomnaill) transcribed from the book of Lughaidh Ó Cléirigh (Irish Texts Society) 1948.
9. Readers might also like to consult Standish O'Grady (ed.), *Pacata Hibernia; Ireland Appeased and Reduced (1633)* (1896), an English version of the campaign against Hugh O'Neill which includes letters between George Carew and Don Juan de

Aguila as well as a list of the Gaelic nobility who left Ireland as a result of the Battle of Kinsale. It was compiled by Sir Thomas Stafford from Carew's enormous collection of Irish documents, of which the Lambeth Library holds thirty-nine volumes and the Bodleian four.

10. *Journalism* (1996), introduction by Terence Brown.
11. Robert Welch (ed.) *Oxford Companion to Irish Literature* (1996).
12. *The Poems of J.J.Callanan* (1847, 1861) and R. Welch, *A History of Verse Translations from the Irish 1789–1897* (1988).
13. A letter quoted by Charles Smith in his *Antient and Present State of the County and City of Cork* (1774).
14. For further reference to *The Book of Lismore* see Brian Ó Cuiv, 'Observations on the Book of Lismore', *Proceedings of the Royal Irish Academy 1883*; for the *Annals of the Four Masters*, see Paul Walsh, *The Four Masters and their Work* (1944).
15. Smith, op. cit.
16. Frank O'Connor, *The Big Fellow* (1937); Leon O Broin, *Michael Collins* (1980); Tim Pat Coogan, *Michael Collins* (1990).
17. Lady Mary Carbery, *West Cork Journals* (1995).
18. Janet Dunbar, *Mrs G.B.S. A Biographical Portrait of Charlotte Shaw* (1963).
19. ibid.
20. ibid.
21. The Revd James Coombes, *Utopia in Glandore* (1970).
22. Translation by Thomas Kinsella in *An Duanaire* (with Seán Ó Tuama), 1981; note also Seamus O'Neill, *Gaelic Literature* in Robert Hogan, *Dictionary of Irish Literature* (1996).
23. Samuel Johnson, *Lives of the English Poets* (1779, 1963).
24. A comprehensive account of Swift's time in Cork and of the matter of the Freedom of the City is given in *Jonathan Swift and Contemporary Cork* by Gerald Y. Goldberg (1967).
25. Somerville and Ross, *Irish Memories*.
26. Gifford Lewis, *Somerville and Ross, The World of the Irish RM* (1987). Geraldine Cummins (1890–1969) the Cork-born novelist and playwright, was co-founder with Edith Somerville of the Munster Women's Franchise League. A noted feminist she married the poet Austin Clarke but their marriage was extremely short-lived. Her interest in and use of psychical research was another bond between herself and Somerville, who turned to spiritualism for comfort on the death of Violet Martin and who afterwards insisted that the novels written after Martin's death were still collaborations. Cummins herself collaborated on her plays with Suzanne Rouvier Day (1890–1964), also of Cork, and the Abbey Theatre presented their *Broken Faith* (1913) and *Fox and Geese* (1917); active in local politics, Day was also co-founder of the Women's Franchise League with Cummins and Somerville.
27. Michael Holroyd, *Bernard Shaw*, vol. 2 (1989).
28. Somerville and Ross, *The Real Charlotte*.
29. Declan Kiberd, *Inventing Ireland, the Literature of the Modern Nation* (1995).
30. Somerville and Ross, *Irish Memories*.
31. Patrick Hickey, 'Famine, Mortality and Emigration' in *Cork, History and Society* (1993).
32. Patrick Hickey, ibid.
33. See Brigitte Anton, 'Women of The Nation' *History Ireland* 1, (1993).
34. Kevin Corcoran, *West Cork Walks* (1996).
35. Erik Haugaard, *The Complete Fairy Tales and Stories of Hans Andersen* (1974).
36. The novel *The Killeen* (1985) by Mary Leland takes these burial grounds as its theme.
37. Smith, op. cit.
38. Thomas Davis, 'The Sack of Baltimore' from *The Cork Anthology* (1993).

39. Smith, op. cit.
40. Michael Hayes (ed.), *The Fantastic Tales of Fitz-James O'Brien* (1977); Francis Wolle, *Fitz-James O'Brien, a Literary Bohemian of the Eighteen-Fifties* (1944).
41. Wolf Mankowitz, *Dickens of London* (1976); *The Extraordinary Mr Poe* (1978).
42. Tom Dunne, *Theobald Wolfe Tone: Colonial Outsider* (1982), or biographies by Henry Boylan and others.
43. Gaye Shortland, *Mind that 'tis My Brother* (1995); *Polygamy* (1998).
44. See Marianne Heron, *The Hidden Gardens of Ireland* (1996).
45. The several spellings all sound more or less the same; Beara is the name given most often to the district, Beare is that of the chiefs of the O'Sullivans.
46. Philip L. Marcus, *Standish O'Grady* (1970).
47. A.L. Rowse, introduction to *The Two Chiefs of Dunboy* (1969).
48. Gearóid Ó Crualaoich, 'Continuity and Adaptation in Legends of Cailleach Bhéarra' (*Bealoideas*, 1988, 1994).
49. ibid.
50. O'Connor (tr.), 'The Old Woman of Beare' op. cit.
51. Thomas Kinsella (tr.), *An Duanaire*.

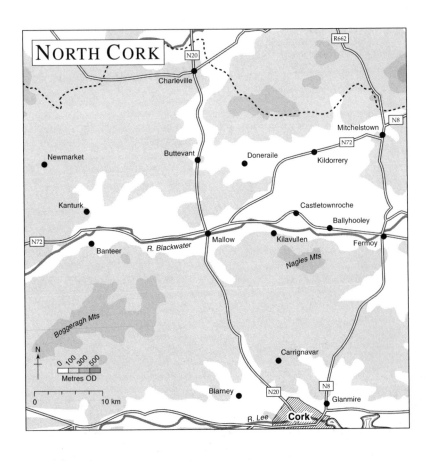

NORTH CORK

From the city via Carrignavar to Kilavullen, Castletownroche, Ballyhooley, Fermoy, Mitchelstown, Kildorrery, Doneraile, Buttevant, Mallow, Charleville, Newmarket, Kanturk, Banteer, Blarney and Cork

I raise my eyes, I peer into the shimmering distance. Along the sky-line of the far-off hills, I look for a clump of trees, gapped in the middle. A hundred motley fields of roots, of pasture and corn, lead up to it; and set haphazard among these fields, clutching them together, grouping them, are thriving farmsteads with trees and hay-barns – a homely landscape, its slope, its thoughts, its heart, one would surely think, set always upon this neighbouring city of Cork ... Hidden in that far-off clump of trees are the white walls of a tiny hamlet, Whitechurch by name. To the left, as I look, lies Blarney, and near-by runs the road to Dublin ... For me, to gaze thus into that trembling distance, where the little wind-swept hamlet, trees and all, fades into the light of the sky, is to sink softly, and with, perhaps, some gathering wistfulness, into the Gaelic world of the eighteenth century.[1]

*D*aniel Corkery makes it clear in *The Hidden Ireland* that this Gaelic world cannot be approached without an introductory journey through the centuries of Irish literature that had preceded it. Wistfulness, by the way, is not the tone of a book which, despite the errors inevitable at the time of its writing in someone coming late to the literature he was determined to rescue, survives to this day as a significant text. Visionary at the time of its publication, that text is also a clarification of a teeming landscape that is spiritual as well as geographic.

It is a landscape which unites Edmund Spenser, Edmund Burke, Mary Wollstonecraft, Anthony Trollope, Canon Sheehan, Elizabeth Bowen, William Trevor – even Samuel Pepys can be accommodated here at something of a literary stretch, as can Queen Elizabeth I if geographic flexibility is accepted. But these are latecomers.

The land they found and wrote about or read about is not the Gaelic world conjured by Corkery and established by scholars who preceded him. As our chapter on Cork city will explore, Corkery was a contentious figure for most of his long life, and in his book *Repossessions*[2] Sean Ó Tuama, one of his UCC students, examines and explains the conflicts aroused by Corkery's cultural philosophy.

Facets of that conflict are quarried in the journeys of this chapter as stone is quarried from the living rockface of the land. For as Corkery reveals his hidden Ireland, we hear the layers of other voices, louder through the course of history, laid like a moraine over the very landscape he sings and we visit.

To those of us who read *The Hidden Ireland* as an angry elegy (very far from wistful, indeed!) the voices piercing the shale are poignant because of the depth at which they are buried. There is a danger of piety in attempting to make clear, for anyone travelling towards Whitechurch and Blarney and those other townlands of North Cork the differences understood by the natives between the filidh, the bardic schools and the courts of poetry.

Encouraged by the ebullient hedgerows of this still-pastoral landscape we will take that risk, knowing that Frank O'Connor uses broader terms and a less reverent pen to describe important literary, indeed historic, distinctions. If we get above ourselves, he will cut us down to a size appropriate to Cork.

The German scholar Kuno Meyer (1858–1919)[3] was a hugely significant influence on Celtic studies in Ireland and abroad (although the Freedom of the City of Dublin conferred on him in recognition of his services to the Irish language was later rescinded because of his pro-German campaigning in America during the First World War). To him Ireland was 'the earliest voice from the dawn of Western European civilisation'.

That voice had escaped the influence of Rome (at least until the arrival of St Patrick and Christianity) and its native culture had survived uncoloured by European civilisation.

For Rudolf Thurneysen (1857–1940),[4] who pioneered during his teaching career at the universities of Jena, Freiburg and Bonn the application of historical and comparative linguistics to the ancient Irish language, that voice represented the earliest form of a Celtic tongue available to scholars.

One of Thurneysen's students was the Cork-born Osborn Bergin (1873–1950) who left his position as lecturer in Celtic studies at what was is now University College Cork in order to study first in Dublin and then in Freiburg. A towering figure in native scholarship, expanding Kuno Meyer's School of Irish Learning into the School of Celtic Studies and knitting the resources of universities and academies into powerhouses both of research and preservation, Bergin explained in 1912 that the Irish bardic order existed in prehistoric times, the social status of the bards well established in the earliest tradition.

'We must remember', he said, in a lecture concentrating on compositions from the periods known as Later Middle Irish and Early Modern Irish, or from the thirteenth to the seventeenth centuries –

> that the Irish file or bard was not necessarily an inspired poet. He was, in fact, a professor of literature and a man of letters, highly trained in the use of a polished literary medium, belonging to a hereditary caste in an aristocratic society, holding an official position therein by virtue of his training, his learning, his knowledge of the history and traditions of his country and his clan.[5]

We must remember this description of Bergin's, for the tradition he presents vanished; its unmourned, even unnoticed, loss is what drove Corkery's polemic.

In the same paper Bergin explains too why, although verse arrives before prose in the literatures of the world, in Ireland poetry was the sustained medium.

> The misfortune is, I think, that this state of things lasted too long ... although the early writers had full command of an admirable medium for plain, vivid narrative. Unhappily it was not developed.[6]

That, he proposes, might have been because prose was seen as common property, no one thought of claiming a narrative as a personal accomplishment. 'If we want the personal note of the conscious literary artist we must go to the verse.'[7]

To the verse he goes, and to the schools which trained the versifier over seven years and which, grouped around a particular poet or professor (*olamh*), provided the nearest things in Ireland to university life. The schools were independent of the Church, having existed in some form before Christianity, although later their mutual interests merged. They also provided a sustained dignity of style, an awareness of theme and a metrical convention which has distressed as much as it has invigorated scholars.

'Too much has been said about the difficulties of Irish metre', announces Bergin. 'What is wanted is less amazement and more attention. The requisites of an Irish stanza are, curiously enough, often ignored by those who write about them.'[8]

No, the real difficulty was that practically all bardic poetry was written in one standard literary dialect, which remained almost unchanged for 500 years. Because local dialects were diverging more and more, the trained poets set an artifical standard by normalising the language and admitting into their verse only such forms and usages as had the sanction of earlier poets of high repute. Adaptation was not in their style; professional pride was too strong and the bards refused to pay the price of popularity.

It was not all formality. Seán Ó Tuama explains that 'noble Irish families, of whom there were many hundreds, had maintained hereditary poets with great honour and ceremony, and there was intense (if mixed) poetic activity.'[9]

Formal eulogy and elegy apparently made up most of this verse, but Ó Tuama believes that the aristocracy encouraged a wider variety of work –

> otherwise it is hard to account for the corpus of delightful, non-formal syllabic verse which survives from the same period, or for the sudden emergence of other types of verse, apparently fully-fledged, in the era after Kinsale; learned accentual verse, sophisticated folk poetry, lays and lyrics of the Fianna.[10]

Like Ó Tuama, Bergin notes how even an official poet could write simply when his own feelings were touched. He quotes an elegy by Gofraidh Fionn Ó Dálaigh (Ireland's arch-professor of poetry who died in 1387 and who is believed to be a native of this district of Duhallow) who was lamenting the death of his son by addressing the cross which marked the grave.

> O cross yonder upon the hill that art the cause of my weeping, whoso-ever is glad at thy completion, thy setting up is my casting down.
>
> It is thou, my beloved son's cross, that hast made me cheerless tonight: o firm cross by which I mourn, it is thou that shall quench my joy ...
>
> This cross which I see overhead is the cross of one who was best at winning goodly prizes: this cross, that is viewed like a banner, conceals the very flame of art ... [11]

It is perhaps too smooth a leap to attach that image, the very flame of art, to the vision of Daniel Corkery's elegy written 600 years later and about the poets who replaced the bards schooled by such as Ó Dálaigh. The continuum may be in the fidelity to art itself, although in Ó Dálaigh's era it was trapped in a convention which could not bend when the prevailing wind changed to a tempest.

According to Ó Tuama, verse, during these centuries, had a wider function than it has today, being often used where we might consider prose more appropriate. For poets of great intellectual energy and skill verse was the natural vehicle not only for the obvious subjects of poetry – passion, atmosphere, mood – but also for social, historical and other rational discourse.

Such discourse was rendered socially meaningless after the defeat of the Irish at the Battle of Kinsale in 1601: within the next 100 years 85 per cent of the land was transferred to English ownership. The native aristocracy fled or were dispossessed, and 'the native institutions which had hitherto supported Gaelic poetry – the whole educational, legal, religious and economic continuum – virtually disappeared.' [12]

This reduction was a tragedy which cannot be over-estimated: the poets, their schools, their learning and status within their own community, meant nothing to the conquerors. Gradually, more and more of the poets, 'isolated within a political and social system which was both alien and repressive', died in 'despair or abject poverty, many refusing to consider seriously any way of life but that of the poet-scholar.' [13]

After Kinsale, although the language was not dead, its practitioners had to adapt to a wholly new cultural environment in which their own value, not to mind their actual values, were of no account. 'When the change came', says Bergin, 'it came suddenly. The old Gaelic world went to pieces, and numbers of highly trained educated men found that their once honourable profession had disappeared.'[14]

Yet Bergin's description of the bards is not inappropriate to some of those who displaced them: they depended on patronage, their work, is 'addressed exclusively to members of the upper and educated classes. They sometimes lack genuine inspiration, but they are always dignified in style and carefully finished.'[15]

An example of the later use of such a convention could be offered by 'A Winter Campaign' composed by Eochaidh Ó hEóghusa (1560–1612), head of a learned Ulster family and *ollamh* or chief poet to the Maguire chieftains of Fermanagh.

His patron Hugh (Aodh) Maguire has joined the campaign of Hugh O'Neill, Earl of Tyrone, against the Elizabethan forces led by Lord Carew in Munster in 1600. Safe in Fermanagh, Ó hEóghusa imagines the furious winter weather assailing his patron in the south; in fact Maguire was killed by Sir Warham St Leger in a skirmish outside Cork city – although not before fatally wounding his enemy.

> Fuár liom an adhaighsi dh'Aodh,
> cúis tuirse truime a ciothbhraon;
> mo thrúaighe sein dár seise,
> neimh fhúaire na hoidcheise …
>
> Gémadh fiaidhmhiol a bhfiodhbhaidh,
> gémadh éigne ar inbhiormhuir,
> gémadh ealta, is doiligh dhi
> soighidh ar eachtra an úairsi …

These, the first and fourth verses of the poem, are translated by Bergin:

> *Too cold I deem this night for Hugh;*
> *the heaviness of its shower-drops is a cause of sadness;*
> *woe is me that this is our comrade's lot –*
> *the venom of this night's cold.*
>
> *Though it were a wild hare in the wood,*
> *though it were a salmon in an estuary,*
> *though it were a flock of birds –*
> *it is grievous for them to venture abroad at this time.*[16]

They are given, somewhat more loosely, by Frank O'Connor:

Too cold this night for Hugh Maguire,
I tremble at the pounding rain;
Alas that venomous cold
Is my companion's lot ...

One thinks of the hare that haunts the wood,
And of the salmon in the bay,
Even the wild bird, one grieves
To think they are abroad ...[17]

Simplified in this way these extracts do not give an indication of the allusive classical ornament and imagery distinguishing most of the bardic poetry. Unswerving from old traditional standards, the poems form a great linguistic storehouse of classical Gaelic, unimpeachable in vocabulary, morphology and syntax, a reservoir whose importance for the social history of Ireland cannot be exaggerated.

That social history enveloped the townlands we are looking towards here, on the northern outskirts of Cork city, indeed close both to the home and to the university of Seán Ó Tuama, former professor of modern Irish literature at UCC and working still in the Irish language.

It is close – only a crow-flight to the east – to the home at The Glen on the Ballyhooley Road of a former professor of music at UCC, the late Aloys Fleischmann. In his immense and accomplished compilation of *Sources of Irish Traditional Music* (1999)[18] Fleischmann tracks the origin of the earliest song on record having an Irish text found, as Bergin notes, in Queen Elizabeth's virginal book: *Callino Casturame*.

Bergin decodes the title through Scots Gaelic, catching the use of the phrase in Shakespeare's *Henry V* when Pistol, asked by his French captive for his credentials as a gentleman offers the only foreign phrase he knows, the name of a song, 'Calen O custure me!' For Bergin the words represent the first line of a 'waulking-song' published in the *Macdonald Collection of Gaelic Poetry* (1911): 'Chailin óig an stiúir thu mi?' or Maiden, will you be my guide?[19]

For Fleischmann, having worked through a multitude of cross-references in a fifty-year endeavour which outlasted his career at UCC, this is not Scots Gaelic but Irish: Cailín ó cois tSiúire mé – I am a young girl from the banks of the Suir.[20]

Language, song, the verses that last as literature, the filaments connecting a landscape with its singers – although Bergin insists that the bards made poems, not songs – melt eerily together among the shadows of this landscape. A vanished order is measured by Bergin:

We may regret the class prejudices of the bardic order. We may wish that their horizon had been widened by the freshening influences of the renaissance ... (but) They stood for the independence of the Gael, and they fell with it ... To serve one's own day and generation may not be the highest ideal for a man of letters, but it is an ideal worth attaining.[21]

The first book in Irish to be printed in Ireland was a Protestant catechism in 1571; the great Irish annals, histories and genealogies existed in manuscript form only. The prose tradition had been for centuries the chariot of the sagas, with the first existing Irish manuscript written in Ireland composed by a monk who died in 1106.

The copying and preservation of texts such as these became the work of those poets who remained from the courts of poetry: in Cork city Donncha Ó Floinn (1760–1830) of Carrignavar, scholar and scribe, worked above his shop in Shandon Street on the sixteenth-century *Book of Lismore*. This collection of manuscript folios had been made by Aonghus Ó Callanáin for Finghin MacCarthaigh Riabhach (MacCarthy Reagh) of Carbery, one of the three great MacCarthy lords, and was found at Lismore Castle in 1814.[22]

Ó Floinn's friend and colleague, poet Micheál Óg Ó Longain (1766–1837) of Dun Bolg in Carrignavar worked for fifty years as a scribe, was himself the son of a scribe and the father of three sons who assisted his work as both teacher and copyist (two of them eventually working for the Royal Irish Academy as scribes).

According to Frank O'Connor, Irish prose had a brief enough flourish:

From the eighth to the twelfth century Ireland had a most remarkable literature. It had a fine poetry and an even finer prose, which was not equalled until the rise of the Icelandic story-tellers in the thirteenth century. By this time Irish poetry was in a bad way and Irish prose was dead.[23]

This characteristically sweeping assertion needs no dissection here, for it is already obvious that whatever the verdict on Irish prose (and O'Connor was not far wrong) Irish poetry recovered its impetus and its status, changing most noticeably with the changes which followed the Battle of Kinsale in 1601.

For while, with Corkery, we can follow the miles to the courts of poetry which succeeded the bardic schools, we must remember now that those miles were from then on familiar to the horses of other poets, the carriages of another culture and another literature altogether.

The old Irish aristocracy which had supported the poets was gone, beaten into exile, ground to a fugitive detritus; O'Connor says that by the eigh-

teenth century it hardly existed at all, the few remaining poets living as out-
laws (some of the more famous of whom have been immortalised in song as
Seán Ó Dhuibhir an Ghleanna or Eamonn an Chnoic), and professional
poetry remaining only as a peasant imitation. Indeed, O'Connor asserts,
'unlike Daniel Corkery, who wrote a very lyrical and wrong-headed book on
it, I can see nothing to admire in Irish eighteenth-century poetry.'[24]

O'Connor is mistaken – this judgement may be the irascible expression of
his disenchantment with Corkery and his fear that Corkery's fervent cultural
nationalism might prevail in an Ireland in which the books of O'Connor's
peers (and of O'Connor himself) were being banned.

It is time, however, to leave the disputes and to enter the landscape,
choosing a century of admission which coincides with that period of
immense change but choosing also a townland which remained for a considerable time untouched by it.

An easy day's drive will embrace these otherwise unlinked territories.
Short journeys, or holidays of easy walks, spent exploring the roads crossing
the countryside between Kanturk, say, and Blarney, embrace also a distilla-
tion of language and culture in a process which, despite the work of active
and inspired scholars, had been left unremarked by popular history and literature alike until 1925, and the publication of *The Hidden Ireland*.

Carriganavar

We begin aslant of Blarney, at Carriganavar, near Kilcully, so close to Cork city as to be virtually a suburb. The last streets peter out beyond Blackpool, and we swerve west and north and ignore the traffic heading for Limerick. The rural hinterland takes over beyond Kilcully. The signs to the left indicate Blarney and eventually Mallow, from which Buttevant and Charleville can be reached easily, and beyond them to the west Kanturk and Newmarket. The road directly ahead rises: we cross the route designated the Blackwater Way (for hill-walkers tracing the river's rise near Ballydesmond to its estuary at Youghal in East Cork) and the Nagle Mountains on the right frame a view completed by the Ballyhouras to the north. We are looking into the barony of Duhallow; to the west, close enough for the skirmishes which speckle the history of these townlands, is the barony of Muskerry. Those names, applied now to foxhunts and golf clubs, were once the portents of the clash of arms, the seizure of cattle, the honed stanzas of poetry.

The little hamlet of Whitechurch lies to the north and east of Blarney, Carrignavar a very few miles to the east of that again. It is to this territory and its people that the bardic school of Blarney which had flourished under the MacCarthy lordship was transferred when the MacCarthys had been swept aside and the great MacCarthy castle at Blarney was left in the ruin we visit today.

To understand the impact of that devastation, we recall the incident quoted by John A. Murphy, emeritus professor of Irish history at UCC. He describes the reaction of a noblewoman of the exiled MacCarthy clans urged to her window in France to watch the triumphant homecoming of Louis XIV, the Sun King. 'I have seen The MacCarthy enter Blarney' she said without stirring, 'and what can Paris offer to rival that?'[25]

Those few poets who remained took to farming (one, Eoghan Ó Caoimh (1655–1726) assisted the poet-priest Conchúr Mac Cairteáin (1658–1737) in the translation of the Latin catechism into Irish before being ordained himself and ending his life as parish priest of Doneraile) and their most obvious successor was Liam Mac Cairteáin (Liam an Dúna 1668–1774) who served with a regiment of horse for James II. With the defeat of the Jacobite cause he went home to Whitechurch, a village which had escaped the worst effects of the Williamite wars largely because of the remaining influence of the Mac-Carthys. The MacCarthys were said once to have owned a million acres of Munster; their connection with this district lasted until 1924, when the last of the family left their estates in Carrignavar, their house being taken over by a religious order and run as a school – which it is to this day.

Whitechurch was also the home of Fr Mathew Horgan (1776–1849), a convivial Gaelic scholar whose parties inspired the painting 'Snap Apple

Night' by Irish painter Daniel Maclise; Horgan was a friendly acquaintance of Sylvester Mahony (Fr Prout).

In this settled community the shattered bardic school was replaced by a court of poetry, one of the *cúirt éigse* which developed in several townlands throughout the country. Liam an Dúna was succeeded as head of the court first by Liam Rua Mac Coitir of Castlelyons (near Fermoy, to the north-east) and then by his own pupil Seán Ó Murchú na Ráithíneach (1700–62), whose people came from Ráithín near Bandon. Seán na Ráithíneach left the largest collection of Irish manuscripts of his time, including notebooks from 1720 to 1745. On his death the Whitechurch court of poetry came to an end; with it faded the last gleams of the Blarney bardic school.

That does not mean that there were no more poets in Carrignavar and Whitechurch. There were: among them Micheál Ó Longain (1720–70) and his son Micheál Óg (1766–1837), poets and scribes, farmers and teachers, maintained the tradition until close to the middle of the nineteenth century; Donncha Ó Floinn (1760–1830) spent the last thirty years of his life in Shandon Street on the north side of Cork city – not far at all from the main road to Whitechurch and Carrignavar.

Their work and that of others was conserved and revived through the scholarship and determination of Tadhg Ó Donnchadha ('Torna', 1874–1949) poet and translator and professor of Irish at UCC from 1916 to 1944. Born in Carrignavar while Irish was still heard as the language of the older people of the district, and educated at the North Monastery in Cork city, he became a devout member of the popular revivalist movement, the Gaelic League, working in Dublin before taking up tenure in Cork.[26]

His brother Eamann (1876–1953) also wrote poetry and succeeded Osborn Bergin as lecturer in Irish at UCC. And no discussion of Carrignavar could be complete without mention of the parish priest who worked tirelessly for the Irish language throughout his life: Fr Tadhg Ó Murchú (commonly known in Cork and elsewhere as an tAthar Tadhg) was chairman of the committee which produced, in 1962, a souvenir history of the court of poetry at Carrignavar.[27]

Also born in Carrignavar and influenced by its immense heritage was Patrick Sarsfield O'Hegarty (1879–1955), historian and journalist and father of Seán Sairséal Ó hÉigeartaigh (1917–67) founder of the Dublin publishing house Sairséal agus Dill, dedicated to the promotion of Irish-language writers.

If North Cork is stretched a little eastward then Glenville, between Carrignavar and Fermoy, introduces historian and genealogist Mark Bence-Jones (1930–) who has written novels as well as biographies such as *Clive of India*. He is most recently renowned for his best-seller *Twilight of the Ascendancy*

(1986) and for his mammoth reference book *Guide to Irish Country Houses* (1988). He is married to the Suffolk poet Gillian Bence-Jones (née Pretyman), whose collection *Ostrich Creek* appeared in 1999.

As these laden acres fall away behind us the Nagle mountains hover in marshy, rocky folds to the east. We are travelling through the space enclosed by an almost perfect geographic triangle formed on one hand by the main road from Cork to Mallow (and Limerick), on the other the main road to Fermoy, and completed by the Blackwater and its attendant hills.

We are extending the geometry to take in Mitchelstown as our extreme beyond Fermoy, and Charleville as our ultimate beyond Mallow. Our five fixed points are the towns of Cork, Fermoy, Mitchelstown, Charleville and Mallow. This is not a difficult terrain, and it is made even easier by local groups eager to welcome visitors to a landscape not often promoted by mainstream tourism interests.

This hint of another hidden Ireland brings us back to Corkery:

> ... a poor Munster peasant, a labourer, a wild rake of a man, Eoghan Ó Súilleabháin. He had misbehaved himself whilst in the service of the Nagle family, whose place was not far from Fermoy, and enlisting in the Army was his way of escaping the consequences. From Fermoy he was sent to Cork, transferred to the Navy, and straightaway flung into England's battle-line, thousands of miles away. [28]

Rake is putting it mildly: there is a suggestion that his attempt to make love to a woman while recovering from fever brought on a relapse which was fatal. Thus died, in poverty but not without hope, the poet of the sweet mouth, Eoghan Rua Ó Súilleabháin (1748–84).

Born in the Sliabh Luachra district of Kerry, famed as the birthplace of poets, Ó Súilleabháin roamed throughout the southern counties after his discharge from the forces, working both as teacher and labourer. Many of his best compositions take the form of the *aisling*, covert political poems in which extravagant love is declared for a female vision whch represents, according to date, either Ireland herself or the Jacobite cause. But as a journeyman teacher and labourer he had time to think of other things, as in this extract from a request to his friend Séamas FitzGerald for a decent spade:

> Séamas, light-hearted and loving friend of my breast,
> Greek-Geraldine-blooded, valiant and terrible in arms,
> supply in good order one smooth clean shaft for my spade
> and, to finish the show, add tastefully one foot-piece.

When you have done, and my weapon's in elegant order,
since the learning won't pay in a lifetime to drown my thirst
I'll not pause in my going till I've brought my spade to Galway
where daily I'll get my pay: my keep and a sixpence ...

This translation by Thomas Kinsella[29] goes on through the verses in which the poet promises to entertain his foreman with stories of Troy, of Samson, of Alexander and the Caesars and of the great Irish heroes and heroines, and ends with his promise to drink with his friend Séamas and never save a halfpenny till the day of his death.

The location of the misdemeanour of this rollicking character was the home of a branch of the Nagle family, the Annikissy Nagles, where he was employed as a teacher. The Nagle territory is all around us now.

The Blackwater Valley is one of the most beautiful regions in Ireland; Edmund Spenser lived there and it is the landscape of *The Faerie Queen*. The view from the ruins of Monanimy Castle looks across the Ballyhoura hills to the country of FitzGibbon, the White Knight of Irish history. To the east the peaks of the Galtee mountains strain to link up with the Knockmealdown mountains of Waterford. Southwards are the undulating hills, known as the Nagle mountains at the base of which stands the graceful seventeenth-century castle of Sir Richard Nagle of Carrigacunna ... For young Edmund, the view from his school must have had complex and powerful associations.[30]

The tumbling stream surges still around the old Nagle stronghold at Monanimy; the sound of the river we hear today was heard in memory by the man whose life was to end at his house near Beaconsfield in England. On his death George Canning wrote: 'There is but one event, but it is an event for the world. Burke is dead.'

Although this is disputed by his politically cautious matriculation entry at Trinity College, Dublin, the tradition that Edmund Burke was born among his mother's people, at the house of her uncle James Nagle at Shanballymore, is accepted by Conor Cruise O'Brien in *The Great Melody*.[31]

For in those times when the Penal Code was the law of the land an ambitious young man did not declare his Catholic background, and Burke's mother, Mary Nagle, remained a practising Catholic throughout her life. At six years of age Edmund Burke was sent to live with his mother's brother Patrick Nagle at Ballyduff. In places such as this valley and parts of Tipperary the apartheid laws were not applied, despite the animosity of the great landlords at Mitchelstown and Doneraile.

Burke was sent from the largely Protestant society of his father's home in Dublin to a Catholic stronghold, and was given his early education – until he was eleven – at a hedge school. Because these were the only places in which Catholics could be educated they were illegal, and they although they taught Latin and Greek, the common language was Irish. (A somewhat romantic but dramatically useful version of the hedge school is presented in the play *Translations* by Brian Friel.)

This Blackwater school was in the grounds of the ruined Nagle stronghold of Monanimy. The shadow of the keep would have fallen across the young scholars, who must have heard how Ellen, the eldest daughter of David Nagle of Monanimy, had married Sylvanus, eldest son of Edmund Spenser. They must have heard how Sir Richard Nagle of Carrigacunna Castle on the Blackwater at Kilavullen had been appointed attorney general for King James II and had followed him into exile in France after the Battle of the Boyne. And they must have heard too how, in 1641, John Nagle of Monanimy had been killed at Mallow during the Confederate War which was to have its bloodiest day at Knockanuss, near Kanturk, in 1647.

> To be brought up in Ballyduff, and to love his Nagle relatives, as Burke did, was to share directly in a considerable part of the experience of the Irish, Gaelic-speaking Catholic people and to be at least somewhat affected by Irish Catholic interpretations of history, and aspirations for the future.[32]

It should be mentioned here that O'Brien (the title of whose book is taken from the tribute to Burke by William Butler Yeats in his poem 'The Seven Sages') credits that early education as the foundation of Burke's sustained interest in the Irish language and its literature, leading for example to his discovery in the library of his friend Sir John Sebright of some very important early Irish manuscripts. Sebright later presented these to Trinity College Dublin, where they provided the foundation of the library's Irish manuscript collection.

As L.M. Cullen says of this district, 'To have provided a haven for Ó Súilleabháin, to have coloured indelibly the outlook of Burke and to have produced the founder of the famous brandy house is a large contribution by one small region to the story of the eighteenth century.'[33]

The brandy house is Hennessy, founded by Richard Hennessy whose family were tenants and relations of the Nagles, themselves the most powerful of the Catholic families surviving the penal era in this valley. Burke and Hennessy were contemporaries, brought up for several years within a few miles of one another and acquainted as young men; the Hennessy family lived at Ballymacmoy, but without the success or security of the extended Nagle holdings Richard Hennessy made his way to France where other members of his family had already begun to operate. Need it be added, he settled in Cognac.

That French connection was only one of the influences on Edmund Burke as a parliamentarian and orator; his great melody encompassed America, Ireland and India. Burke's literary legacy is not easily abridged for a book such as this. *The Oxford Companion to Irish Literature* [34] describes him as the architect of modern British conservative thought, the leading principles of which he shaped in his reflections upon the great questions of his time.

Burke remembered many things from his Cork background and remained loyal to it in many ways, apart altogether from his great parliamentary and philosophical preoccupation with the Irish issues of his time. Among his domestic loyalties was that of discreet but reliable support for his cousin Nano Nagle in the foundation of her convent for the education of Cork's poor. He was a generous patron to the irascible Cork painter James Barry, whom he encouraged to travel to London and abroad; despite his achievement as the only artist to be expelled from the Royal Academy Barry's reputation as a painter survived and he is buried in Westminister Abbey next to his friend Sir Joshua Reynolds. [35]

Also buried in the Abbey is Edmund Spenser. But before we reach the pastures in which most of *The Faerie Queene* was written and which with the mountains and rivers of this territory are mutated beyond geography to a mythical resonance, we must turn a little to the east.

The ideal turning-point (advised with the promise of a return journey via the good high road on the northern bank of the river) is the southern side of the bridge over the Blackwater at Ballyhooley Castle. The castle itself towers over the water-meadows; a Roche fortress destroyed in the wars of 1641–52 it was originally restored by the Listowel family, who also lived in the now ruined Convamore near Castletownroche. The old Bridgetown Abbey, at the junction of the Awbeg and the Blackwater, is less than two miles away.

Fermoy

The deeply hedged road here and there retains the high walls of old estates. These are broken in many places and the gaps allow views across long fields of plough, corn or stubble according to the season; in autumn the golden acres stretch down to the invisible but ever-present river and its flanking woods; the landscape opens out like a bowl, its rim the western Ballyhouras, the grander eastern slopes of the Knockmealdowns. The road wanders into the town of Fermoy on the southern side; to continue along the main street would be to take a delightful route towards Lismore in Co. Waterford; instead the left-hand turn over the bridge brings us back to the river.

About the year 254, Fiach Muillethan, King of Munster, bestowed the greater part of this country on the Druid, Mogruith, from whom it obtained the name of Dal-Mogruith. The druid, on coming into possession of this country, converted it into a kind of sanctuary, and on the high land which bounds it erected a number of altars and places of worship, some of which yet remain, hence called it *Magh Feine* or the sacred plain.

The inhabitant was called *Fier Magh Feine*, or the man of the sacred plain, or *Fier Magh*, whence Fermoy.[36]

James Roderick O'Flanagan, BL (1814–1900) was born and died in Fermoy, whose history he gives in some romantic detail in the best known of his books, *The River Blackwater in Munster*. Combining his legal career with his literary life he published several novels as well as anecdotes of the Irish bar. His delightful book on the Blackwater, although moderately outdated and also moderately inaccurate, traces the river from its source in the Kerry hills to the sea at Youghal in Co. Cork, as inviting a prospectus as any offered in Ireland.

Modern Fermoy, however, is the creation of a Scot, John Anderson, who had settled in Cork and bought the bulk of the estate including the town in 1791; he designed it as a garrison town to suit the needs of the British army of the time, but it also grew a middle and merchant class which today gives Fermoy a distinct solidity and character. One of its more noticeable buildings is St Colman's College, where the poet Thomas MacDonagh (1878–1916) taught for five years.

Leaving Fermoy in 1908 MacDonagh went to teach at St Enda's, founded by Patrick Pearse in Dublin. His play *When the Dawn is Come* was presented at the Abbey Theatre in Dublin, and the pupils who attended it returned 'yearning for rifles', according to the school journal. When he lectured in English at University College Dublin MacDonagh, who joined the nationalist Irish Volunteers in 1913, is remembered by the poet Austin Clarke as teaching a class on 'Young Ireland' with a revolver on the lectern. A signatory of the Proclamation of the Irish Republic at Easter 1916 MacDonagh, commander of a unit of Volunteers, was captured and executed in May of that year.[37]

St Colman's was still a new school when it housed, for a while, John Stanislaus Joyce, grandfather of James Joyce; at ten years of age the youngest boy in the school he was particularly befriended by the Rector Dr Croke, later archbishop of Cashel; during his year in Fermoy Joyce had special tuition in music and singing but was taken back to his family home due to continuing poor health.[38]

A later student at St Colman's was the young Patrick Sheehan of Mallow (1852–1913). As Canon Sheehan of Doneraile his posthumous novel *The*

Graves of Kilmorna (1913) centres on the Fenian rising of 1867, an event which had a special resonance for Sheehan with the death in Kilcloney Wood of Peter O'Neill-Crowley, leader of the Fenians of East; besieged both by British soldiery and police his only comfort was the last rites brought by a priest from Mitchelstown.

Sheehan as a boy saw, and never forgot, the subsequent funeral.

The Graves of Kilmorna is not an optimistic novel; its literary importance lies not so much in its revelation that at the end of his life Sheehan was not hopeful for the future role of the Catholic intellectual in Irish nationalism, but in its vision of what that nationalist Ireland might be. 'He seems', writes Terence Brown,

> at the end of this dark and prescient work to prophesy, in the death of its hero at the hand of his own people, a period when the role of the Catholic intellectual in Ireland, and of a clergy culturally as well as spiritually endowed, would be overshadowed by the kind of cruel dialectic of revolutionary violence and reaction which destroyed Myles Cogan. [39]

At the end of the novel the graves of Kilmorna contain two Irish rebels and martyrs. The last words of the oration delivered by a priest close the book: 'There they lie, and with them is buried the Ireland of our dreams, our hopes, our ambitions, our love. There is no more to be said ...'

There is more to be said about Canon Sheehan and we will say it when we reach Doneraile. But for the moment other names must be invoked, including that of the third Earl of Desmond, Gearóid Iarla, thirty of whose poems are contained in the *Book of Fermoy*. The earliest of these vellum pages dates from the fourteenth century; as a whole the book, which also contains bardic poems and religious and medical texts, was compiled for the Norman-Irish Roche family whose term as lords of the Fermoy area ended *c.* 1694 with the death of the 10th Viscount Fermoy. [40]

Novelist and playwright Una Troy (1918–) was born here; four of her plays were produced by the Abbey Theatre, and she began to publish novels after the 1950s. Her sister Siobhan also won attention as a modern poet publishing in Ireland.

Mitchelstown

Leaving Fermoy for Mitchelstown there is a left-hand junction a few miles to the north: follow the signs for Glanworth faithfully – the temptation to digress is difficult to resist – and the road leads to this small village where the river Funshion is forded by a thirteen-arch bridge. Be careful: it is old and too narrow for anything but one-lane traffic. The cliff-top remains of an old Roche castle dominate the approach, and the mill on the river has been converted into an inn where each bedroom is decorated according to the themes of local writers from William Trevor to Canon Sheehan. (This village is also the Irish exterior location for Atom Egoyan's film of Trevor's 1996 novel *Felicia's Journey*.)

Turning up the hill and left-handed out of the village again the traveller finds, without much ceremony, the largest and best of Irish wedge-tombs. This is Leabacalla, reputedly the burial place of the daughter of the druid who named Fermoy. His grave is said to be on the hill south of Fermoy itself; a crow flying from here would have that hill in its sights. The mystical geography of the townland is forceful among the lush fields, with the brown river stirring below the road, and the timeless stone slabs leaning against one another at the edge of the wall.

Before the junction at which this diversion can be taken, the main road passes a gaunt grey tower on the right: Cloghleigh, near the village of Kilworth, was built by the Norman Condons who feuded and married with their rivals the Roches through several hundred years. Their support for the Desmond rebellion cost them this castle of Cloghleigh which went to the Fleetwood family and eventually became the home of the Moores, later Barons Kilworth and Earls of Mount Cashell. By 1781 the Mount Cashells had built Moore Park on these Kilworth acres. The house is now gone, the acres used by a national agricultural research institute.

Kilworth was the home of John Edward Pigot (1822–71), barrister, friend of Thomas Davis, a song-writer and poet and founder member of the Society for the Preservation and Publication of the Melodies of Ireland. He assisted Eugene O'Curry in the publication of his *Lectures on the Manuscript Materials of Ancient Irish History* (1861). Pigot left his collection of Irish music to the Royal Irish Academy.

The wife of the second Earl of Mount Cashell was Margaret King, one of the twelve children of the second Earl of Kingston. The Kingstons built modern Mitchelstown, originally a holding of the Condons who were related to the FitzGibbons or White Knights and thus to the FitzGerald Lords of the Decies; by 1614 these old lordships had all come down to one Margaret FitzGibbon, whose daughter married Sir John King, later Lord Kingston of Mitchelstown.

In 1786 a later Margaret King received her lessons in Mitchelstown Castle from Mary Wollstonecraft (1759–97) who had written, but not yet published, her *Thoughts on the Education of Daughters* (1787). The revolutionary feminist was to marry the radical William Godwin but neither revolution nor radicalism could save her from the old-fashioned septicaemia which killed her after the birth of her daughter Mary (1797–1851). The younger Mary married Percy Bysshe Shelley and wrote *Frankenstein, or The Modern Prometheus* (1818).

Although Mary Wollstonecraft only stayed with the Kings for two years her impact was considerable. The fourteen-year-old Margaret was enthralled by her and was later to develop, to the dismay of her husband from whom she eventually separated, an eccentric political philosophy of her own which allowed her to support Republican and other causes in Ireland and abroad. In Italy Margaret became a friend of Shelley and his wife Mary.

The author of *A Vindication of the Rights of Women* (1790) may also have had an influence on the career of Margaret's sister, Mary Elizabeth. In 1797 she eloped with a Colonel Henry FitzGerald whose ineligibility was due not only to the fact that he was already married and the father of two children, but that he was her mother's illegitimate half-brother. They were pursued and the colonel was shot dead in Kilworth by Mary's father, then Lord Kingsborough and shortly to inherit the earldom; he was subsequently tried and acquitted by a jury of his peers in Dublin, but died within a year of his trial. Mary married, apparently happily, George Meares of Co. Longford.[41]

His experience as agent for the Kingsborough estates at Mitchelstown did much to disabuse Arthur Young (1741–1820) of any notions he might have held about the efficiency of Irish landlords. His travels in Ireland were enough in themselves to convince this agrarian reformer and economist that neither landlord or tenant could, or would, work successfully together under the system he observed in action; lethargy, improvidence and the practices of middlemen and agents encouraged by absentee landlords were all evils he evaluated in terms of their social and agricultural implications. Yet he believed that despite the effects of the Penal Laws and the generally apathetic society, Ireland had the resources for improvement and general social betterment within its grasp. Even his time in Mitchelstown did not defeat that conviction which is expressed in his *A Tour of Ireland* (1780) and also in his autobiography (1898).[42]

Born in Mitchelstown, Arthur O'Connor (1763–1852) was a United Irishman who left the country after acquittal on a charge of high treason. He rose in Napoleon's army to rank of general and died at Bignon; his letters and addresses were published, some compiled with Thomas Addis Emmet and William James McNevin. His brother Roger (1761–1834) was chief director of the United Irishmen in Cork. He published the *Chronicles of Eri* which purported to be the history of the Irish people as found in and translated from manuscripts in the Phoenician dialect of the Scythian language (1822). *The Dictionary of National Biography* says that the book is mainly if not entirely the product of O'Connor's imagination.[43]

From Kilworth and Cloghleigh a little road to the right leads to the secluded Araglin valley and Ballyderown, another Condon castle. By the time Richard, the last of the Condons, was killed by a fall from his horse in 1671, Ballyderown had been attached to the holdings of Francis Fleetwood. Fleetwood's son Thomas had married Dorothy Kingmill. After the death of Thomas, Dorothy Fleetwood married again and had a daughter, Elizabeth St Michel who, aged fifteen, married Samuel Pepys the admiralty secretary and diarist.

That slender link may not be reason enough for a detour from the main road; it is supported only by the attraction of the course of the Araglin river as it cuts through this steeply wooded valley on its way to the Blackwater.

At Mitchelstown the castle was considered too small for the third earl, known locally as 'Big George'. It was demolished and replaced by an enormous building designed by the Pain brothers, beggaring the family. George's son Edward, Viscount Kingsborough (1795–1837) was an antiquarian who published, at a personal cost of £32,000, *The Antiquities of Mexico* (1830); he died from typhus while imprisoned as a bankrupt in Dublin's Marshalsea only two years before he would have inherited the family estate.

The great castle of Mitchelstown was burned down by the IRA in 1922, its stone taken for the building of the abbey of Mount Melleray at Cappoquin in Co. Waterford, its very site now marked by a large creamery:

> In virtue of this being a garden party, and of the fact that it was not actually raining, pressure was put on the guests to proceed outside ... Wind raced around the Castle terraces, naked under the Galtees; grit blew into the ices; the band clung with some trouble to its exposed place.
>
> It was an afternoon when the simplest person begins to anticipate memory – this Mitchelstown garden party, it was agreed, would remain in everyone's memory as historic. It was, also, a more final scene than we knew. Ten years hence, it was all to seem like a dream – and the Castle itself would be a few bleached stumps on the plateau. To-day, the terraces are obliterated, and grass grows where the saloons were ... The unseen descent of the sun behind the clouds sharpens the bleak light; the band, having throbbed out God Save the King, packs up its windtorn music and goes home.[44]

Thus, in *Bowen's Court*, Elizabeth Bowen remembers the first day of the First World War when, at fifteen years old, her only anxiety was whether or not the Mitchelstown party would be cancelled.

Something of that elegiac visitation also pulses through the short stories of William Trevor Cox (1928–) of Mitchelstown, whose father's career as a bank official gave him a touch-down in several other Co. Cork towns. Educated at boarding school in Dublin and at TCD, Trevor worked first as a sculptor, a discipline which may account for the precision of his prose.

For most of his working life Trevor has lived in England, but when he writes about Ireland there is no sense of any other than objective distance. It might be said that the duality of his work, largely praised and widely rewarded, is almost as important as what he writes about.

Several of his novels concern England and the English only; others migrate between England and Ireland. Short stories treat these countries separately and more concisely. His style has evolved as seamless yet masterful, its economy controlling plot and atmosphere with an accuracy sometimes almost unsettling to the reader. His plays for stage, radio and television reflect a consciousness which has only deepened through the years, although the effect has become lighter, more sparing, in touch. Since his novel *The Old Boys* won the Hawthornden Prize for Literature in 1964 the honours have accumulated; he is a Member of the Irish Academy of Letters, and was awarded an honorary CBE in 1977. The *Collected Stories* were published in 1992 and his most recent novel is *Death in Summer* (1998).

Kildorrery

The road westward from Mitchelstown to Kildorrery edges the river Funshion, the Nagles to the south and the Ballyhoura hills shadows in the northern distance. This is the territory of Bowen's Court, of which nothing at all remains now except, up the little avenue at Farahy, the church dedicated to St Colman where, every August, a memorial service for Elizabeth Bowen is held. This was the family church for the Bowens; the very roads around it were laid by her grandfather.

Re-built in 1720, the church was the site of the deanery of Cloyne (described in a letter of 1736 by Dean Swift of Dublin as a hedge-deanery – 'we have many such as them in Ireland ...') until 1851; its records go back to 1225. William Maziere Brown, author of *Clerical and Parochial Records of Cork, Cloyne and Ross* (1863) served here before converting to Catholicism and going to the Vatican where he became lay vice-chamberlain.

Elizabeth Bowen is buried, with her husband Alan Cameron and many of her ancestors, in the churchyard although not in the old Bowen vault. The big square house could be reached by the adjoining avenue, more often in summer by the track across the fields. That too is gone, although the old mass-path through Bowen's Court land has survived the changes in ownership and the demolition of the house.

The Farahy Addresses, edited by Éibhear Walshe (1998), is a collection of the talks given here by critics such as historian Roy Foster, biographer Victoria Glendinning, essayist Hubert Butler, political advisor Martin Mansergh; each August the gathering sings again what Elizabeth Bowen called the 'loud confident Protestant hymns' of her childhood.

Bowen remained intellectually committed to Christianity despite a colourful romantic career which included Sean O'Faolain and the Canadian diplomat Charles Ritchie. She understood the world of love through an intuitive fusion of her brain and her senses; in a way given to few of the Ascendancy class – perhaps to few of any class – she understood the world of the Anglo-Irish. Her family had begun its time in Ireland as Cromwellian settlers; it ended on the clear-eyed modern assessments she could make in fiction and in fact.

But Ireland, and North Cork, were not Bowen's only territories. She is claimed here because of the psychic geography of a landscape we cannot but recognise in her words. Powerful though it may be to us, it is not her only landscape.

Nor is it exclusively hers although from her time on she will be a part of it. Walking these acres, knowing that the road ahead leads to Sheehan's Doneraile and Spenser's Kilcolman, the recognition grows that the ground beneath our feet, the hills, the timber, the cattle and horses in the fields, the modern bungalows and the old dilapidated gateways speak to us not through a crust of years but of imagination. The land has been translated from one time to another as if from one language to another:

> It was already falling twilight as we turned in the back gate of Bowenscourt [sic] whose austere Italianate limestone front rose against the mountains beyond. There in that great open field, under the great screen of trees, we found a double row of tents – the army on manoeuvres, or the Volunteers in training, I do not know which. Long before I saw this house (genealogically as old as Spenser) I had read Elizabeth Bowen's lovely novel *The Last September*. As we drove past the tents I remembered how the company, in that story, sat on the steps of the house before us, hearing in the crooning noise beyond the demesne walls the sound of pigeons, and then going indoors and bolting the windows as they realized that it was really the sound of a patrolling armoured-car. That was the last autumn of the old regime. Here is the new. After dinner we sat on the steps and heard the voices of young men singing, and saw the lights of the tents through the trees.
>
> I went into the library and got a Spenser and we searched for the famous fragment on Mutability ... For a while we talk of things as they arise, and then a sudden bugle-call goes wandering through the woods. The 'Lights Out'. The singing stops ...
>
> The fields are dark. From nowhere is there a sound. We, too, turn in. From my room I hear the iron bar falling across the door, and the great chain being hung in its place. A few steps sound through the house. I can see over the tree-tops the ghosts of the tents.
>
> Far away to the right over the screens, beyond the fox-covert, across the dark bogland, towards Doneraile, he too may well have sat up late

and on such a night as this. And at some lines like: '*The day is spent, and commeth drowsie night* ...' looked up over the sleeping land of Cork, yawned, stretched his arms, and, as I do now, laid down his pen.[45]

Doneraile

Spenser, says O'Faolain, was one settler whom the Irish never made their own. To find his 'waste where I am quite forgot', the road leads on to the long elegant main street of Doneraile straddling the Awbeg. This town with 3,000 acres was granted to Edmund Spenser, whose Irish career included the role of clerk to the English Council of the Plantation of Munster (and later that of sheriff of Cork) to which he was recommended by his support of the fierce suppression of the Desmond rebellion by his patron Lord Grey of Wilton. His political and military experiences understandably influenced his appreciation of Irish life, but more particularly of the obligations of authority, the role and likely fate of the plantations, and the influence of the surviving native lordships.

He was deaf – deliberately so it seems – to the tradition of Irish language and poetry, yet the twenty years he spent in Ireland saw the creation of his own most dazzling verses, including the *Amoretti* and *Epithalamion* written to celebrate his courtship of and marriage to the widowed Elizabeth Boyle of Kilcoran, near Youghal, in 1594. She was his second wife – his first was Machabyas Chylde – and was to outlive him, later marrying Sir Robert Tynte.

A friend of Sir Philip Sidney, whose sister Mary Herbert, Countess of Pembroke, is the 'Urania' of *Colin Clout*, Spenser had worked for Sir Robert Dudley Earl of Leicester. He was a friend too of Robert Devereaux Earl of Essex who paid, in the end, for Spenser's funeral in 1599 (not so long before his own). And he was a friend of Sir Walter Ralegh, to whom he dedicated *Colin Clout*.

Here Spenser sat:

... as was my trade,
Under the foot of Mole, that mountain hore;
Keeping my Sheep amongst the cooly shade
Of the green alders, by the Mulla's shore.
There a strange shepherd chanc'd to find me out,
Whether allured with my pipe's delight,
Whose pleasing sound yshrilled far about;
Or thither led by chance, I know not right.
Whom when I asked, from what place he came?
And how he hight, himself he did ycleep,
The shepherd of the ocean by name,
And said he came far from the main sea-deep ...[46]

But Spenser felt himself to be unfortunate; although acclaimed as a poet he was not well rewarded financially and his hopes of preferment were disappointed. Then the campaign led by Hugh O'Neill of Tyrone (which was to prove disastrous for Essex as well) flared up in Munster. Kilcolman Castle, which had belonged to the Desmonds before Spenser's arrival, was attacked and burned in 1598, Spenser's young son dying in the flames.

For ordinary readers of Spenser the contradictions between the minor statesman actively engaged with the coercive violence and his other persona as a poet of classical culture are difficult to accept. Ann Fogarty, in her essay 'The Colonization of Language' believes that the differences between his prose treatise (*A View of the Present State of Ireland*) and his epic poem are perhaps so glaring and obvious that the simalarities are often ignored.

> Often, Spenser's political views are simply discounted or discarded. In particular, they are seen as an embarrassment or an impediment for the reader of 'The Faerie Queene'. Not infrequently, Spenser's work is protected by a grim determination to keep the role of poet and Elizabethan colonist permanently distinct.

That false separation of aesthetics and politics masks the vital interconnections in the work of 'this Elizabethan functionary'. Fogarty's premise is that both tract and poem should be seen in a continuum, as mutually defining intertexts rather than as conflicting expressions of a divided mentality. Also it is evident to her that

> ... all of Spenser's work evinces a passionate concern with the mediatory function of language and with the shaping and thereby political force of rhetoric ... [writing] is the medium through which the social world is explored and contained.[47]

And still Kilcolman, its lake and marshy fields now a wildlife refuge, lives forever in his poetry; the Awbeg becomes the Mulla, the Ballyhouras supply Mole, 'that mountain hore'. Sean O'Faolain admits that 'I never can – such is the force of a truly creative mind, a powerful and affective imagination – travel across this wide limestone plateau of North East Cork, between the Nagles and the Galtees, without seeing it all, north and south, in the light and under the imprint of that swooning, sensuous, silvery poem *The Faerie Queene*.'[48]

Doneraile town was sold by Spenser's son to Sir William St Leger, and the St Legers became the manorial family, their house of Doneraile Court (now in the care of the Irish government) surrounded by splendid parkland which is open to the public. The house is closed as yet, but within it is the alcoved room surviving from the original seventeenth-century castle where Elizabeth St Leger was discovered during a Masonic meeting; her father was faced with the choice of having her discreetly put to death or admitting her as the only woman Freemason in Ireland.

Elizabeth survived to become Lady Aldworth and is commemmorated at St Fin Barre's Cathedral in Cork city. Discreet murder was also the choice facing friends of the fourth Viscount Doneraile: a famed rider to hounds, he was bitten by a pet fox and although spending time in Paris to avail of the new anti-rabies treatment there, he returned to Doneraile without a cure. As the disease took hold his friends gathered; as its violence increased and they realised he would have to be restrained like a lunatic until he died, they met by his bedside and, each man with a hand on the pillow, smothered him in a collective act of euthanasia.

Or so the story goes, in Doneraile.

It was in Doneraile that Tadhg Ó Duinín, the last olamh or poet of the Bardic School centred on the MacCarthys of Blarney, died in 1726.

Francis Barry Boyle St Leger (1799–1829), a grandson of the first Lord Doneraile, was a very popular novelist in his day and especially successful with *Tales of Passion* (1829).

There was some association haunting everything, inexpressibly sweet, but so vague, so elusive, he could not define what it was. The fields in the twilight had a curious colour or cloudland hanging over them, that reminded him of something sweet and beautiful and far away; but this memory or imagination could never seize and hold. And when, on one of those grey days, which are so lovely in Ireland, as the light falls sombre and and neutral on all things, a plover would shriek across the moorland, or a curlew would rise up and beat his lonely way, complaining and afraid, across the ashen sky, Luke would feel that he had seen it all before in some waking dream of childhood; but all associations had vanished.[49]

Patrick Augustus Sheehan was born in Mallow in 1852 and died parish priest of Doneraile in 1913. His novels were full of feeling and emotional detail – but almost as if it couldn't be helped. In fact they were written with a purpose, a feature which did not at all deter his readership which was only too ready to enjoy the buttressed Catholicism and nationalism he seemed to purvey. Yet the novels transcend this evangelism; the author's creative idealism could not always bow to the intellectual imperatives. Perhaps the author knew what the priest denied – that his books were read not so much because they declared Catholicism and nationalism as thoughtful and important subjects for the novelist but because they touched the common, imaginative, chord.

'Throughout his career', writes Terence Brown, 'Sheehan had indicated in his fiction that nationalism as a social and cultural movement of his idealism could provide an intellectually aware priesthood with the means whereby it might achieve the leadership of the people in a worthwhile, ennobling cause.'[50]

Sheehan lived with his people through a time of tremendous change. The defeat of landlordism, the expansion of capitalism, the dawn of socialism, and, in Ireland, the undercurrents of revolution – these were the connected circumstances which engaged his mind and to which he set his pen.

The fascinating thing about his novels is that they were written so directly to a particular readership, deliberately 'popular' – and yet they were demanding, challenging, polemical texts, widely translated stories of priests and people in Irish towns and villages, using as background still-familiar agitations, rebellions and causes.

As a priest Sheehan was loved by his parishioners for whose economic as well as spiritual welfare he worked tirelessly. Buried in Doneraile, his statue stands outside his church, and his house stands across the street from the walls of Doneraile Court with whose owners, Lord and Lady Castletown, he campaigned for civic improvements.[51]

Although born in Melbourne, Australia, Colonel James Gove-White of Kilbyrne, Doneraile, (1852–1938) was one of Cork's most famous antiquarians. Having completed thirty-two years of military service he returned to lead an active farming life on the family estates in Cork and Waterford and was a founding member of the Cork Historical and Archaeological Society, of which he later became President. His *Historical and Topographical Notes on Buttevant, Castletownroche, Doneraile and Mallow* was published in two volumes in 1924.

Isabella Creagh Shawe was a member of an Anglo-Irish family from Doneraile. She met William Makepeace Thackeray in Paris; their marriage (1836) was tragic; of their three daughters the second died in infancy and with the birth of the third, in 1840, Isabella suffered a complete mental breakdown and spent the rest of her life detained in a private nursing home.

This third daughter Harriet (Minnie) was to marry Leslie Stephen; after her death in 1875 Stephen married Julia Duckworth, the mother of Virginia Woolf and Vanessa Bell. In *Night and Day* Woolf portrayed Thackeray's elder daughter Anne, later Lady Ritchie, as 'Mrs Hilbery'; Lady Ritchie was herself a novelist and an acknowledged influence on her step-niece.[52]

Arch Bridge crossing the Blackwater at Mallow by R.L. Stopford, 1849

Mallow

Thackeray leads to Trollope as Doneraile leads (admittedly with a little loop) to Mallow:

And she undid the bundle at her back, and laying the two babes down on the road showed that the elder of them was in truth in a fearful state. It was a child nearly two years of age, but its little legs seemed to have withered away; its cheeks were wan, and yellow and sunken, and the two teeth which it had already cut were seen with terrible plainness through its emaciated lips. Its head and forehead were covered with sores; and then the mother, moving aside the rags, showed that its back and legs were in the same state. 'Look to that', she said, almost with scorn. 'That's what the mail has done – my black curses be upon it, and the day that it first come night the counthry.' And then again she covered the child and began to resume her load.

'Do give her something, Herbert, pray do,' said Clara, with her whole face suffused with tears …

Herbert Fitzgerald, from the first moment of his interrogating the woman, had of course known that he would give her somewhat. In spite of all his political economy, there were but few days in which he did not empty his pocket of his loose silver, with these culpable deviations from his theoretical philosophy. But yet he felt that it was his duty to insist on his rules ... It was a settled thing at their relief committees that there should be no giving away of money to chance applicants for alms. What money each had to bestow would go twice further by being brought to the general fund – by being expended with forethought and discrimination. This was the system which all attempted, which all resolved to adopt who were then living in the south of Ireland. But the system was impracticable, for it required frames of iron and hearts of adamant.[53]

In *Castle Richmond* Anthony Trollope (1812–82) wrote what could be ironically called a romance of the Great Famine. His rival families are named Fitzgerald and Desmond in a confusion of the native titles: set on the banks of the Blackwater, between Mallow and Kanturk, with the Duhallow hunt and the hounds of Muskerry baying in the dim background, Castle Richmond

> ... stood in a well-timbered park duly stocked with deer – and with foxes also, which are agricultural animals much more valuable in an Irish county than deer. So that as regards its appearance Castle Richmond might have been in Hampshire or Essex; and as regards his property, Sir Thomas Fitzgerald might have been a Leicestershire baronet.

Not so the Desmonds:

> But, nevertheless, the Desmonds were great people, and owned a great name. They had been kings once over these wild mountains; and would be still, some said, if every one had his own.

The novel concentrates on heirs, wills and poisoned genealogy with heroes and heroines uncharacteristically, for Trollope, of ambivalent status. But the sub-text is the famine, glossed as an examination of the relationship in terms of mutual working priorities betweeen the Catholic and Protestant clergy.

Trollope has been criticised for his handling of Irish themes; his reflections on the politics and issues of the day burden many of his novels, and while this is also true of *Castle Richmond* (written in the year of his departure from Ireland) the famine scenes themselves have a descriptive anger which reveals not only his own immediate contact with such suffering but also his questioning of the official reactions to the disaster itself.

He would have observed the end of the famine and considered its effects from his home on the High Street in Mallow town where he had moved from Clonmel with his wife Rose and their two sons. He had already written his first novel – *The Macdermots of Ballycloran* (1847) – his income had increased, he was still minded by his Irish groom Barney, he could hunt while continuing his work with the Post Office; Mallow, in fact, saw him enjoying to the full the first real satisfactions of his adult life. In his autobiography he makes it clear: 'From the day on which I set my foot in Ireland all these evils went away from me. Since that time who has had a happier life than mine?'

Canon Richard Chester (1811–83) of Ballymagooly House near Mallow was rector of Ballyclough; his sermon 'The Potato Blight' (1846) was printed and circulated, and may have reached Trollope. Certainly in his descriptions of the famine in *Castle Richmond* Trollope wrote as one who had seen and heard enough to recognise the national scale of the disaster as well as its intimate detail:

He stood for a time looking round him till he could see through the gloom that there was a bundle of straw lying in the dark corner beyond the hearth, and that the straw was huddled up, as though there were something lying under it. Seeing this he left the bridle of his horse, and stepping across the cabin moved the straw with the handle of his whip. As he did so he turned his back from the wall in which the small window-hole had been pierced, so that a gleam of light fell upon the bundle at his feet and he could see that the body of a child was lying there, stripped of every vestige of clothing.

For a minute or two he said nothing – hardly, indeed, knowing how to speak, and looking from the corpse-like woman back to the life-like corpse, and then from the corpse back to the woman, as though he expected that she should say something unasked. But she did not say a word, though she so turned her head that her eyes rested on him. ...

'Was she your own?' asked Herbert, speaking hardly above his breath.

' 'Deed, yes!' said the woman. 'She was my own, own little Kitty.' But there was no tear in her eye or gurgling sob audible from her throat.

'And when did she die?' he asked.

'Deed, thin, and I don't jist know – not exactly;' and sinking lower down upon her haunches, she put up to her forehead the hand with which she had supported herself on the floor ... and pushing back with it the loose hairs from her face, tried to make an effort of thinking.[54]

There is something universal in that gesture, the apathetic hand to the forehead, the effort of thinking; it is a contemporary gesture, familiar to us from Ethiopia and Rwanda and elsewhere. Familiar too is the tone in which Trollope notes how fruitless were individual acts of relief: 'But his efforts in her service were of little avail. People then did not think much of a dying woman, and were in no special hurry to obey Herbert's behest.'

People since then have thought more and more, and with more anger than irony. Among them would have been William O'Brien (1852–1928), the politician, novelist and journalist who was alive to the origins of his native town as a FitzGerald foundation long before the advent of Sir John and his brother Sir Thomas Norrys; the Norrys were particular friends of Queen Elizabeth, who counted Elizabeth Norrys, daughter of Sir Thomas, among her many god-children. It is believed that the herd of white deer which still roam the park at Mallow Castle descend from the harts given to Sir Thomas. Descended from the Norrys line the Jephsons continued as proprietors of Mallow Castle until the middle of this century; Robert Jephson (1736–1803) was a playwright of some status, his work including *The Count of Narbonne* (1781), a stage adaptation of Horace Walpole's *Castle of Otranto*.[55]

O'Brien quickly became a political activist and a close friend of Charles Stewart Parnell, leader of the Irish Parliamentary Party and MP for Cork in 1880.

Imprisoned for organising a rent strike (on the Kingston estate) O'Brien wrote *When We Were Boys* (1890) while in jail; his parliamentary career lasted from 1883 to 1918. At his London wedding in 1890 to Sophie Raffalovich of Paris (author of *Rosette, a Tale of Dublin and Paris* (1907) and of several books of reminiscences) there were no fewer than eighty-two members of the Irish Party, led by Parnell himself. The celebrant was Dr Croke, archbishop of Cashel. O'Brien's several novels include *A Queen of Men* (1898), and his *Recollections* (1908) and *The Irish Revolution* (1928) provide reflections on a career which encompassed some of the most important events and people of modern Irish history.

O'Brien is buried in Mallow which is the native town of John Crawford Wilson (1825–90), poet and novelist and of Evelyn Bolster (1925–) a member of the community of Sisters of Mercy in Cork. A historian and teacher, Bolster is author of *The History of the Diocese of Cork* (1972). Canon Sheehan's birthplace is now called William O'Brien Street. Born before either of these writers however was Thomas Davis (1814–45), founder, with Charles Gavan Duffy and John Blake Dillon, of *The Nation* (1842) – the weekly journal which lasted in its first, fiery phase until 1848.

Gavan Duffy, John Mitchel and Davis himself wrote influential essays and reviews, debates on the critical issues of the time reported along with events in the Houses of Parliament, and the popular songs and speeches of the day were also carried to a readership reputed to have reached 250,000 by 1848.

In its character it reflected the personality of Davis whose enthusiasms were widespread even while centred on nationalism, the Irish language, and romantic interpretations of Irish history and mythology. Its contributors included many minor poets of both sexes as well as more established or weighty writers.

After the suppression of *The Nation* the nationalist press took several different forms; its writers produced collections and anthologies and by 1849 a second series of the journal appeared, lasting until 1896. In the meantime Davis had died of scarlet fever. It was the enormous attendance at his funeral that attracted the attention of Jane Francesca Elgee later Lady Wilde to Davis, his work and the columns of *The Nation*. In the tribute lecture to mark his centenary in 1914 W.B. Yeats recalled Speranza of *The Nation*:

> Lady Wilde once told me, in that darkened room of hers where no ray of light was admitted to shew where time had withered, that once when she was a young girl and walking through some Dublin street she came upon so great a crowd that she could go no further. She waited in a shop that it might pass but it seemed unending … She was so struck to find so many people honouring a poet and one she had never heard of, that she turned Nationalist and wrote those energetic rhymes my generation read in its youth.[56]

Davis had quickly gained a reputation as an inspiring and independently minded orator; his own poetry was rousing and rhythmic:

> 'Did they dare, did they dare, to slay Eoghan Ruadh O'Neill?'
> 'Yes, they slew with poison him they feared to meet with steel.'
> 'May God wither up their hearts! May their blood cease to flow!'
> 'May they walk in living death, who poisoned Eoghan Ruadh!'

He was also composer of 'Clare's Dragoons' the song which used to be known to many an Irish schoolchild, when, up to twenty or so years ago, they still learned 'by heart':

> When, on Ramillies' bloody field,
> The baffled French were forced to yield,
> The victor Saxon backward reeled
> Before the charge of Clare's dragoons.
>
> The flags we conquered in that fray,
> Look lone in Ypres' choir, they say,
> We'll win them company today
> Or bravely die like Clare's dragoons.
> Viva la, for Ireland's wrong!
> Viva la, for Ireland's right!
> Viva la, in battle throng,
> For a Spanish steed and sabre bright!

Yeats understood what the ballads were about: 'All who fell under his influence took this thought from his precept or his example: we struggle for a nation, not for a party, and our political opponents who have served Ireland in some other way may be the better patriots.'

It was a theme acutely perceived on the very occasion of the tribute lecture, which was organised by the Gaelic Society at Trinity College Dublin but which was banned when the authorities, in the person of Dr J.P. Mahaffy, philosopher and classicist, realised that 'a man called Pearse' was to be one of the speakers.

The revolutionary teacher Patrick Pearse was as yet unknown to Mahaffy, who must not have been paying much attention to the campaign against recruitment for the British army then being conducted by nationalists in Dublin. The society refused to cancel Mr Pearse and was suppressed by Mahaffy, the centenary lecture going ahead instead in the Antient Concert Rooms in Dublin in November.

Also on the platform that evening was economist and poet Professor Tom Kettle who despite his support for the nationalist cause was in favour of recruitment – so much so in fact that he died on the Somme. Yeats could have had no foreknowledge that within two years both Pearse and Kettle would be dead, when he told his audience of his sorrow that Professor Mahaffy was not present:

> I am not more vehemently opposed to the Unionism of Professor
> Mahaffy than I am to the pro-Germanism of Mr Pearse, but we are here
> to talk about literature and about history. In Ireland, above all nations,
> it is necessary to keep always unbroken the truce of the Muses.[57]

Davis believed in that truce; born the posthumous son of an English army doctor who died on his way to Portugal to take over management of a military hospital during the Peninsular War, his mother a member of the famous house of O'Sullivan Beare, he almost embodied the fusion of disparate but accommodating cultures.

Brought to Dublin from Mallow while still a child he grew up in a Unionist environment; his career, until the years he spent with *The Nation*, was not particularly brilliant. Yet this man, Yeats said, could 'show forth the service of Ireland as heroic service worth a good man's energy ...' As T.W. Rolleston wrote, it was difficult for those remembering Davis in 1914 to realise the state of things which prevailed in his time:

> The people in general – even those who passed for educated – National-
> ist and Unionist alike, could not ... have told whether the Battle of
> Benburb came before or after the Battle of Clontarf, or whether Owen

Roe O'Neill was a naked savage armed with a stake or one of the most accomplished soldiers in Europe.

Davis, Rolleston believed,

knew well of what a number of ancient and admirable stocks the modern Irish nation is composed, and no son of any of them, from the Phoenician to the Cromwellian, was a foreigner to Davis … Still, he recognised that the root-stock of the population was Celtic, and he was the first Irish public man, I think, to turn the minds of the people with special reverence towards their Celtic ancestry … [58]

Mallow was visited by Sir Walter Scott, travelling with his son-in-law and biographer John Lockhart, in 1825; at that time the town still had the name of being the Irish Bath. The curative reputation of its hot mineral springs gave it a social prominence which did not survive much beyond the time of Scott's visit.

It would have been only a civic memory when Sidney Royce Lysaght (1860–1941) was born nearby. A novelist and literary journalist his elegant prose was hijacked by polemic; his best work is considered to be *My Tower in Desmond*.

Lysaght died in Mallow, which still has associations with his son Edward (1887–1986), the historian and genealogist educated at Oxford and at University College Cork. Imprisoned by the British during the Irish War of Independence Edward preferred to use the Irish form of his name – MacLysaght; a senator in the new Irish government from 1922 to 1925 he travelled widely, farmed and worked as a journalist before his appointment as chief genealogical officer and keeper of manuscripts at the National Library of Ireland from 1943–55.

Chairman of the Irish Manuscripts Commission, MacLysaght was also a historian, but his most significant publications were those of genealogical interest, such as the *Guide to Irish Surnames* (1964) which appears in subsequent editions as *The Surnames of Ireland*. *Irish Families: Their Names, Arms and Origins* (fifth edition 1985) continues to be popular. He wrote novels in both English and Irish and his autobiography – *Changing Times: Ireland since 1898* – was published in 1978.

Ballyclough, close to Mallow town, is now widely recognised as the site of an important creamery; it was also the birthplace of Sir Redmond Barry (1813–80) whose legal career began at Trinity College, Dublin but subsequently took him to Australia, where he was a founding father of Melbourne University and Public Library as well as being presiding judge in the trial of Ned Kelly.

Mallow is the home too of poet and novelist Martina Evans (1961), whose most recent publications are the novel *The Glass Mountain* (1997) and the poetry collection *All Alcoholics are Charmers* (1998).

Buttevant

Buttevant is the next town from Mallow on the Limerick road; it is halved by the main carriageway and the Awbeg river is hidden from the high street through which the traffic moves too quickly for an appreciation of this old settlement. The surrounding pastoral landscape gives little indication now that Buttevant was a much-disputed holding of the Barrys, an Anglo-Norman family whose spread took in territories throughout Cork from east to west.

Although this is disputed, the town's name probably stems from the French word for a defensive buttress – *botavant*; more popular is the belief that it is merely a corruption of a Barry (subsequently Barrymore) rallying-cry: *Boutez en avant!* – used to such good effect that it is still inscribed as the Barry motto on the gates of one of the last Barry demesnes at Fota, in east Cork.

Buttevant (originally Cill na Mullach) was a walled town and famous for its monasteries, largely founded by the Barrys; David Barry, lord justice of Ireland under King Edward I is buried in the Franciscan abbey he had built here, and there are memorials to more Barrys, to FitzGeralds and Nagles and O'Keeffes, all of whom held or claimed property in the area. Even earlier than the Franciscan abbey is Ballybeg, just outside the town to the east, an Augustinian foundation from 1237. Close by, on a cliff over the river, is a ruined Barry castle.

Clotilde Inez Mary Graves (1864–1932) was born in Buttevant, a cousin of Alfred Percival Graves, the anthologist and poet; under her pseudonym Richard Dahen she wrote plays with some success – *Nitocris* (1887) appeared at Drury Lane in London, and *The Lover's Battle* (1902) was among several performed both in London and New York. She also published more than twenty novels and collections of short stories including *The Doctor Dop* (1910) and *A Well-Meaning Woman*.

William B. Guinee (d. 1901) journalist and parliamentary reporter in London who also published novels, poems and songs, was born in Buttevant.

Charleville

The main road from Buttevant to Charleville – a town close to the border of Co. Limerick – intersects the Ballyhoura Way, a scenic diversion with many streams and copses winding on to the foothills of the Galtee mountains, touching castled Liscarroll in Cork and Kilfinnane in Limerick. Charleville itself was largely built by Roger Boyle, Earl of Cork, and named in honour of Charles II, whose name replaced the old title of Ráth Luirc – although this is still often in use.

Archbishop Daniel Mannix (1864–1963) was one of Charleville's most famous sons. Ordained in Maynooth he went to Australia in 1911 where he published many essays and speeches on Irish issues.

The Revd William Reeves (1815–92), the antiquarian who acquired *The Book of Armagh*, a Latin manuscript from 807, for Trinity College Library in Dublin, was born in Charleville. Appointed bishop of Down and Connor in 1886 his own work is best remembered for his *Life of Columbus* (1857). The Revd Michael Barry (1820–73) also came from Charleville. A doctor of divinity and professor of All Hallows College he is gratefully (or sometimes perhaps not) remembered as the first to abridge Shakespeare for use in schools.

John Martin Anster (1793–1867) was born here; at Trinity College Dublin he became regius professor of civil law but he also gained a reputation as a poet, particularly for his verse translation of Goethe's *Faust* as *Faustus: A Dramatic Mystery* (1835).

Another law professor born in Charleville was Daniel Anthony Binchy (1899–1989), professor of jurisprudence and Roman law at University College Dublin. A Gaelic scholar who also worked with the diplomatic service and at Corpus Christi College in Oxford, Binchy was senior professor at the School of Celtic Studies in the Dublin Institute for Advanced Studies, his particular field being Gaelic law in Ireland. His greatest work is his *Corpus Iuris Hibernici* (1978), but he can also be met with as an essayist and historian, and his name recurs time and again in modern Irish scholarship especially in relation to the work of Osborn Bergin whose biography he published in 1970.

While Rath Luirc was being transformed into Charleville one of its natives was Seán Clárach Mac Dónaill (1691–1754):

My cattle are shelterless,
My team, unfed, thrive ill,
In misery my people dwell,
Their elbows through their clothes;
A price is on my head,
At the landlord's will;
My shoes are tattered,
And no wherewithal to make them good.[59]

Described by Seán Ó Tuama as a poet, scholar and strong farmer, Seán Clárach spent his life at Kiltoohig where he presided over the court of poetry which met here and sometimes in Bruree, Co. Limerick. He was said to have had a classical education, and in one of his best-loved songs the disguised Jacobite allegiance takes on a reference he would have expected his audience to understand:

Is é mo laoch, mo ghile, mear,
Is é mo Shaésar, gile mear,
Ni thuaras féin an suan ar séan
O chuaidh i gcéin, mo ghile mear ...

My hero, Living Brightness mine!
My Caesar, Living Brightness mine!
No sleep I've known since he has flown
Far from his own across the brine! [60]

It is this Duhallow territory too which was the home of Gofraidh Fionn Ó Dálaigh (d. 1387), the annalist and poet whose lament on the death of his son is quoted in the introduction to this chapter.

Newmarket

South-west of Charleville is Newmarket, once a holding of the MacAuliffes; after the Williamite wars the exiled sons of the family led the MacAuliffe Regiment under the flags of Spain. One of their Newmarket castles was in the demesne of that Sir Richard Aldworth who married Ireland's Lady Freemason, Elizabeth St Leger of Doneraile. The town, given its patent as a market in the reign of Charles II, was home to Revd Denis Murphy, SJ, (1835–96), professor of history and English at University College Dublin, who edited *The Annals of Clonmacnoise* (1848) and *Beatha Aodha Ruaidh Uí Dhomhnaill*. Newmarket, also the birthplace and, at Priory Glen, the first home of John Philpot Curran (1750–1817), whose warning that 'eternal vigilance is the price of freedom' has passed into the history of the spoken word. An eminent barrister (he defended the patriot Wolfe Tone and other members of the United Irishmen) and parliamentarian, he was appointed master of the rolls in Ireland, a position from which he retired in 1814. [61]

One of his children, Sarah (1780–1808), is buried here in Newmarket beside Curran's mother, Sarah Philpot; the younger Sarah had engaged the love of the insurgent Robert Emmet and on his abortive rebellion (1803) letters which he had been reluctant to burn brought the militia to her father's house in Dublin from which she was speedily banished to Cork.

Her subsequent marriage and early death did nothing to soften her father's outraged heart and he refused to allow her burial near the family home in Dublin. Instead she was laid here; her monument, however, was built by the poet and song-writer Thomas Moore (1779–1852) in whose verses she lives as the heroine of revolution and romance.

Moore was a friend of Curran and must have known all the facts of Sarah's life (including the elopement of her mother with a clergyman after

twenty years of marriage) and of Curran's behaviour, yet his songs glory in
inaccurate pathos:

> She is far from the land where her young hero sleeps,
> And lovers around her are sighing.
> But coldly she turns from their gaze, and weeps,
> For her heart in his grave is lying ...

The poet and novelist Henry Grattan Curran (1800–76) was John
Philpot's illegitimate son.

Kanturk

Southwards the town of Kanturk sits between its two rivers, the Dallua and
the Allow; a busy and prosperous town it is the birthplace of Gillman Noo-
nan (1937–) the journalist and writer of short stories. He has published *A
Sexual Relationship* (1976) and *Friends and Occasional Lovers* (1982). A centre
of the Duhallow hunt Kanturk is also distinguished by having, on its southern outskirts, one of the finest ruins in Ireland. Travellers taking the route
back to Cork which crosses the shallow foothills of the Boggeragh mountains will pass Kanturk Castle.

Smith in his *Antient and Present State of the County and City of Cork* (in 5
volumes, 1749) records that the town had belonged to a branch of the
MacCarthys:

> In Queen Elizabeth's time they erected a most magnificent pile near
> this place, the walls of which remain intire [sic]. It was a parallelo-
> gram, being 120 feet in length by 80 in breadth, flanked with four
> square buildings. This structure was four stories high, and the
> flankers five, all the window frames, coigns, beltings and battlements
> were of hewn stone, and the whole made a most grand and regular
> appearance.

A MacCarthy castle, it is said to have been the ambitious work of Donagh,
or MacDonagh, of the Duhallow MacCarthy chieftains. Start dates are uncertain, given the somewhat unsettled nature of both the area and the times,
but Smith says that it was begun in the reign of Queen Elizabeth I. James N.
Healy, the historian of the castles of Co. Cork, believes that it was the work
of Dermot MacOwen MacCarthy who was disputing the MacCarthy lordship
with Donagh, and that it was not begun until after the accession of James I.

Whichever was the monarch, the size and superiority of the building was
seen as a threat rather than a tribute to the serenity of Duhallow, and the
Lords of the Council in London ordered that it be stopped.

The coloured glass which was to have been used for windows and sky-lights was thrown into the nearby stream (now called the Blue Pool); the corbelling still awaits the parapets; fireplaces still decorate the internal walls; the empty windows and untenanted doorway all remain in place. 'Thus it remains still in the same condition, the walls having braved all the injuries of time,' wrote Smith in 1749 in a comment which is still true today.

John Christmas Deedy (1849–84), a prolific if short-lived poet was born in Kanturk; a contributor to *The Nation* and known as 'The Poet of Duhal-low', he died in Banteer. Kathleen Daly, writing as Margaret Hasset, was author of the novels *Educating Elizabeth* (1937) and *Beezer's End* (1949).

Near Kanturk are several old castles: Lohort at Cecilstown is a fifteenth-century MacCarthy towerhouse and a good excuse for an exploration of an almost unchanged pastoral landscape.

The Magners of Castlemagner had had their differences with the English crown, and it was probably with this history in mind that Oliver Cromwell visited Richard Magner, asking, as they walked through the graveyard behind the castle, who was buried there. The family graves included those of Magner's father, grandfather and granduncles. These might have been great men in their time, observed Cromwell, but he was able to walk over them now. This may have been meant as a timely warning to his host, but Magner was not easily intimidated and retorted that it was easy for a live dog to walk over dead lions.

The road running south now skirts the Allow which meets the Blackwater at Banteer (the road from Banteer to Mallow keeps company with the pic-turesque Blackwater). Poet Bernard O'Donoghue (1945–) was born at Cullen, near the Cork/Kerry border town of Rathmore; now teaching at Oxford Uni-versity, O'Donoghue published his collection *Poaching Rights* in 1987; *The Weakness* (1991) was short-listed for the Forward and Whitbread Poetry prizes, and *Gunpowder* won the Whitbread Award in 1995. His latest collec-tion *Here Nor There* appeared in 1999.

The road rises to the hills, allowing a view westwards to the mountains on the Kerry border where the Blackwater rises near Ballydesmond, and then, after the village of Nead an Iolair (Nad; the eagle's nest) south to the valley in which Blarney stands.

Blarney

'The more we know of the Lords of Muskerry, or the Earls of Clancarty, to whose castle at Blarney we now turn, the more we feel disposed to esteem them', writes Revd C.B. Gibson in his *History of the City and County of Cork* (1861). The old castle at Blarney was the stronghold of the MacCarthys of Muskerry, a great keep surrounded now by long flat pastures and rocky wood-

land. Cormac Laidir MacCarthy built this castle *c*. 1460 in a resounding statement of the family's provenance and power.

Cormac Laidir (the strong) buttressed his holdings along the valleys of
the Lee and the Bride – Kilcrea Abbey and castle are among his foundations –
as a defence not merely against the invasion of his territory by the advanc-
ing Anglo-Normans but as a protection too against the family feuds; he died
at the hands of his brother Eoghan in 1494. Eoghan was slain by his nephew
three years later.

For generations the MacCarthys were embroiled in wars with themselves, the Desmond overlords and the crown (both for and against). The
family spread throughout Cork and split into rival factions, losing and
regaining territory with the MacCarthys of Muskerry being created Earls
of Clancarty.

It is never the end of the story, however. The Clancartys fell foul of
William of Orange and finally lost their Muskerry estates, the last Earl dying
in Hamburg in 1734. The town, castle and 1,400 acres of Blarney eventually
went to Sir James Jeffreys, appointed by William as governor of Cork, and
then through marriage passed to the Colthurst family who now live in the
Victorian mansion nearby.

The castle's reputation as a source of eloquence (for those who kiss
the stone under the battlements) dates from Elizabethan impatience
with a verbose Lord Muskerry; it was celebrated by the insertion, in a
poem by Richard Milliken, of the lines by Francis Sylvester Mahony
(Fr Prout):

There is a stone there,
That whoever kisses,
Oh! he never misses
To grow eloquent.
'Tis he may clamber
To a lady's chamber,
Or become a member
Of parliament;
A clever spouter
He'll sure turn out, or
An out-an-outer
'To be let alone';
Don't hope to hinder him,
Or to bewilder him;
Sure he's a pilgrim
From the Blarney stone![62]

The lilt of Mahony, and Milliken, is a thin echo of the kind of poetry which made this townland renowned. Equally weightless now seem the verses of The Revd James Delacour (1709–81), a native of the village.

For here at Blarney was one of the country's longest-surviving bardic schools; before it came to an end Dónal MacCarthaigh, (*fl. c.* 1540) was entertaining his audience with his skilful observations on a love-affair:

> ... I dream of breasts so lilylike,
> Without a fleck,
> And hair that, bundled up from her back
> Burdens her neck
>
> And praise the cheeks where flames arise
> That shame the rose,
> And the soft hands at whose touch flees
> All my repose ...
>
> I am a ghost upon your path,
> A wasting death,
> But you must know one word of truth
> Gives a ghost breath –
>
> In language beyond learning's touch
> Passion can teach –
> Speak in that speech beyond reproach
> The body's speech. [63]

This translation by Frank O'Connor strays at times quite far from the original according to Sean Ó Tuama, but 'captures much of its lyrical quality.' These excerpts omit the poet's plea for comfort both to the Blessed Virgin and to the virginal subject of the poem. The rapid accentual flow of the original verse and the 'personal passionate pulse' intensify the underlying mood to such a degree that, for Ó Tuama, 'it is not too fanciful to imagine it being recited, to the accompaniment of a bronze-stringed harp, in the great hall of the MacCarthy castle in Blarney, County Cork.'[64]

The mighty keep of the castle still stands, attracting tourists in their thousands. It makes a dramatic picture on its rock. From its battlements the pleasant pastures stretch across the valley. The druid stones still lurk in the dolmen close. The mist of the town veils the trees. In the distance the thicker haze spells the city of Cork, where this journey began.

Notes to North Cork

1. Daniel Corkery, *The Hidden Ireland* (1925).
2. Sean Ó Tuama, *Repossessions* (1995).
3. Kuno Meyer: see Sean Ó Luing, *Kuno Meyer 1858–1919* (1992).
4. Rudolf Thurneysen (1857–1940), *Die Irische Helder-und Konigsage* (1912).
5. Osborn Bergin (1873–1950), 'Irish Bardic Poetry' (*Journal of the Ivernian Society*, V, 1912). David Greene and Fergus Kelly (ed.) Dublin Institute for Advanced Studies, 1970, Foreword by D.A. Binchy
6. ibid.
7. ibid.
8. ibid.
9. Sean Ó Tuama and Thomas Kinsella, *An Duanaire* (1981).
10. ibid.
11. Bergin, op.cit.
12. Ó Tuama and Kinsella, op. cit.
13. ibid.
14. Bergin, op. cit.
15. ibid.
16. ibid.
17. Frank O'Connor, *Kings Lords and Commons* (1962).
18. Aloys Fleischmann, *Sources of Irish Traditional Music* (1999).
19. Bergin, op. cit.
20. Fleischmann, op. cit.
21. Bergin, op. cit.
22. See Briain Ó Cuiv, 'Observations on the Book of Lismore', *RIA Proceedings* (1983).
23. Frank O'Connor, *The Backward Look* (1967).
24. ibid.
25. John A. Murphy, in O'Flanagan, Buttimer, *Cork, History and Society* (1993).
26. 'Torna' also translated *Rubaiyat of Omar Khayyam* (1920).
27. Faiche na bhFili, *Souvenir History of Court of Poetry at Carrignavar* (1962).
28. Corkery, *The Hidden Ireland*.
29. Ó Tuama and Kinsella, op. cit.
30. Conor Cruise O'Brien, *The Great Melody* (1992).
31. ibid.
32. ibid.
33. L.M. Cullen, 'The Blackwater Catholics and County Cork Society in the Eighteenth Century' *Cork, History and Society* (1993).
34. Robert Welch (ed.), *The Oxford Companion to Irish Literature* (1996).
35. Mathew Arnold (ed.), *Letters, Speeches and Tracts on Irish Affairs*, with a new introduction by Conor Cruise O'Brien, (1988); also Paul Langford *The Writings and Speeches of Edmund Burke* (1981).
36. J.R. O'Flanagan, *The River Blackwater in Munster* (1844 and 1975).
37. Johann Norstedt, *Thomas MacDonagh: A Critical Biography* (1980).
38. Richard Ellman, *James Joyce* (1959).
39. Terence Brown, *Ireland's Literature: Selected Essays* (1988).
40. Now at the British Library.
41. E.C. McAleer, *The Sensitive Plant, a biography of Lady Mount Cashel* (1958).
42. M. Bentham-Edwards (ed.), *Autobiography of Arthur Young* (1898).
43. See John de Courcy Ireland, 'The Irish Sword', vol vi, no. 25, Winter 1964; and James Colehman, 'General Arthur O'Connor', *Journal of the Cork Historical Society*, Series 2, vol. x, 1904.
44. Elizabeth Bowen, *Bowen's Court* (1942, 1998).
45. Sean O'Faolain, *An Irish Journey* (1940).
46. Edmund Spenser, *Colin Clout's Come Home Againe* (1595).

47. Anne Fogarty, 'The Colonization of Language', in Patricia Coughlan (ed.), *Spenser in Ireland* (1989).
48. O'Faolain, op. cit.
49. Canon Sheehan, *Luke Delmege* (1901).
50. Terence Brown, op. cit.
51. Herman Heuser, *Canon Sheehan of Doneraile* (1917).
52. Winifred Guerin, *Anne Thackeray Ritchie* (1981).
53. Anthony Trollope, *Castle Richmond* (1860).
54. ibid.
55. M.S. Peterson, *Robert Jephson* (1930).
56. *Thomas Davis Centenary Lecture 1914* (1965).
57. ibid.
58. T.W. Rolleston, *The Irish Book Lover* (1914).
59. Translation: Daniel Corkery, *The Hidden Ireland*.
60. ibid.; see also Risteárd Ó Foghlú (ed.), *Sean Clarach* (1932).
61. The bibliography of Thomas Davis includes *The Life of J.P. Curran* (1845) and *The Speeches of J.P. Curran edited with a memoir and historical notes* (1845); also Leslie Hale, *Biography of J.P. Curran* (1958).
62. Richard Milliken, *The Groves of Blarney*.
63. Frank O'Connor, op. cit.
64. Sean Ó Tuama, op. cit.

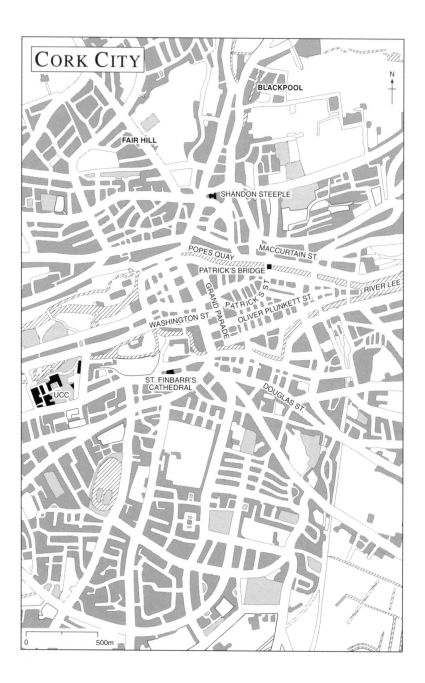

CORK CITY

BLACKPOOL

FAIR HILL

SHANDON STEEPLE

POPES QUAY

MACCURTAIN ST.

PATRICK'S BRIDGE

PATRICK'S ST.

RIVER LEE

GRAND PARADE

OLIVER PLUNKETT ST.

WASHINGTON ST.

ST. FINBARR'S
CATHEDRAL

DOUGLAS ST.

UCC

N

0   500m

CORK CITY

Places of trade, however important to the prosperity of a country, seldom possess attractions for strangers who may visit them on other than mercantile pursuits; nor will the origin of the name Cork excite expectations, its supposed derivation being from the Irish word Corcagh or Curkig, signifying a swamp or morass ...[1]

Cork's folklorist T. Crofton Croker (1798–1854) could not be said to have been a devout citizen; his life was in London where his congregation included such Cork exiles as clustered around *Fraser's Magazine*. They were not addicted to reflections on the status (as opposed to the personality) of their native city and, despite the sentimental ballad of the pseudonymous Fr Prout, were comfortable with their dismissive distance until Croker himself revealed the imaginative possibilities of its legends.

The history of the town was no more or less bloody than other Irish settlements emerging from the mists of Celtic time. First as a shoreline access point, then as a centre of trade and of commerce, the harbour produced the settlement from which the city developed. The monastic origins proclaimed in the name of its patron St Finbarr remain to this day the popular seventh-century foundation date, but from Ptolemy's map-making to the legends of Milesius, from the early belief that Britons retreating from the Roman invasion took refuge in southern Ireland, from the channels used by the earliest inhabitants of the water-logged estuarial town to the saintly journey along the course of the river Lee, Cork's first histories coincide in a kingdom.

The division of the province of Munster among the Eoganacht dynasty, displacing the earlier Iverni, began probably before the birth of Christ; by the time of St Finbarr the tribe of Corca Laighdhe shared the Eoganacht dominance, but the emerging city was already the seat of territorial lordships elevated into kings.

The annals and histories refer to the city under different names, but the first Eoganacht king of Cashel in Munster was Corc and from his descendants came the eventual kings of Desmond. Corcaigh Mor was the great marsh of Cork; a king of Corcaigh, Diarmuid Mor, was involved in the Battle of Gabhra AD 283, and the royal identity of the settlement – largely at first an island – was established by the end of the fourth century AD.

Scholarship has now concluded that the role of Finbarr in the founding of the (relatively) modern city of Cork properly belongs to one or several of the disciples of a Connacht saint who is himself unlikely ever to have visited Cork at all. His legendary connection with the city arose largely in response to twelfth-century ecclesiastical territorialism. The diocesan rivalries of the time – immediately before the arrival of the Normans – involved land titles and tribal allegiances in which the connections with Rome were exploited more subtly by some factions than by others.

Elizabeth Fort and Old St Finbarr's, Cork, 1796 by John Fitzgerald

It was believed that a saint, cult, shrine and school could add to the Corkonian claims and by 1199 the diocese of Cork was taken under the protection of the Holy See and its rights, privileges and possessions were confirmed. This was largely achieved by the production of a convincing '"Life" of the Saint', which also (with equal conviction and success) gave prominence to the power and influence of the MacCarthy clans in the county of Cork.

Evelyn Bolster explains in *A History of the Diocese of Cork* that in approaching the sources for a life of Bairre of Cork one is immediately confronted with a complete lack of contemporary documentation:

> While there is no gainsaying that miracles and anecdotes have made Irish hagiography a labyrinth of legend and wonder ... the very legend itself enhances the prestige of the person around whom it has developed. The commonplace never becomes legendary ...[2]

Listing the sources from which lives of St Finbarr have been written and re-written, Bolster mentions two Cork manuscripts: the oldest complete Irish version copied by Donall Ó Duinnín at Cork in 1629 for Francis Ó Mathgamna, provincial of the Friars Minor in Ireland, the second being a copy of this work, also made in Cork in 1629 by Brother Michael O'Clery in the house of the Friars Minor. As Finbarr's biographer Pádraig Ó Ríain of UCC explains, 'The saint himself is, of course, a casualty of the life; he is merely the peg on which the various claims are hung.'[3]

The antiquarian Dr Richard Caulfield identified Finbarr's first Cork settlement (or at least the foundation attributed to him) as Gougane Barra, the legendary Lough Irce. By the year 606 or thereabouts a plot of land on a hill to the south-west of the river port of Cork was offered to the saint or his followers by Aedh Mac Cair, a tribal relative of Corc, king of Cashel. It is from here, either at Gill Abbey rock which became a prominent medieval monastery, or at the nearby site of the Church of Ireland Cathedral of St Fin Barre, that the history of the city of Cork is popularly related.

Such a provenance is not without its critics, one of the most significant among them being the Cork historian William O'Sullivan:

> ... it may be asked, was Cork, that is modern Cork, founded at all in the ordinary meaning of the word, as used when considering the foundation of a monastery, where direct succession and traditions may be maintained for centuries? ...
>
> St Finbarr founded a monastery. The Norse, influenced by certain motives, founded a settlement in a marsh around the river. The existence of Cork today, as a city of substantial dimensions and commercial

importance, is due to circumstances to which the two latter incidences contributed little or nothing, even though its location has been very materially influenced by the site of the Ostman settlement.[4]

Earlier records support O'Sullivan's economic pragmatism:

Corke is an ancient cittie in the province of Mounster, and builded (as it should appear) by the Easterlings or Norwaies. It standeth now in a marsh or bog, and unto it floweth an arm of the sea, in which are many goodlie receptacles for ships, and much frequented as well for the good-lie commodities of fishings therein, as also for the trade of merchandize, by the which the cittie is chieflie maintained, for the inhabitants are not onlie merchants and great travellers themselves, but also great store of strange merchants do dailie resort and trafficke with them.[5]

Although politically and economically transfigured by the Normans from 1172, the city retained a degree of independence which distinguished it from other Irish cities in the path of the colonial advance.

By Royal Charter the Kingdom of Cork was granted to Robert FitzStephen and Milo de Cogan ... a present of very doubtful value. It may be compared to a present of a hive of bees, which in the process of being made really useful, might occasionally involve the recipients in nasty complications, which in fact it did.[6]

The ensuing process of assimilation, of intermarriage and communality, produced a citizenry which seemed cohesive enough to withstand everything until the Reformation. Different remembrancers, Caulfield's own records and modern historians delineate the affairs of the city with sometimes colourful, sometimes confusing or contradictory detail; through all these accounts runs the importance of the port and harbour in bringing Cork to its contemporary status.

A name so intertwined with the scholarship of local history and antiquarian research in the past century, that of Richard Caulfield (1823–87), is the constant repeated source of fact and anecdote relating to his native city. His particular study – and passion – was archaeology but gradually the literary and genealogical aspects of his research took precedence, especially where these were related to ecclesiastical subjects. He edited the *Autobiography of Sir Richard Cox of Bandon* (1860) and, also working from original manuscripts, the *Life of St Fin Barre* (1864). He is most widely known – and quoted – however for his *Council Book of the Corporation of Cork* (1876) which, with similar publications for Youghal and Kinsale and their appendices, annals and indexes provide an invaluable record of civic life from the early seventeenth century. Honoured during his life-time, joint editor for some years of the *Journal of the Royal Historical and Archaelogical Society of Ireland* and a fellow of similar societies in London, France and Spain, Caulfield was appointed librarian to Queen's College, Cork, in 1876.

Great national events did not begin or end in Cork although their traces marked streets and waterways; the great national heroes passed through – Daniel O'Connell at the courts, Charles Stewart Parnell electioneering outside the Victoria Hotel in Patrick Street, Michael Collins lodging in Oliver Plunkett Street before his fatal last journey to West Cork. But this was not a city central to government, church, the arts or commerce, although its own commercial life was distinct and, in Irish terms, unique.

Again, that had much to do with its port: the ships lying safe aground at what is now Castle Street brought in wines and took out woolpacks, brought in foreigners and took out exiles. The harbour hosted fleet after fleet of British ships, warfare made Cork's merchants wealthy, its butchers and tanners meeting the needs of army and navy for more than two centuries. Milk and butter established the streets around Shandon as an international marketplace. It was as a commercial rather than a political centre that Cork developed its identity; its wars were local, its factions fierce but domestic, and when the tide of great events washed over the city as with the Siege of Cork in 1690 or the Civil War in 1922 it left, on its retreat, a town largely unimpressed and even unchanged.

The intimate geography of Cork city is decided by the division of the river to the west, near the cliff on which University College now stands, near the Gill Abbey site of the ancient monastery. The city's north side begins at two bridges spanning the north channel flowing east towards the sea and uniting with the south channel below the spur of Custom House Quay.

There are now five bridges leading north, but only Patrick's Bridge and the North Gate Bridge are the historic fords of what was once a settlement in itself, at odds with the burghers of the walled town below Shandon. For several centuries only one bridge linked the reluctant neighbours of north and south, of hillside and marsh.

As the bogs on which Cork was built were gradually reclaimed the fords followed; reclamation and drainage in turn imposed on developers or owners the duty of bridging. When the river's streams were arched over during the eighteenth and nineteenth centuries the wider streetscape emerged and the islanded city was banked into the centre we know today.

Inevitably, a growing population, the spread of suburbs to include nearby villages and even towns, building developments and new roads and bridges have altered the physical city. Yet old divisions still linger as geographical identities, offering a perspective more intimate, more surprising, than might

Northgate Bridge by Nathaniel Grogan (the elder)

seem likely. An alley, a flight of steps, a hill will have a name originating in ancient usage or function. Keyser's Hill recalls the Danes; Half Moon Street is named for a ship plying the American routes which tied up here at Lavitt's Quay. Like other cities, Cork is a place memorialised by its artists, and the modern writers are as drawn to its images, its neighbourhoods and their histories, as any older school of singers might have been. There is the immediacy, for example, of Michael Davitt 'Will I meet myself again/Among the crowd in Patrick Street ...'[7] or of Greg Delanty '... Our one-time, dark/side streets and alleys are now trendy shopping thoroughfares;/ Paradise Place, French Church Street, Half Moon Street/Carey's Lane ...'[8]

As Seán Dunne has noted, the plays of Patrick Galvin echo with Cork accents, his poems ringing with the memories and manifestations of Cork characters.[9] And even Francis Sylvester Mahony took as his alias the name of Fr Prout, a priest from the Cork village of Watergrasshill; although a confidant of some of the great literary names of the day in London and Paris, Mahony is best remembered now as the author of verse enshrining the hill, the steeple and the bells of the Cork church in whose cemetery he is buried.

Cork-born novelist Alan Titley (1947–) has chosen to write in the Irish language; his novels include *An Fear Dána* (1993) based on the life of the medieval poet Muireadhach Albanach Ó Dálaigh (*fl.* 1220) whose title 'Albanach' is witness of his time in Scotland where he found refuge after murdering a steward. Titley's play *Tagann Godot* was produced at the Abbey Theatre in Dublin in 1992, and his collection of short stories *Eiriceachtaí agus Scéalta Eile* appeared in 1987. It is as the observer and critic of modern writing in Irish however that he is included in this introduction, for he both evaluates and exemplifies a strong current in the river of Irish literature; many modern writers of Cork city and county are sweeping that current to national prominence.

When the Irish language 'revival' began at the end of the last century, it was always seen as holding out an ideal for the entire country. Although the Gaeltachtaí were extremely important, the language did not exclusively belong to them. The language was a powerful force in repossessing consciousness and binding up historical wounds now openly recognised in most postcolonial criticism. The literature was to be an expression of this consciousness in all its plenitude, and so it has proved in the more than 100 years of modern Irish writing.[10]

Noting that there have been more collections of poetry in Irish produced annually during the last twenty-five years than in any comparable period and that there were more Irish-language novels written in the 1980s than in any other decade, Titley gives University College Cork a crucial date-stamp in that entire process:

> What happened in 1970, however, was a revolution. Unbidden, unheralded, and unexpectedly, a group of young poets started their own literary magazine in University College, Cork. It was initially a broadsheet but has since become the single most important poetry journal in Irish. The group of poets quickly became known as the *Innti* poets after the name of their publication. The idea was that of an undergraduate student, Michael Davitt. He edited the first edition ... [and] quickly gathered round him like-minded spirits, and together they have changed the face and nature of Irish poetry in the last twenty-five years.[11]

As a novelist and short story writer Titley doesn't ignore his own work in this overview, although in terms of prose in Irish there is less for him to write about with reference to Cork authors. Yet there is a resurgence in creative prose, even if the fortunes of the short story in Irish are not so rosy when compared to those of new novels. Welcoming the appearance of committed and reputable literary scholarship concentrating on work in Irish, Titley has added significently to that genre himself, with *An tÚrscéal Gaeilge* (1991), an important reference source to the books of his peers and colleagues throughout Ireland.

The birth of *Innti* at UCC in the 1970s must have had much to do with writers and academics working then at the university college, including poets such as Seán Ó Riordáin, Seán Ó Tuama, Seán Lucy, John Montague and Tomás Ó Canainn. Those credits are offered generously by graduates now; less discernible is the provenance of Cork's earlier writers, novelists, poets and balladeers, the makers of mild short stories, the composers of plays and sermons, the collectors and editors and diarists whose voices are now almost indistinguishable under the layers of centuries or the lapse of publication.

Eaton Stannard Barrett (1786–1820), for example, was a Cork-born lawyer practising in London where his verses 'All the Talents' satirising the Whig cabinet of the day were published under his pseudonym 'Polypus' (1807), winning him instant success. Plays of a comic character, parodic verses and journalism added to his popularity.

Another Cork lawyer was barrister Michael Joseph Barry (1817–89) whose *Echoes from Parnassus* is an anthology of Cork poets published in 1849. Politically affiliated to the Young Ireland movement Barry also worked as a journalist, writing leaders for *The Times* at one stage. His poetry is collected as *The Kishogue Papers* (1872).

Tragic Thomas Delaune (1635–85) was befriended by Daniel Defoe in England, where he had gone on leaving his Catholic Cork background for the Baptist church, and where, unable to work or write, he – and his family – died from starvation while imprisoned for debt. He was his own hero, though: *A Plea for the Non-Conformist* (1683) and *A Narrative of the Sufferings of T.D.* (1804) tried to draw attention to his plight – his release from jail could have been purchased with £67.

Brothers Isaac (1812–68) and Ralph (1820–86) Varian wrote ballads and collected native Irish songs: Ralph, whose pseudonym was 'Dunkathel' was married to the poet Elizabeth Willoughby (Lizzie Twigg). In a curious bi-lingual pun the songs and poems of Lizzie Twigg were published, with an introduction by Canon Sheehan of Doneraile, in 1905 as the work of Eilís Ní Chraoibhín.

Hester Sigerson (d. 1898) was a sister of Ralph and Isaac Varian and the wife of Dr George Sigerson; she wrote many poems and the book *A Ruined Race: or The Last MacManus of Drumroosk* (1890).

Britsfieldstown near Carrigaline is now almost a suburb of the city, but was the birthplace of Sir Randal Howland (1837–90) who served as a special correspondent in the Franco-Prussian War, winning the Iron Cross of Prussia for Valour. He concentrated later on sporting journalism and produced several novels, including *Curb and Snaffle* (1888). The poet John Augustus Shea (1802–45) worked as a clerk in the brewery of Beamish and Crawford before emigrating to America; his poems were published posthumously in 1846, his historical romance *Clontarf; or The Field of the Green Banner* having appeared in 1843.

Crofton Croker himself gives credit to James Cavanah Murphy of Blackrock (1760–1814), the bricklayer who travelled to Spain and Portugal and became an architect; his studies of the Moorish decorative style were enormously influential in the British and Irish architecture of the period, and Sir Richard Morrison in particular has left evidence of Murphy's *Arabian Antiquities of Spain* (1815) in several of his great Irish houses.

James Sheridan Knowles (1784–1862) was born in Anne Street; he abandoned a career in medicine for poetry, fiction and the London stage, his wide-ranging choice of subjects including Brian Boru, Alfred the Great and Mary Magdalen. His *The Elocutionist* (1822) was a popular compilation of material for recitation, but his contemporary fame rested on the immense success of *William Tell* in London. His novels were written after he had become a Baptist preacher. His son Richard Brinsley Knowles (1820–82) was a journalist and novelist; Richard Brinsley Sheridan was a cousin.

Ministering to his Presbyterian congregation in Princes Street was The Revd Thomas Dix Hincks (1767–1857), later professor of Hebrew and oriental languages at the Royal Belfast Academical Institute. Among his talented offspring born in Cork was his son, the The Revd Edward Hincks (1792–1866). Although working for most of his life as a clergyman in the North of Ireland Edward Hincks is commemorated now by a marble bust at the entrance to the Cairo Museum. He was an accomplished Sanskrit scholar and Egyptologist, a pioneer of Assyrian hieroglyphics and discoverer of the Persian vowel system. He never visited the countries of these languages; apart from some months spent at the British Museum in London all his work was carried out through textual copies and casts of ancient inscriptions. He is buried with his wife Jane at Killyleagh Church in Co. Armagh.

Not all the writers whose names have been submerged in the city are as distant as Delaune or Twigg or Murphy. Donal Giltinan (b. 1908–), for example, was a customs and excise officer until he decided to concentrate on writing plays for radio and television, as well as producing over 600 radio programmes. His play *Goldfish in the Sun* was presented at the Abbey Theatre in 1950 which also staged three more of his plays, and his novel *Prince of Darkness* was published in 1955.

References to Eileen Gould (1900–88) are usually made via studies of the life and work of her husband Sean O'Faolain. But this young Cork woman had ambitions of her own, necessarily – although this must be debatable – abandoned for the sake of O'Faolain's work. Publishing as Eileen O'Faolain, she wrote several novels for children including *The Little Black Hen* (1940) and *High Sang the Sword* (1959). Her most important work, however, is in her knowledgeable and creative treatment of Irish legends: *Irish Sagas and Folktales* (1954) and *Children of the Salmon and Other Irish Folktales* (1965), which are English-language classics of the genre. Her daughter Julia O'Faolain is a well-known novelist.

One of several priests whose names will be forever associated with Cork city was Fr James Christopher O'Flynn (1881–1962), affectionately remembered as 'Flynnie', whose service to the north side of the city has been recorded in *Like a Tree Planted* (1967) by Richard O'Donoghue. Not a writer himself, Fr O'Flynn was a literary enthusiast whose special love was Shakespeare; this led to the creation of an amateur theatrical society known as 'The Loft' after the little attic premises in which rehearsals were held near the church of St Anne's, Shandon. For many years these were the only performances of Shakespeare available to Cork where Fr O'Flynn established a tradition which continues to this day. The Loft was also responsible for the production of several of Ireland's leading actors, including members of the Abbey Theatre in Dublin.

Born in Cork, the poet Aidan Murphy (1952–) lives in London; his most recent collection, *Stark Naked Blues* was published in 1997, and other publications include *The Restless Factor* (1985) and *The Way the Money Goes* (1987).

A vocation for journalism seems to have been part of the personality of The Revd James Good, DD (1924–) who served in several Cork city parishes including that of the Lough. He was also a lecturer in ethics, philosophy and theology at UCC. The controversy aroused by the publication of the papal encyclical on birth control *Humanae Vitae* in 1968 brought his somewhat liberal views into conflict with his bishop Cornelius Lucey. Ordained in 1948, Dr Good wrote widely for leading academic journals as well as for national and provincial newspapers, and was one of the most significant mediators for modern theology in Ireland until controversy encouraged him to go abroad. He worked for nearly twenty years in Kenya (where he was briefly joined by Cornelius Lucey) before retiring to live in Co. Cork.

Nigel FitzGerald (b. 1906) was the author of many popular thrillers which included *Midsummer Malice* (1953) and *Affair of Death* (1967), while Stephen Foreman, born in South Terrace in 1868, was the author of verse collections and at least two novels, *The Terrible Choice* (1909) and *Fen Dogs* (1912). Frank Gallagher (1893–1962) used several pseudonyms including David Hogan and David O'Neill for his short stories while working for *The Irish Press* as editor in chief from 1931–35 and head of the Government Information Bureau from 1940; he joined the National Library in 1954. His grand-niece is Patricia Finney (1958–), the London-born novelist.

Con O'Leary (1888–1959) was also a barrister; while writing novels and plays (some of which were produced by his friend Daniel Corkery, he worked as a journalist for *The Manchester Guardian*.

Eoin Neeson (1927–) has written plays for stage, radio and television as well as histories and biographies, including *The Civil War in Ireland* (1966); his translations are collected in *Poems from the Irish* (1986).

Gerald Hanley (1916–) had a career which spanned ranching in South Africa and service with the Royal Irish Fusiliers in Burma; he became a scriptwriter for the BBC's European service and wrote *The Consul at Sunset* (1946) and *Gilligan's Last Elephant* (1962) with at least six other novels.

Other Cork-born novelists include Sheila Flitton (1935–) who has also written the play *For Better, For Worse* (1982); her most recent publication is *Waiting in the Wings* (1996); and Kathleen O'Connor (1934–) writer of *Stepping Stones* (1990).

Cork is also well-served by its memorialists, including Declan Hassett, arts editor of *The Examiner* newspaper, author of *All Our Yesterdays* (1998) and *The Way We Were* (1999). Walter McGrath, a former journalist on the same newspaper, is a local historian and a prolific contributor to journals such as the *Cork Historical and Archaelogical Society*, the *Military History Society of Ireland* and the *Irish Railway Record*.

Born in Anglesea Street close to South Terrace in 1912, Gerald Yael Goldberg is the son of a Lithuanian refugee who had been put ashore in Cork although hoping to reach America. Solicitor, antiquarian, governor of the National Gallery of Ireland and former lord mayor of Cork, founder with his wife Sheila of the Cork Orchestral Society and patron of art, literature and music, Gerald Goldberg is the author of the study *Jonathan Swift and Contemporary Cork* (1967).

He is also the uncle of David Marcus (1924–), barrister, former literary editor and novelist. As founder of 'New Irish Writing' for *The Irish Press* in 1967 Marcus was crucial to the emergence of young writers in Ireland. This avocation began as early as 1946 when with Terence Smith he edited *Irish Writing* until 1954, while also editing *Poetry Ireland* from 1948 to 1954. His first novel *To Next Year in Jerusalem* was published in 1954, but it was more than thirty years before another novel *A Land Not Theirs* appeared (1986) which was followed by *A Land in Flames* (1988). Married to the novelist Ita Daly, Marcus will always be remembered in Ireland for the dedication and enthusiasm with which he pursued and recognised new literary talent. He has edited numerous anthologies of Irish writing, including *Mothers and Daughters* for Bloomsbury (1998).

The later novels by David Marcus concerned the history of Cork's Jewish community, giving it an epic resonance in the life of the city (where now the community has been reduced to a few remaining families). He could be said to represent those modern vigorous authors who contribute to a city's mythology as surely as do the letters and diaries of visitors such as John Betjeman or the travel journals of Thackeray – although these too, as in the poems of Augustus Young (1943–), are the stuff of modern literature.[12]

Daniel Laurence Kelleher (1883–1958) Cork-born teacher, journalist and playwright, was another traveller, one whose journeys ended at home. Educated at Queen's College Cork and a collaborator of T.C. Murray on *The Last Hostel* (1918), his own plays were also produced at the Abbey Theatre: *Stephen Grey* in 1910 followed by *A Contrary Election*.

But Kelleher's historical sketches (and several radio plays) and sentimental or humorous verse have left a different legacy, ripe and over-written, perhaps, yet full of the inspired imagery which lodges in a city's collective consciousness. In *The Glamour of Cork* (1919) Kelleher recreates St Finbarr: 'A traveller, a scholar, a gentleman ... Such is Finnbarr, the Connaughtman, whom we meet now. Businesslike, as a Saint should be, daring, original, ambitious, but with a difference.'

Perkin Warbeck peers through these pages, with Sir Walter Scott and Patrick Sarsfield, Lord Macaulay, Charlotte Brontë on honeymoon; Edmund Mortimer, Earl of March, dying at the monastery of St Mary's of the Isle at Christmas in 1381, Prince Rupert of the Rhine leaping Cork's puddles in

1649, St Malachy and Lord Mountjoy, Oliver Cromwell and Oliver Gold-smith, or Justin MacCarthy leading Mountcashel's Brigade to glory at Piedmont.

To these perspectives the later visitors add their weight: Robert Graves before the news cameras at UCC, displaying the purple petals of herb Robert in his lapel. Anthony Burgess spreading breakfast marmalade in Tom McCarthy and Catherine Coakley's high-windowed flat on Wellington Road, silenced by the view if by nothing else. John Heath Stubbs sitting at his ease in the company of Evelyn Montague and her husband John in their house on Grattan Hill. Alan White, chairman of the Methuen publishing company, living at Hayfield House on Perrott Avenue, and killed in a traffic accident on the Western Road.

The commonplace, says Evelyn Bolster, does not attract legends. But common experiences acquire a sheen from such incidents. With time the common names and landmarks, the milestones of a city's tumbled history unite like the river to provide the shared provenance of landscape and literature. In his poem 'A Nocturne for Blackpool' Theo Dorgan writes that the unicorns of legend are the donkeys of childhood, 'nobody/Knows that better than we know it ourselves ...'

> We are who we are and what we do. We study indifference in a hard
> school
> And in a hard time, but we keep the skill to make legend of the
> ordinary.[13]

A City Location:
The North Side, beginning at Half Moon Street

I am only a few streets away from Half Moon Street and my sleep. All I hear is my own heel-tapping, or Shandon above us all on the hills grinding out a few more grains of time as it has done for so many generations of enduring poverty, quiet resignation, selfish ambition, and smug content. Oh all those damp and cloying nights! Oh breeding time of wild dreams, and smothering anger and terror of defeat! Oh my youth! Oh my city! I have loved, admired, feared and hated no city so much as you.[14]

For twenty-six years of his life Cork was Sean O'Faolain's shadow – 'and no man jumps off his own shadow'. It was his life – 'and one does not spit life out of one's mouth.'[15] No indeed – yet it was these characteristics, singly and together, which O'Faolain (1900–91) was to challenge throughout his subsequent career as a writer. Poverty, dreams and anger, ambition and complacency, resignation and content – these were the enduring material of his fiction and even, in an excercise decoded by his biographer Maurice Harmon, of his autobiographical work.

Not everything in *Vive Moi!* (1963/1993), says Harmon, happened as O'Faolain describes: writing of the imagination at work in that book Harmon says that O'Faolain himself

identified it as histrionic and attributes its presence to the twin influences of the Cork Opera House and the church of Saints Peter and Paul, both of which he attended frequently as a boy ... It was not only that the real became part of the unreal, but that theatre and church seemed part of the same unreality.

What was unreal? Perhaps it is the imagined construction of a city which is the real one, or at least the one which somehow remains recognisable. Both O'Faolain and his friend and rival Frank O'Connor have left in their work portraits of their native city which their successors as citizens and as writers accept as historically accurate and even, dismayingly, sometimes immediate. And both have left a portrait not only of each other but also of their mentor, patron and friend Daniel Corkery; although many other personalities weave through the mesh of these three lives, the biographical coincidence first of their friendship and then of their conflict still echoes with a profound literary resonance.

This attempt to describe the conflict, to measure the resonance and to assess the work of all three must be abridged by the nature of this book, but some attempt is necessary, if only for the sake of a row which was important at the time – and which has left its mark.

Not least on Sean O'Faolain, who lived until his young manhood in one of the tall houses of Half Moon Street. This is the street which runs behind the Opera House and art gallery to the river, facing the stage door of the theatre (a sports shop and a garage now take up most of the block).

It was an ideal location for the theatrical boarding house run by Mrs Whelan, as Sean O'Faolain's mother would have been known in those days before it was politically and culturally popular to change one's name into the Irish language. His father Denis was a constable in the Royal Irish Constabulary; the atmosphere in the house was a combination of fantasy, glamour and exoticism on one hand, civic order and ritualised religion on the other.

Behind Sean O'Faolain's home here lay much of the city: between these lanes and the main thoroughfare of Patrick Street ran Paul Street and Browne Street leading on to Castle Street – itself a former water-way, gated and guarded and visible with its freight of ships in the old maps – and thence to the market area of the Coal Quay and North Main Street.

This street is (with South Main Street) the major residual element of the early walled town; archaeology has revealed its buildings as standing on the grids of other buildings; its church, now restored as a sympathetically designated municipal 'vision centre', stands where the early maps show a church to have stood since the maps were made.

The important church of O'Faolain's youth was SS Peter and Paul's, which is situated in the narrow curved alley linking Paul Street to the Grand Parade end of Patrick Street (Peter and Paul's Place):

> Its pulpit of carved pine, spired by a tapering fretted pinnacle, was, we believed, the tallest pulpit in the world. The church was lit by trident-like gas standards held by a row of carved angels along each aisle. We were told that a former parish priest, in showing these to a stranger, informed him that they were the work of a German woodcarver.
>
> 'Not so' said the man. 'They were carved by John Hogan'.
>
> The priest smiled unbelievingly. 'I know whom you mean, the famous Irish sculptor. But Hogan never did anything as fine as these angels.'
>
> For answer the stranger led the priest to one of the angels, drew out a carved quill from one of the wings and showed, carved thereon, the signature John Hogan, saying: 'I am John Hogan.'[16]

In 1940 O'Faolain collaborated with the Irish artist Paul Henry on *An Irish Journey*; in what amounts to an ascerbic elegy for his native city O'Faolain

Dalton's Avenue (Cornmarket Street) by William Harrington

views its parishes and suburbs as if rooted here, on the pavement of Half Moon Street, looking southwards as helplessly as looking northwards.

> There is only one tune for Cork. It is one of those towns you love and hate. Some wag said that in Cork you do not commit sin; you achieve it. You do not, likewise, enjoy life in Cork; you experience it. For it is a town with a sting, inhabited by the Irish Gascons, the most acidulous race we breed ... To a stranger entering Cork I would say: Be on the defensive. These soothering, Blarnying folk have the mountains of Cork and Tipperary to the North of them, the sea to the South of them, the wilds of West Cork and Kerry at their backs, and as for the valley to the East down to Youghal, it seems to be asleep, and I always found it asleep, but since it is part of Cork it is safer not to believe for a moment that it *is* asleep.

Railing against creeping gentility he suggests a literary pantheon for the poor:

> It is odd that these folk, so rich of life, of language, of emotion, of history, have hardly ever been treated in literature. Some of the best things Daniel Corkery ever wrote were a few sketches of the Cork poor at the end of his first book of short stories 'A Munster Twilight'. Frank O'Connor's 'The Saint and Mary Kate' is the only real tribute they have received. Beside it I would put his play 'Time's Pocket', a play genuine to the core ...[17]

Like *Vive Moi!*, *An Irish Journey* was written in exile: only Dublin, but far enough. Its remembered geography is appropriate still. Although O'Faolain returned to his native city with increasing reluctance through the years and eventually wouldn't come at all, these are his streets, his playgrounds, the architecture and geography of his young life. To stand here close to the quayside is to remember that Emmet Place was once a dock, the Crawford Gallery a former custom house:

> My father-in-law who lived away at the farthest, western end of the city, in Sunday's Well, an old sailor, used hurl it all back on me when, as he lay bedridden in the heel of his days, he would suddenly cock an ear and say – 'There's a ship coming up the river.'
> And I would lift my head, and ever so faint and far away, out of the little, poky, stuffy sick-room, down the valley of the city, down the river between its mudflats or on its first loch, I would hear the gentle hoot of a siren, a cock-crow of triumph for safe entry from the sea. The arms of

Cork record that endless adventure – a ship entering between two castles. Statio Bene Fida Carinis. The first Latin I loved to mouth ...[18]

This was territory O'Faolain shared, actually and as a resource for fiction, with other writers. It was a territory he transformed creatively, but it also had a creative power of its own:

Last night I was in Cork: the climate was Italian; I lay on the steps of the square in Patrick Street ... and Pigott's front was just two immense doors from roof to pavement in black and gold lacquer, and Egan's the jeweller's had a hallway of great size surrounded by walls covered by lifesize brass repousse goddesses and gods and warriors designed by Harry Clarke ... Suddenly Jack Hendrick and Kitty O'Leary appeared. Jack wore a lieutenant's uniform, Irish army ... and then, lo, and how exquisitely beautiful it was, he flung himself down beside me, threw down the army cap, and Kitty curled up too ... and my God how he laughed and how Kitty laughed, and we were all young again and full of joy and to-hell-with-the-world feelings, and life was our oyster, and Ireland was the world the way it used to be. What woke me up was crying because in my heart I knew it was only a dream I was dreaming.[19]

The tears of that dream rippled under the crust of his experience both of Cork and of the world until then – a dream recalled in this letter of 1953. Pigott's cluttered, resounding music store, Egan's the jewellers and religious outfitters in one of whose great windows a monstrance would glitter against an embroidered cope while in the other emeralds nestled on ivory velvet and pearls gleamed from a case of inlaid ebony. And Jack Hendrick, like Nancy McCarthy and Seamus Murphy an enduring figure of this Cork life, was known as Seán Hendrick and would marry Kitty O'Leary.

Enduring also were the local wars and disappointments. O'Faolain's frustrated hope of becoming professor of English literature at University College Cork, for example, and the not unrelated fissures in the most complicated engagement of his life in Cork, that uniting him with his friend Michael O'Donovan – the writer Frank O'Connor – and with Daniel Corkery (1878–1964), who won the chair of English denied to O'Faolain.

In his essay 'After the Revival: Seán Ó Faoláin and Patrick Kavanagh' Terence Brown sets the early O'Faolain novels in the context of a city environment dominated intellectually by Corkery and therefore, for a time at least, dismissive of Yeats:

The young writers coming into their own in the early 1930s, inheritors of the post-civil-war disillusionment, could agree with the Yeats of the later poetry that the Irish Free State in no real sense re-established the values of the old Gaelic order, but they could not agree with him that the Literary Revival provided an adequate model of how such a re-establishment might be effected ... they knew the drab, unadventurous, unromantic, puritanically Catholic, English-speaking, economically-prudent reality ... the antithesis of art. [20]

No wonder they yearned to escape it! No wonder, either, that O'Faolain tried to describe it – first in *A Nest of Simple Folk* (1934) and then in *Bird Alone* (1936) and *Come Back to Erin* (1940).

And no wonder, in the end, that it was with Corkery's publication first of *The Hidden Ireland* (1924) and then, more controversially because it seemed as if the finger of national exclusivity was being pointed at them, of *Synge and Anglo-Irish Literature* (1931) that O'Faolain and O'Connor finally shook off the last shreds of Corkery's patronage.

Forgivingly, O'Faolain writes of Corkery in *Vive Moi!*:

Some defensive reaction is inevitable in every writer whom the gods drop into an antipathetic environment, a threat against which the artist must sooner or later concoct an anodyne to preserve his personality ... He decided that the remnants of the old, pre-conquest Ireland, the apparently lost but actually merely hidden traditional Ireland was a medieval world, to be sought and still to be felt in our fields, farmhouses, lone islands, small towns and villages, with all their traditional rustic ways, especially when expressed in the already vanishing Irish language ... In his old age he devoted himself wholly to the enthusiastic support of the Irish language-revival movement and a stern disapproval, expressed in forcible English, of the unpatriotic practice of writing in English. He also ceased to be creative.

One sighs. There is none of us who does not make some lunatic misjudgement about the nature of his circumstances ...[21]

Forgivingly – yet that sigh is dismissive. What was eventuallly to divide the three writers and to resolve their relationship as two against one, the younger against the elder, is caught in Terence Brown's essay in which he describes Corkery's commitment to the 'doctrine of national distinctiveness where the only authentic national life was certainly Gaelic, and possibly Catholic as well ...'[22]

The visitor may find it hard to understand why in Cork this controversy is still alive – and kicking with all its might. Perhaps its literary importance lies in the timing: in these three writers the critical cultural renaissance of the new Ireland – post-civil war, post-literary revival – was embodied. In the end each representative of rival ideologies – Corkery on one hand, O'Faolain and O'Connor on the other – dismissed and despised the rival positions.

Patrick Maume writes of all this with authority in his study of Corkery, *Life that is Exile*. This was a battle which embraced all the issues – language, religion, racial identity, history and cultural heritage, literature, provincial complacency and social realism, O'Faolain's editorship of *The Bell*, Corkery's contempt for Dublin modes, O'Connor's restless lifestyle. For decades they wrote against and about one another in journals and newspapers, pamphlets and books, often with a sneer which seems typically Irish. From their contest the literature of modern Ireland was born in both Irish and English.

Tilting against Corkery and inspired by O'Connor, O'Faolain argued that the pre-Conquest Gaelic society proselytised by Corkery was instead a decadent aristocratic world refusing to move with the great European forces of change and revitalisation. According to Maume, O'Faolain's thesis was that the modern Irish nation only began when the Irish peasantry freed themselves from the Gaelic shadows and followed Daniel O'Connell's campaign for Catholic Emancipation in a vision of social as well as religious liberty.

To the end of his days Daniel Corkery remained committed to the ideal of an Irish-speaking Ireland; although professor of English at UCC he only visited England twice. Appointed to the Irish senate in 1951 he never spoke there; appointed to the Arts Council he attended only fifteen of the forty-three meetings of his term. He would not have the names of O'Connor or O'Faolain mentioned in his hearing; passing Frank O'Connor unexpectedly on a Cork street he exclaimed: 'Well, if it isn't Mr. Frank O'Connor, who only writes for American magazines now?', and walked by. It was, says Maume, their last meeting.[23]

If that was the row, who, after O'Faolain, were these people?

He lived in a small suburban house on Gardiner's Hill with his mother and sister, surrounded by books and pictures. Over the mantelpiece was a large water colour of his own of a man with a scythe on Fair Hill overlooking the great panorama of the river valley. Inside the door of the living room was a bust of him by his friend, Joe Higgins which – if my memory of it is correct – is the only likeness of him that captures all his charm.[24]

It is a very short distance from Emmet Place to Patrick's Bridge, from where a seeking eye will discern the still-wooded eastern slopes of the suburb of Montenotte above the crowded avenues of Summer Hill, Wellington Road, Gardiner's Hill, Grattan Hill. All these hills look downwards to the river, the city port, the railway station (arches and steps lead from the slopes to the Lower Road where the modern Kent Station operates). On Summerhill it is still possible to see, behind St Patrick's Church, the site of the old railway terminus used by those fleeing the Great Famine.

Montenotte is the suburb which intervenes between the city, the road to Mayfield and the river-bank route to Tivoli and Glanmire. From the flat of the city it is marked by two spires: first, at the end of Summerhill on Mac-Curtain Street, by that of Trinity Presbyterian Church, and then after the climb past the first tiers of tall houses, past the entrances to the iron-railed and stone-built passages back down to the Lower Road, by that of St Luke's Church of Ireland which gives its name to this district, St Luke's Cross. Montenotte begins here at the right hand turn beyond the church; the left-hand turn leads back to the city via Wellington Road, or up again to the military barracks via Military Hill. The main road continues directly north to Dillon's Cross and Mayfield, the Old Youghal Road and the roads to the countryside of Ballyvolane and Ballyhooley.

At St Luke's Cross the position and atmosphere of Henchy's public house made it a general gathering place for the writers and artists living in or visiting the locality. A turn to the right almost immediately beyond the cross opens into Gardiner's Hill. Daniel Corkery was born in a thatched cabin here at the foot of this hill.

All Corkery's schooling was through the medium of the English language. It was not until he became a monitor, and then a teacher, that he began to explore writing, and thinking, in Irish and to discover the *Gaeltacht* (Irish-speaking) districts of Munster. As a young man he wrote for nationalist and socialist journals, joining the Gaelic League and gradually developing his personal philosophy of an Irish cultural heritage which was most comprehensively expounded in his book *The Hidden Ireland*.

A founder member of the Cork Dramatic Society (1908) Corkery was a close friend of Terence MacSwiney (1879–1920), who was later to become lord mayor of Cork and to die on hunger strike in Brixton Prison. Both men wrote plays which were produced by the company – although with some difficulty on occasions: according to Patrick Maume one of Mac-Swiney's plays could not be staged because it had five female parts and the CDS had only four actresses. 'MacSwiney was asked to rewrite it; he gave it six female parts.' [25]

MacSwiney's tendency was for revolutionary or socialistic plays: *The Holocaust* (1910) was based on a bitter local trade union dispute (a theme Corkery himself used later in his play *The Labour Leader* 1917). As a one-act piece it had a better chance of production than *The Revolutionist* (1910–11) which required eighteen changes of scenery. None of this theatrical work survived MacSwiney's immolation in the politics of the time from which his literary legacy rests with his philosophical declaration *The Principles of Freedom* (1921).

In a letter to MacSwiney's grieving sister Annie, Corkery described the dead man as 'almost superhumanly perfect – not only as a patriot but as a man'. And in a tribute published after MacSwiney's death Corkery described him as having 'practised literature for the sake of Ireland', writing 'the noblest propaganda that perhaps ever was written.'[26] In a way this is what Corkery wanted all his friends and protégés to do; inevitably the two most famous of them resisted, resented and fled.

Corkery, who was also a musician, a carpenter like his father and brothers, a choral conductor and a painter worked consistently as a writer, producing plays and short stories. Others who would later achieve fame were encouraged by the light he shed in the CDS: the teacher T.C. Murray of Macroom left Cork in 1912 to become one of the Abbey Theatre's most popular playwrights, having been encouraged by Corkery to write his first play.

Lennox Robinson had his play *Patriots* (1912) produced at An Dun, the CDS premises over a livery stable; it was, says Maume, the work which 'first showed the young Sean O'Faolain the life around him could provide subject matter for literature.'[27]

Teaching at St Patrick's national school at St Luke's Cross (the building has been demolished recently, but stood inside the wall at the bus-stop near Henchy's pub, almost directly opposite Gardiner's Hill) Corkery lived at Ashburton on Gardiner's Hill until his appointment at UCC; then he moved to the rural surroundings of Ballygroman House at Kilumney in Co. Cork. On retirement he went to Myrtleville on the coast and then to Passage West on the shore of Cork harbour.

He wrote four collections of short stories, several plays, three cultural histories, a novel and countless articles. It is accepted, however, that by the time of his appointment to UCC his best work was already done; it was from Gardiner's Hill that his influence was to spread most profoundly to other Irish writers and artists.

His many short stories ('The Wager' (1950) and 'Nightfall and Other Stories' (1987) are selections from publications from 1916 to 1939), his novel *The Threshold of Quiet* (1917), his plays, poems and literary criticism make up an impressive body of work of varying quality. Yet the work for which he remains best known in Ireland is *The Hidden Ireland* (1924) which expounds the literary theories forged both by his extensive reading of Irish-language material and the tragic tumults of the first twenty years of the century.

But Corkery's greatest friend was Sean O'Faolain, who was three years older than I and all the things I should have wished to be – handsome, brilliant, and, above all, industrious ... Once the three of us met on Patrick's Bridge after Corkery and O'Faolain had attended a service at the cathedral, and when O'Faolain went off in his home-spun suit, swinging his ash-plant, Corkery looked after him as I had once seen him look after Terence MacSwiney and said: 'There goes a born literary man!' For months afterwards I was mad with jealousy.[28]

This succinct paragraph conveys something of the perceived intellectual status of Corkery and of the tensions shared by those who felt or valued that influence.

I do not blame myself for not understanding and sympathising with what was happening to him, because it was precisely the opposite of what was happening to me. He was a man who, by force of character, had dominated physical difficulties, family circumstances and a provincial environment that would have broken down anyone but a great man ... Nowadays I remember how his mind seemed always to brood on self-control, as when he described how he had written his novel, getting up each morning at six, or wrote to me when I was in prison, quoting Keats on the beneficial effect of a shave and wash-up when one's spirits were low, or praised Michael Collins, who had made himself leader of the whole revolutionary movement because he was up answering letters when everyone else was in bed ... He would gaze at me gloomily, and predict in his harsh unmodulated voice that I would go through life without ever finishing anything, and then add 'like Coleridge', awarding me a valuable second prize ...[29]

Frank O'Connor (1903–66) remembers with a forgiving grace a friendship which was to end in a triangle of bitterness. Its original importance can be estimated, however, from O'Connor's own explanation of his part in the Irish Civil War: 'To say that I took the wrong side would promote me to a degree of intelligence I had not reached. I took the Republican side because it was Corkery's ...'[30]

It was around these sloping streets that all three men, two young, one middle-aged and lame, walked together in their arguments; this was the territory they all used in their fiction, and which appears and reappears, disguised or otherwise, throughout their writing lives. And there is a point worth making about O'Connor in particular: in certain stories, notably 'The Idealist' and 'The Duke's Children' he describes exactly the response of the imaginative Irish child denied access to fiction by Irish writers and reared instead on the English periodicals and popular novels of the time. (Indeed 'The Duke's Children' is also the title of a novel by Anthony Trollope in the Palliser series.) O'Connor records the ironic complications of the Irish child determined to obey the British notions of fair play and schoolboy honour and the limitless possibilities of foundling status; these, when introduced to an uncomprehending social circle, are found to be inadequate ... This is not what Corkery meant, but it is acknowledgement of a kind.

Born Michael O'Donovan in Douglas Street on the south side of the city O'Connor has left his own witness in his short stories to the north side squares and hills where he was reared.

In his two-volume autobiography he explains the geography of his early life and makes it clear that this is also the geography of his imagination. The interconnections of street and story, of shop and school, convent and suburb and character are clear to those who read the early stories especially with some idea of the lie of this urban landscape.

The long flight of stone steps leading to St Patrick's Church, for example, is portrayed in 'The First Confession'; the railway station, the city stores, the squares and little gardens, the clubs and public houses, all are drawn and re-drawn in his fiction and live in them as if in Cork's collective memory. As his own life developed, as he travelled and discovered himself as a writer, and as what Sean O'Faolain called the radius of his experience expanded, the scenery changed: the little locations of the city or of West Cork gave way to broader thoroughfares and bigger ideas.

Too big for the censorious Ireland of his times: his novel *Dutch Interior* (1940) was banned, as well as two collections of short stories – *The Common Chord* (1947) and *Traveller's Samples* (1951). Also forbidden to the the Irish people was his translation of the explicit and sexually affirmative Gaelic poem *The Midnight Court* (1940) by Brian Merriman (?1745–1805). As a suc-cessful contributor to *The New Yorker* by 1944 O'Connor was growing closer to America and went there to teach in 1951.

But he had created a life for himself in Dublin by that time: he had been a librarian, a broadcaster and a writer, a director of the Abbey Theatre, a colleague of W.B. Yeats with whom, determined to oppose censorship by providing a rational and scholarly forum for writers, he founded the Irish Academy of Letters. His untidy personal life was what would be considered tumultuous in Ireland and led to some difficulties in his professional career; after the death of Yeats his measurement of friendship and functional loy-alty changed:

> With Yeats permanently gone, I began now to realise that mediocrity was in control, and against mediocrity there is no challenge or appeal ... I felt that as a result of the death of Yeats I was left alone with a group of men not one of whom I should trust ... I knew then, as I know now, that this kind of infighting and intrigue was something I could not carry on alone.

Their terms were those of the Nationalist-Catholic establishment – Christmas pantomimes in Gaelic guying the ancient sagas that Yeats

Cork from Shandon – Northside, 1981 by Brian Lalor

had restored, and enlivened with ... Gaelic versions of popular songs and vulgar farces. One by one they lost their great actors and replaced them with Irish speakers; one by one, as the members of the Board died or resigned, they replaced these with civil servants and lesser Party politicians.[31]

O'Connor is writing about why he left the Abbey Theatre – but in a sense he is writing about why he left Ireland.

Having abandoned formal education before he was fourteen, O'Connor had a passion for scholarship. His teaching career in American universities was renowned – so much so that Sylvia Plath is believed to have made her first attempt at suicide because she failed to get into one of his classes. While there he met and married Harriet Rich (who, after O'Connor's death, married their mutual friend Maurice Sheehy) and in 1960 he returned with her to live and work in Ireland.

Frank O'Connor's academic life was also the background to his works of literary analysis: *The Mirror in the Roadway* (1956) on the novel and *The Lonely Voice* (1962) on the short story. Perhaps it was in *The Backward Look* (1967) however that he most satisfied his craving for affiliation with the great themes and scholarship of Irish literature. This was his last book and it is written with a self-denying humour, as if there were no longer any need to be as reverent as he was inclined to be:

One effect of this oral tradition was particularly regrettable. The development of the memory at the expense of the intelligence paralyses the critical faculty, since the critical faculty depends as much on what it forgets as on what it remembers. The mass of information that was fed into the memory of an Irishman of the professional classes could produce nothing but a brainstorm.[32]

Again, O'Connor is addressing the absence of a critical apparatus (as opposed to scholarship) in the early Irish literary tradition, but the sentences scan as if ruefully applicable to O'Connor's contemporaries.

In pursuit of this Gaelic world and – perhaps this was the priority – its interpretation as faithful to the social, emotional, political and spiritual circumstances from which its literature developed and was handed on, O'Connor himself became a translator. He produced *Kings, Lords and Commons* in 1959 and in collaboration with David Green, professor of Irish at Trinity College Dublin, edited the anthology *A Golden Treasury of Irish Poetry 600–1200* (1959).

He was tilting against the decorum of the received translations, and his racy style punctured the veneration of people such as Daniel Corkery. He also enjoyed decoding the provenance of different sagas; based on a series of lectures delivered at Trinity, the book debunks accepted verdicts on both Irish and Anglo-Irish writing but is faithful to the rights of practitioners up to, literally, O'Connor's own end: '... it becomes my own story ...'.

In this work Edgeworth, Yeats and Synge lead to Seán O'Casey, Liam O'Flaherty, Sean O'Faolain, Patrick Kavanagh, Austin Clarke, Mary Lavin and Thomas Kinsella. It is a fascinating, funny, provocative and profound book which even O'Connor might now admit to be out of date in its denunciations, but only just.

By the time O'Connor left for America the man he called a prince of scholars was dead. Osborn Bergin was born in Cork in 1873 and educated there at Queen's College, also becoming a member of the Gaelic League. This organisation was developing rapidly as a country-wide Irish language revival movement; its use of social gatherings, concerts and dances made it an invaluable meeting-place for the young people of the towns and cities, among whom it fostered an interest in the countryside as the source of their native culture.

Although its original determination was to remain politically inactive, the League's various campaigns for cultural resurgence and independence led to predictable allegiances and it was an important influence on the policies of the Ireland which emerged after 1922.

Bergin, however, was essentially a scholar and went to study in Germany with Kuno Meyer, an experience which coloured the lectures delivered in Dublin in 1912 on Irish bardic poetry. Appointed a professor at the School of Irish Learning, Dublin, in 1907 and at University College Dublin two years later he was briefly the director of the School of Celtic Studies in 1940.

With R.I. Best he produced what is still accepted as the authoritative edition of *The Book of the Dun Cow*, a collection of Gaelic manuscripts some of which were written on vellum, or cow-hide.

Originating in the twelfth century the volume contains early versions of the Ulster cycle of legends and poems, including one described as written by the epic hero Fionn Mac Cumail. Bergin and Best together identified the different writers and sources for the book in an edition which has been distinguished as 'a landmark in Irish palaeographical studies'. [33]

Bergin, who died in 1950, befriended Frank O'Connor in Dublin, or was befriended by him. Gatherings which included George Russell, R.I. Best and Osborn Bergin met regularly to discuss the work of German scholars, the influence on such writers as Yeats of the rediscovery of Old Irish and the ensuing Gaelic studies, schools and academies. Or at least they all met when all were on mutual speaking terms. These were devout, testy and beleaguered men in a new Ireland which wasn't quite living up to their expectations. Their rivalries, while linguistic, were intense: Bergin, according to O'Connor, was a fiercely emotional and possessive man with a dislike of George Moore, a distrust of George Russell and a detestation of Yeats – all based on philological inaccuracies or discourtesies.

Devoted to accuracy in translation even at the expense of poetry Bergin insisted to O'Connor that the old Irish verses were in fact as untranslatable as an ode of Horace. He reverenced their authors as aristocrats and scholars, loving, according to O'Connor, their neatness, order and the feeling these produced of an Oxford common-room.

That strongly donnish note existed in Irish poetry from the beginning, but in these poems it is at its strongest because the world they knew was collapsing in ruin about its authors. I think Bergin liked to remember that even in the days when earth was falling, 'the day when earth's foundations fled', these Irish professional poets continued to count their syllables, and admitted no word, no grammatical form, which their masters of two hundred years before would not have approved. Like other artists, he identified himself with his subject, for he was one of the last of a great generation of scholars in a country where scholarship was no longer regarded.[34]

There is a remarkable persistence in the habit by which rows begun in Cork were transported to Dublin where they flourished. Not even rows: disagreements, doubts, resentments carried forward like a balance in a ledger and put to uneasy use. As in the case of Edward Dowden (1843–1913), Cork-born son of a linen-draper and librarian, professor of English literature at Trinity College Dublin, close friend of John B. Yeats and mentor of his son William Butler Yeats.

A Victorian classicist in a city and a university in which loyalism and literature were practically consanguineous, Dowden was described by W.B. Yeats in his autobiography of 1915 as a gracious example of the ungracious realities of Victorian ideals as expressed in Dublin life. Yet Dowden himself was aware of Dublin's deficiencies; his ambition to become a poet faltered under the weight of an early marriage to a woman ten years older than himself and (although his poems were published in 1876 and again in 1914) he settled instead for the academic life.

His *Shakespere: His mind and Art* appeared in 1875; his awareness of and engagement in the philosophical and scientific debates of the Victorian world are revealed in *Studies in Literature: 1789–1877* (1878) which, as Terence Brown has commented, '... amount to a cultural history of nineteenth century thought ...'[35]

Corresponding with Walt Whitman, promoting Ibsen, biographer of Shelley, Southey, Browning and Montaigne and a friend of Samuel Ferguson,

Dowden nevertheless distrusted the fervour of the literary revival led by W.B. Yeats. Dismissive of the fashion, he ignored the achievements. Thus the first professor of English literature in Ireland, teaching for forty-six years in Trinity College, misread the single most important literary movement he was ever to witness in his own country.

Dowden lived in Dublin the life of the English scholar and critic. Other Cork writers avoided Dublin altogether and made London their capital city of ideas, of letters, of professional life and of the companionship of genius.

Men such as Francis Sylvester Mahony (1804–66):

> Born in Ireland, I know not if O'Mahoni is descended from the Count of that name, but to the spirit, the prejudices, to the system of the Count, he adds the fanaticism, the dissimulation, the intrigue, and the chicane of a thorough Jesuit! ... Irish and Scotch Catholics have about them a smack of the Spanish Catholics; they love to sniff the reek wafted from the funeral pyre of the doomed wretches who have declined to hear mass. The Society designs to place O'Mahoni, later on, at the head either of colleges or congregations ...

The society invoked by the Abbé Martial Marest de la Roche-Arnaud (in 'Les Jesuits Moderns') was the Society of Jesus, by whose Order the young Francis Sylvester Mahony hoped to be accepted, having been educated by them in Ireland, at Amiens, and for two years at the Jesuit seminary in Paris. Born into a Cork woollen-milling family, the boy known at home as Sylvester became a brilliant classical scholar with an easy fluency in Italian and French and a profound devotion to Latin. Despite his learning and intellectual vitality however Mahony's personality – the young man had a passionate temper and a gift for acid mimicry – was recognised by his religious superiors as unsuitable for the Society of Jesus. Mahony himself refused to accept that decision and returned to the Jesuit school at Clongowes Wood in Ireland to take up a teaching post.

Unfortunately for his hopes, while appointed master of rhetoric, the young aspirant was also responsible for taking students on country walks. On one such long outing, or 'course', Mahony saw to it that the boys were treated to whiskey punch at the several meals which punctuated the event. While still five miles from the college the master of rhetoric precipitated a major row with his hosts (to his last breath he hated Daniel O'Connell, then the hugely popular apostle of Catholic Emancipation) and led his drunken scholars through the dark and saturated winter roads – with the help of some late-working turf-cutters – to arrive at Clongowes some time after midnight.

This was not the way to convince the Jesuits of a genuine vocation. Released by the order Mahony went instead to the Irish College in Rome after which, in a sequence which remains mysterious, he was ordained a priest for the Cork diocese. The city, on his return, was in the grip of a cholera epidemic; Mahony distinguished himself as a selfless pastor and friend to the afflicted.

Here was something bigger than himself and his opinion of himself; the uncertainties of his temper – 'irascible' is a word which recurs in various descriptions – were allayed for a while, only to irritate him to action again when the civic crisis was over. His next project was to build a chapel of ease to the North Cathedral (St Patrick's Church was the eventual outcome) despite the reluctance of his bishop; it was made clear that he had better find another ministry, and he left Cork for London and a whole new career.

'At what point,' writes Ethel Mannin,

> and by what mental and emotional processes, Francis Mahony came to the conclusion that the Jesuit fathers had been right and he had no real vocation for the priesthood cannot be assessed with any degree of certainty, but two years after the ordination he had so intensely craved and so stubbornly worked for, in spite of all Jesuit counsels ... we find him in London entering upon a journalistic career and no longer functioning as a priest.[36]

Biographers differ: some say his problems with the priesthood lay in his gift for sarcasm and his quick temper, others blame his conviviality. Yet he never abandoned some aspects of the priesthood, saying his office faithfully each day until his death, and he never denied his faith. In fact his contemporary Blanchard Jerrold described him (in his introduction the *Final Reliques of Fr Prout* 1876) as 'a half-pay soldier of the church – minus the half-pay ...'

Fraser's Magazine of Town and Country was founded by Hugh Fraser in 1830 as a Tory journal to rival the dominant *Blackwood's*, the *Quarterly* and the *Edinburgh Review*. When Mahony began to write for it the editor was William Maginn of Cork; on one occasion a gathering of its twenty-seven regular contributors was sketched by Daniel Maclise, also of Cork, a drawing which was to be published with the collection of Mahony's writing for *Fraser's* – *The Reliques of Fr Prout* (1859). The group included Thackeray, Crofton Croker, Coleridge, Southey, Carlyle, Hogg (the Ettrick Shepherd) and other names famous in London's literary society.

It was for *Fraser's* that the character of Fr Prout was invented; Mahony did nothing by halves, and gave Prout the interesting parentage of Dean Swift and Stella, as well a inventing an editor named Oliver Yorke. This intricate joke – begun with the announcement of Fr Prout's death and a description of his obsequies – later gave way to the elaborately detailed hoax on the theme of Moore's melodies and the plagiarism (from the Greek, Latin and ancient French) which Prout alleges was committed by Moore.

Mahony himself of course was composing what Prout describes as the originals: a song attributed to the Comtesse de Chateaubriand, mistress of Francis I, begins 'Va où la gloire t-invite' whose lines are compared with Moore's 'Go where glory waits thee'. And so on – although there was more than intellectual rivalry behind Mahony's savage attack on Daniel O'Connell (whom he called 'the bog-trotter of Derrynane') in his poem 'The Lay of Lazarus' (1845). Written as the first portents of the Great Famine were being recognised, this purported to come from the pen of Mahony's later invention Don Jeremy Savanarola:

> Hark, hark to the begging-box shaking!
> For whom is this alms-money making?
> For Dan, who is cramming his wallet, while famine,
> Sets the heart of the peasant a-quaking.

Set against this contempt for the great popular hero the verses (put to music by Dubliner Morgan D'Arcy) by which Mahony is now remembered chime with nostalgia and wistfulness.

> But thy sounds were sweeter than the dome of Peter,
> Flings o'er the Tiber, pealing solemnly,
> Oh! The bells of Shandon,
> Sound far more grand on
> The pleasant waters of the river Lee.

Mahony's sister Mary entered the North Presentation Convent in Cork in 1832, but apart from such family connections he seems to have preferred to avoid his native city. It's hard to blame him, considering the company he was keeping in London: Robert Browning wrote of meeting him in Regent Street, he was in regular attendance at the brilliant salon of Lady Blessington, he took Fr Prout away from Maginn and over to the *Bentley Miscellany* edited by Charles Dickens in 1837, and within a year of that had begun to travel around Europe, sending poems back to Dickens for publication.

He also engaged in a vicious battle with some of his former friends and colleagues in London, and later involved himself – also from abroad – in the dispute surrounding the appointment of the Catholic Bishop Delaney of Cork; Mahony's favourite for the post was his friend Theobald Mathew, the 'Apostle of Temperance', a tireless worker for the victims of the Great Famine. Sending dispatches as a journalist from Rome to London, and creating the persona of Don Jeremy, Mahony never outgrew his early prejudices:

the expected arrival of Daniel O'Connell in the Holy City was announced with scorn:

> He will find here, in a state of bodily and mental debility equal to his own, at an advanced age, the only living daughter of Curran, the sister of her of whom it is written, in pages that will never die, 'She is far from the land where her young hero sleeps' ... [and] the newly repaired and refreshened epitaph of two Irish chieftains who did not confine their aspirations against the Saxon to mere talk ...[37]

This paragraph is a model of economic reference: Curran was John Philpot Curran, the famous barrister; his only living daughter was Amelia[38], who had made her home in Rome where she was to die; her sister was Sarah, the heroine of the song written by Thomas Moore, Mahony's earlier satirical victim and close friend of John Philpot Curran. 'Mere talk' was a jibe against O'Connell. Neither time nor distance had diluted Mahony's animosities.

> I shall always be grateful to Fr Prout, always ... A very singular person, of whom the world tells a thousand and one tales, you know, but of whom I shall speak as I find him, because the utmost kindness and warmheartedness have characterised his whole bearing towards us ... Not refined in a social sense by any manner of means, yet a most accomplished scholar and vibrating all over with learned associations and vivid combinations of fancy and experience – having seen all the ends of the earth and the men thereof ...[39]

Elizabeth Barrett Browning's enthusiasm may have waned somewhat under the almost daily visitations from Mahony to her home in Florence, but later Browning himself was to describe him as 'the man whom I knew so little and liked so much.' Back in London Mahony re-entered the literary life of his remaining friends, but again a Cork connection roused him to viciously enthusiastic anger.

This was the notice that Dr Edward Vaughan Kenealy (1819–80) was to stand as the Repeal candidate for Dublin University. The news prompted Mahony to wonder if 'Repeal' had become such a common urinal that any blackguard could make it a convenience? He was writing, in 1847, to Charles Gavan Duffy of *The Nation*, a letter which was not for publication but which, in the light of events of which Mahony could have had no foreknowledge, proved an accurate indicator of the later career of the Cork-born barrister, politician, poet, translator and journalist.

Kenealy had begun his journalistic career in London in 1841 under Mahony's patronage and in the pages of *Fraser's Magazine*, but fouled his

relationship with Mahony on the publication of 'Brallaghan' (1845), an inju-
rious skit on the Fraserians, including Crofton Croker and Mahony himself
and copying many of Mahony's attacks, as Fr Prout, on Thomas Moore. It
was a mistake – Mahony's Cork memories were vivid:

'You must surely be aware', Mahony wrote to Duffy,

> that this youth who talks of supporting the established church 'in its
> integrity' is himself the son of a R.C. whiskey shopkeeper who was clerk
> to the late attorney Daltera of Cork whose peasant litigants used to be
> dosed by the clerk with sufficient alcohol to keep up the belligerent
> steam, this youth ministering at the counter ...[40]

Mahony had more immediate London offences to relate: having figured
in a 'pox' case in Cork in which he was sued by his surgeon, Kenealy was
sued in London for legal fees and only avoided expulsion from Gray's 'by
getting Serjeant Murphy to write a whining letter *ad misericordiam*; the serjeant doing so because there is a contingent vote for Cork in the Whiskey
Shop.' Although Mahony's letter was private, Kenealy's candidature was
poorly supported and was withdrawn; elected MP for Stoke-on-Trent in 1875
no one introduced him when he appeared to take his seat in the House of
Commons. Only a few years after Mahony's letter Kenealy was convicted of
such cruelty to his six-year-old illegitimate son that he was jailed for a
month. He was also notorious as the leading counsel for the Tichburne
Claimant (in 1873) during which his violent approach led to calls for dis-
barring; he was in fact disbarred for publishing libels in his newspaper *The
Englishman*.[41]

After this joust Mahony went to Paris as correspondent for *The Globe*, living near the Palais Royal and close to Thackeray, with whom his friendship
had endured (it was Mahony who had found a house in Paris for Thackeray
and his Irish wife Isabella Creagh Shawe when they first married). In these
last years of his life Mahony, usually seen at Galignani's bookshop, became,
in Ethel Mannin's phrase, 'a living part of the city he loved.'

By the time of Thackery's death in 1863 Mahony had the consolation of
his resumed association with his religious profession, but he was also suffering from diabetes and becoming more and more reclusive. An unidentified
American woman who met him in Galignani's became his last comforter,
supplying him with sympathy, writing his letters for *The Globe*, and providing invalid foods until the arrival of his sister Ellen Woodlock from Cork.
Ellen was with him when, having received the last sacraments from his
friend Abbé Rogerson he died in his room on the entresol of the old hotel on
the Rue des Moulins in May 1866. The obituary written in the *Pall Mall
Gazette* was by Robert Browning, who saw him in Paris 'redacting the news

into a letter, easy, pithy, sensible, with a dash of mockery and scholarship about it ...'

Mahony was no common man, wrote Robert Browning: 'He was a Jesuit and a humourist; a priest and a Bohemian; a scholar and a journalist; a wag and a song-writer; a Cork man familiar to everybody in Rome; a Roman Catholic ecclesiastic well known in the convivial clubs of London.'

Browning's opinion has been cobwebbed by time. Instead it is Ethel Mannin's words which now apply: 'When the pyrotechnics of "Fr Prout" were forgotten Francis Mahony would be remembered by one unimportant sentimental song, 'The Bells of Shandon', his one gift to his own country, his one tribute.'

His body was brought back to Cork and his requiem mass was said in St Patrick's Church, the very building of which was the rock on which his religious career was shipwrecked. And his funeral cortège was led by Bishop Delany, whose appointment he had contested on behalf of Fr Theobald Mathew. He was buried in the family vault in Shandon churchyard, a grave which now serves as a goalpost for local children. [42]

'A rattling Irishman, full of quizzicality and drollery, without ill-nature ...' was how historian and biographer Thomas Carlyle described William Maginn (1793–1842); Thackeray recalled that 'Maginn read Homer to me, and he made me admire it as I had never done before ...' [43]

William Maginn was born the son of a schoolmaster in Cork city and having graduated from Trinity College Dublin at the age of fourteen returned to teach at his father's school. As a contributor to *Blackwood's Magazine* he encouraged the publication of the poems of J.J. Callanan, and on his move to London in 1832 was influential in the foundation and editorial management of *Fraser's Magazine*. So much so in fact that he fought a duel in defence of its founder Hugh Fraser, who had published Maginn's damning review of a novel by Grantley Berkeley. One of his most popular contributions to *Fraser's* was his 'Gallery of Literary Characters', and his prolific and ebullient pen allied to his reputation for 'genial dissipation' earned status and friendship, although he is perhaps accurately represented as Captain Shandon in Thackeray's *Pendennis*. Poet and parodist, he was also capable of fine literary scholarship, but drink, debts (he was imprisoned for three months in 1837) and poor health eventually crippled his career.

His life was also darkened by the marriage, and shocking death, of Letitia Elizabeth Landon (1802–38), the poet and novelist who supported herself by writing. She was engaged for a time to John Forster, the friend and biographer of Dickens and literary executor not only of Dickens but also of Thomas Carlyle and Walter Savage Landor. L.E.L., as she was known in the literary journals, was a contributor to *Fraser's Magazine*, a connection from which grew an attachment to Maginn. Even at this distance it seems typical of Mag-

Seandun (Shandon) by Daniel Corkery

inn that L.E.L.'s letters to him were left where they could be found by Mrs Maginn (a Miss Cullen from Cork whom he married in 1823) who brought them to John Foster. In 1838 Letitia married George Maclean, with whom she travelled to an isolated military outpost in West Africa, and died there two months later. The cause of death was reported at the time as an overdose of prussic acid and this, combined with the immediate burial dictated by the climate, with the unreachable (and questionably inconsolable) widower and with the scarcity of reliable facts about her sudden marriage and almost equally sudden death encouraged suspicions of suicide or murder.

Certainly the tragedy was believed to have brought about a profound change in Maginn, who went to live in Walton-on-Thames in order to write a novel. In poverty and again threatened by debt-collectors, he died while trying to finish *John Manesty, the Liverpool Merchant* (1844). It was published posthumously, having been completed by Charles Ollier.

Daniel Maclise (1806–70) was a central figure in the literary circle which grew around *Fraser's Magazine*, without being a writer at all. Born in Cork, the son of a Scots shoemaker, Maclise attracted the attention of Sir Walter Scott by drawing a quick sketch of the writer on Scott's visit to the city. Encouraged to move to London for tuition Maclise prospered there, eventually being offered, and refusing, both a knighthood and the presidency of the Royal Academy.

He was chosen as an illustrator not only by Irish writers such as Maginn, Mahony, Thomas Moore (for his *Irish Melodies* 1845) and Thomas Crofton Croker, but by Tennyson (for the Moxon edition of his poems in 1857 and *The Princess* in 1860), by Bulwer Lytton for *Pilgrims of the Rhine* (1838), by John Barrow for *A Tour Around Ireland* (1838), and by Mrs S.C. Hall for *Sketches of Irish Character* (1854), among many others. Still regarded as the best painter of Irish subject matter he also worked on Shakespearean and epic themes, one of his best-known paintings being the dramatic 'Marriage of Strongbow and Aoife' (1854); a series of his historical paintings was commissioned for the English Houses of Parliament.

The Cork antiquarian John Windele (1801–65) was known to Maginn and Maclise as a friend of Thomas Crofton Croker and poet J.J. Callanan. Modestly successful as a local historian, Windele is best known now for his *Historical and Descriptive Notes of the City of Cork* (1839), although he enriched posterity both by his efficiency as literary executor of Callanan – his memoir of the poet is held with his own manuscript collection at the Royal Irish Academy – and by his presentation to University College Cork of his assembled ogham stones.

Born the son of an army officer in Cork's Buckingham Square and educated locally, Thomas Crofton Croker (1798–1854) was another significant member of the London group formed around Fraser and Maginn. Again, the figure of Thomas Moore lurks amiably in the background of Croker's career in London, to which he was invited by the poet in 1818. A job in the admiralty gave him enough leisure for the indulgence of his antiquarian interests and from these developed his knowledge of Irish folk and fairy-tales. His collection and retelling of these stories provided a new strand of literary awareness; *Researches in the South of Ireland* was published in 1824 and was quickly followed by *Fairy Legends and Traditions in the South of Ireland* (1825–8). His wife was Marianne Nicholson whose distinctive drawings illustrated these volumes and who allowed some of her own work to be attributed to Croker; further publications of folk songs appeared from 1839 to 1847.[44]

Croker's popularity at the time (one publication was dedicated to Sir Walter Scott, another to Wilhelm Grimm) disguised the degree to which he had used much of the local material as fiction, as well as cloaking the problems of interpretation and provenance caused by his own defective knowledge of the Irish language.

Other writers seized on Croker's researches. However flawed, they were alluring material for Irish novelists and playwrights – among them Gerald Griffin, author of *The Collegians* (1829).

> They galloped in that direction. The morning was changing fast, and the rain was now descending in much greater abundance. Still there was not a breath of wind to alter its direction, or to give the slightest animation to the general lethargic look of nature. As they arrived on the brow of the hill, they perceived the crowd of horsemen and peasants collected into a dense mass, around one of the little channels, before described. ... The whipper-in, meanwhile, was flogging the hounds away from the crowd, while the dogs reluctantly obeyed. Mingled with the press were the horsemen, bending over the saddle-bows and gazing downward on the centre.
>
> 'Bad manners to ye!' Hardress heard the whipper-in exclaim, as he passed, 'what a fox ye found us, this morning. How bad ye are, now, for a taste o' Christian's flesh!'

Hardress Cregan discovers, in the small space kept clear in the centre of the crowd, that the prey is a corpse:

> It was for the most part concealed beneath a large blue mantle, which was drenched in wet and mire, and lay so heavy on the thing beneath, as to reveal the lineaments of a human form. A pair of small feet, in Spanish-leather shoes, appearing from below the end of the garment, showed that the body was that of a female; and a mass of long fair hair,

which escaped from beneath the capacious hood, demonstrated that this death, whether the effect of accident of malice, had found the victim untimely in her youth. [45]

From this scene of the hunter and the prey develops the marvellous psychological study which is the core of Griffin's novel. Yet this book is so closely allied in the popular imagination with its companion pieces – *The Colleen Bawn* under which title it was adapted for the stage by Dion Boucicault, or the opera *The Lily of Killarney* – that Griffin's claim to it is often obscured.

More significant is the belief expressed by John Cronin (*Studies*, Autumn, 1969) that Griffin was the first really talented Anglo-Irish writer to emerge from the Catholic middle-classes 'and his career, his temperament, his development and decline, when properly understood, constitute an important point of entry into an entire branch of the Anglo-Irish literary experience'.

Griffin (1803–40) was born in Limerick city and went to London before he was twenty years old, determined to earn his living as a dramatist and poet. His subsequent career brought him many friends – including his patron the novelist John Banim as well Fanny Brawne, the beloved of John Keats, and Fanny Llanos, the sister of Keats – but his success as a journalist was tempered by his initial extreme poverty, his religious scruples and by the continued failure to find a theatre willing to produce his play *Gisippus* (eventually produced to great acclaim by William Macready at Drury Lane in 1842).

Griffin's first notable publications were a collection of Irish stories in *Holland-Tide* (1827) and *Tales of the Munster Festivals* (1827); these were followed by *The Collegians* (1829), *The Rivals* and *Tracey's Ambition* – both also in 1829. His poem 'Eileen Aroon' was admired by Tennyson, but the gradual success of his creative work was not enough to counteract his growing lack of literary conviction, possibly complicated by a friendship, – platonic but troubling – with Mrs Lydia Fisher.

He resolved this complex dilemma by entering the order of the Christian Brothers in Dublin in 1838, first making a bonfire of all his manuscripts, including unpublished material. He was transferred to the North Monastery in Cork in 1839 where he worked, apparently happily, as a teacher. He had begun a novel called *The Holy Island* when he died of typhus in June, 1840; he is buried in the monastery graveyard in a tomb virtually unknown to Cork.

John Cronin draws a tentative comparison between Gerald Griffin and James Joyce – both sons of unsuccessful businessmen of the Catholic middle class, both educated in Catholic schools, both with intense literary ambition:

Griffin failed to survive as artist, Joyce as Catholic ... There is even a special kind of irony in the fact that Griffin sought eventual refuge from the world with the Christian Brothers, the teaching order whose simple pieties the Clongownian soul of Stephen Dedalus both recognised and shrank from ...

The immensity and intensity of Joycean studies preclude any need to be too observant in these pages of the ways in which the life and works are linked to Cork. The evocations are real enough in *A Portrait of the Artist as a Young Man* (1916): 'Mr Dedalus had ordered drisheens for breakfast and during the meal he crossexamined the waiter for local news', and the Cork origins of Joyce's father, John Stanislaus Joyce of Sunday's Well, are thoroughly excavated. Even the original for 'Dante' in *A Portrait* has been comprehensively annotated; she was Mrs Elizabeth Hearn Conway of Youghal who had intended to be a Bride of Christ but who, unexpectedly inheriting a fortune, made a disastrous marriage and suffered for it ever after – to the significant enrichment of Irish literature.[46]

The visit of the young James Joyce to Cork with his father, who was selling off the remaining family properties in the city, included a walk around Queen's College. Now University College Cork, and vastly expanded from the days recalled by Stephen Dedalus, the institution has yielded a worthy harvest of writers: scholars, historians, classicists, anatomists, scientists, lawyers, all listing publication after publication and keeping pace with the poets, dramatists and novelists of the past eighty years.

Among UCC's graduates early in this century was solicitor John J. Horgan (1881–1967). He became one of Cork's and Ireland's most eminent solicitors, internationally famous for a while as the county coroner who brought in a verdict of murder against the German emperor and government for the sinking of the *Lusitania*; an inquest was held in Cork where many of the victims were brought ashore for burial (the mass grave is in Cobh).

Horgan's father Michael Joseph Horgan was also a solicitor and acted as election agent for Charles Stewart Parnell in Cork (Parnell acted as best man at Michael Horgan's wedding). Lawyer, author, scholar and businessman, Horgan was a towering figure in Cork life until his death at the age of eighty-six. Responsible for the registration of the Irish trademark in 1906 and a member of the Gaelic League, Horgan was honorary consul for Belgium and was knighted with the Order of St Leopold in 1956.

Instrumental in the management and success of the port of Cork through his role as a harbour commissioner from 1912 to 1966 (he was chairman of the board for one unbroken stretch of twelve years) he drafted a new system of municipal government for Cork city in 1926; this was later used as the basis of the system of local government introduced for the new state and was adopted also in Northern Ireland in 1942.

Despite his busy practice and his interest in civic and commercial affairs Horgan was also a trenchant journalist: his work appeared in such publications as *Studies*, *The Atlantic Monthly*, the *Hungarian Quarterly*, the *National Municipal Review of New York*. For thirty years he contributed to *The Round Table*; among his books and pamphlets the most important are his *Complete Grammar of Anarchy* (compiled from provocative Unionist speeches of 1916 to 1922, when Horgan himself was a member of Lloyd George's Irish Convention) and the memoir *From Parnell to Pearse* (1948). He also wrote on aspects of Shakespeare, on educational and labour issues and on the Irish language, which he spoke competently.

Horgan's first wife was Mary Windle, daughter of the first president of the newly designated University College Cork. Originally Queen's College was part of the federal organisation of the Queen's University in Ireland (incorporated 1850); this was replaced by the Royal University of Ireland (1882) which in turn gave way to the National University of Ireland (1908). Initially, presidents of the college lived on campus but by the time of the arrival at UCC of one of Ireland's finest writers for children, Eilís Dillon (1920–94), the domestic presidential presence was reduced. Instead the warden of the Honan Hostel was the main observer of student life in the raw (so to speak), and in 1949 this appointment was taken by the professor of Irish (history of modern Irish literature), Cormac Ó Chuilleanáin, who was married to Eilís Dillon.

Dillon came from an academic background, her father graduating in medicine from Cork, and her Cork-born great-grandfather, William Kirby Sullivan, having been professor of chemistry at the college as well as its president from 1873 to 1890. He had also been a reputable Irish scholar, contributing essays on Irish subjects to the 1870 edition of the *Encyclopaedia Britannica*. He wrote a long preface to Eugene O'Curry's *Manners and Customs of the Ancient Irish* (1873), assembled by Sullivan from O'Curry's papers after his sudden death.

Born in Galway and a fluent speaker of Irish, Eilís Dillon is responsible for what is still regarded as the most authoritative translation of the poem 'Caoineadh Airt Ui Laoghaire'. Her immensely popular children's novels include *The Singing Cave* (1969) and *The Island of Ghosts*; while there are many titles under this classification she also produced adult historical novels such as *Across the Bitter Sea* (1973) and *The Head of the Family* (1960). A little less well known perhaps was her unfortunately brief dalliance with detective fiction, as in *Death at Crane's Court* (1953) and *Sent to his Account* (1954).

Fifty people had to be fed three times a day with food to their complete satisfaction ... I devised eight menus, so that there was always an element of surprise – not even the mathematicians worked out why they were never able to guess what would appear on the table ... I applied the same principle to my own house, where I had to think of a housekeeper and a children's nurse and three children, including a baby who was born after we went to live in the Warden's House. When all this was in order, after a tour of inspection of the hostel, by half-past ten in the morning I was sitting at my desk beginning my other life as a professional writer ... I had exactly two and a half hours for this, because at a quarter past one my husband and I went into the students' dining-room and sat at a separate table for lunch, with the College chaplain.

These were the circumstances (described in the essay 'In the Honan Hostel' for *The Cork Anthology* (1993)) in which, in Cork, Eilís Dillon pursued her life as a writer. She was also a cellist and played in the Cork Symphony Orchestra, and a linguist who founded, with her husband and colleagues in the Italian department, the Cork branch of the Dante Alighieri Society. Their life in Cork was also enriched by the company of people such as the Professor of Music Aloys Fleischmann and the sculptor Séamus Murphy and his wife Maighréad, whose house off the Wellington Road became a refuge for the Ó Cuilleanáins. After the death of Cormac Ó Cuilleanáin, Eilís Dillon married Vivian Mercier. [47]

Another important writer of children's books was Patricia Lynch (1898–1972) who was born at Fair Hill on the north side of the city in 1898 and sent to England when her father died abroad. Her mother's restless search for his legacy which would ensure the security of her family are described in *A Storyteller's Childhood* (1947) but with such whimsy as to be both confusing and coy. However, when retold in her writing for children these childhood experiences brought her a well-deserved international status; among her more than fifty titles are *The Grey Goose of Kilnevin* and *The Turf-Cutter's Donkey* (1935). Working as a journalist and an active suffragette she was commissioned by Sylvia Pankhurst to write about the Easter Rising of 1916 in Dublin; first published in *The Workers' Dreadnought*, her observations were collated as *Rebel Ireland* and distributed widely. She married the writer R.M. Fox in 1922 and settled in Dublin from where she built her career as an author.

William Buckley (1859–1937) was an art and literary critic and literary editor of the *Irish Times*; his book *Croppies Lie Down* was published in 1903.

Moving through the city from one location to another, with the college as its cultural centrepoint, it is possible to divide most of Cork's literary history into geographical catchments. But there are those whose earliest addresses are unknown and for whom what is still called the flat of the city provides the most convenient context. Personalities such as the composer Sir

Arnold Bax (1883–1953), who is buried in St Finbarr's Cemetery. Born in London and knighted as Master of the King's Musick, Bax came to Ireland in 1905 and visited continually thereafter, making frequent visits to Cork where he stayed with his friend Aloys Fleischmann. He acted as extern examiner for the music department at UCC to which he bequeathed his piano. As Dermot O'Brien he also wrote poetry, collected as *Seafoam and Firelight* (1909), and an autobiography – *Farewell my Youth* (1943).[48]

Sigerson Clifford (1913–85) was born at Dean Street, next to the Cathedral of St Fin Barre but was reared in Kerry, his parents' native county. Later moving to work in the civil service in Dublin he married Mary Eady from Cork in 1945. His play *The Great Pacificator* was produced at the Abbey Theatre in 1947 – in all he wrote nearly a dozen plays – but he is now best remembered as a writer of ballads (*Ballads of a Bogman* appeared in 1955) and especially for 'The Boys of Barr na Sráide' which is still sung and recited all over Munster.

The novelist and playwright Vivian Connell (1905–81) was born in Cork and produced short stories as well as the hugely successful novel *The Chinese Room* (1943). Other novels included *The Hounds of Cloneen* (1951) set rather irreverently among the fox-hunting society of Cobh in Co. Cork, and among his plays were *Throng o' Scarlet* (1941) and *The Nineteenth Hole of Europe* (1943).

It was Cork-born novelist, journalist, anthologist and politician Justin McCarthy (1830–1912) who, elected MP for Longford in 1879, led the anti-Parnell faction out of the famous Committee Room 15 although he remained on friendly terms with Parnell himself. He was vice-chairman of the Irish Parliamentary Party to 1896, and retired from politics four years later. Three of his very many novels were written in collaboration with Mrs Campbell Praed, including *The Right Honourable* (1886); titles of his own included *Dear Lady Disdain* (1875) and *A Fair Saxon* (1873). Formerly editor of *The Morning Star* and leader writer for *The Daily News*, McCarthy also wrote a five-volume *History of Our Own Times* (1879) and edited the ten-volume anthology *Irish Literature* with Maurice Egan Maguire (1904). His son Justin Huntly McCarthy (1860–1939) was born in London and also combined a parliamentary career with that of novelist.

Rearden (Patrick) Conner (1907–91) was educated at Presentation Brothers College in Cork before leaving for London where he worked first as a landscape gardener and then made his way into broadcasting. His novel *Shake Hands with the Devil* (1933) was a great success and was later filmed in Ireland – the first international film production in the country. *Men Must Live* (1937), *The Sword of Love* (1938) and *The Singing Stone* (1951) all examine themes of Irish life through lively if disenchanted prose; *A Plain Tale from the Bogs* (1937) is an early autobiography. Barbara FitzGerald (1911–82) was born to a Cork clerical family: her father Dr J.A.F. Gregg was bishop of Ossory for five years, archbishop of Dublin from 1920 to 1939 and then primate of the Church of Ireland from 1939 to 1959. Educated first in London and then at Trinity College Dublin she married Michael FitzGerald Somerville of Castle-townshend and with him spent much of her life abroad, mostly in West Africa. Her first novel was *We Are Besieged* (1946) but poor health affected her writing career and her second novel *Footprint Upon Water* was published posthumously in 1983.

John Paul Dalton (1865–1912) first curator of the Cork Municipal Museum had been manager of his father's antique and curio shop on the Grand Parade and attached to Egan's silversmiths in Patrick Street; he illustrated his poems with pen and pencil sketches which were widely published. Also associated with the Grand Parade was Frank Henry Graves (1887–1927), whose *Selected Poems* appeared in 1929.

Combining a career as businessman and popular poet, Denny Lane (1818–95) trained as an engineer and was eventually a railway proprietor, director of the Cork Gas Company and president of the Institute of Gas Engineers of Great Britain. His lyrics were often published in *The Nation*, but of these the one which has survived and is still sung is the plaintive 'Carrigdhoun'.

Both the city and county of Cork are no less usual than other towns and shires in the common transference of their streams to lyric imagery. In Cork the recurrence of tide, flood, river and lake in its literature is commonplace, and its fundamental identity as a harbour and port is another opportunity for metaphor. But not all who have recourse to imagery are creative writers; sometimes a voice can be heard as if from the littoral itself, from the shipyards which once bellowed from the shores near Tivoli on one side or Passage West on the other.

Among the significant families in the city during the nineteenth century were those of several Quaker merchants and businessmen; of these Ebenezer Pike of Blackrock founded the Cork Steamship Company and established a ship-building enterprise at the Brickfields Road near the river. This was close to the shipyard and engineering works of another Quaker, R.J. Lecky, at Penrose Quay. George Robinson and Co. ran the Waterside Dockyards, and downriver Wheeler's dockyard at Rushbrooke stood across the water from the yards at Passage.

There William Brown and Andrew and Michael Hennessy were among the most prosperous shipwrights during the first half of the nineteenth century, when West Indiamen, barques, brigs, schooners and square-riggers built for Cork merchants jostled in the harbour beside the flotillas of the Royal Navy. The navy yard was at Haulbowline island, near Cobh, but it was in Lecky's yard at Penrose Quay that the first iron-hulled vessel was built for

Cork in 1844. Ten years later the yards building iron ships were predominantly those of Robinson and Pike.

These yards and their histories are recorded by W.J. Barry in several works, but especially in his *History of the Port of Cork Steam Navigation* (1917) which is as readable as it is comprehensive, rich in anecdote and recall:

> What a flood of memories the mere mention of Mr Pike's name recalls. I was born within a few thousand yards of Water Street building yard and memory is active now and unbidden brings me back to my childhood's days, with a vivid picture of the building of the 'Ibis' – the hundreds of men coming out of the yard at the sound of the dinner bell – the laying down of the keel on the blocks – the gradual development of the structure of the ship until finally one day a brilliant scene meets my eye – 'tis the day of the launch, and the steamer is a very picture of beauty in her array of flags from stem to stern.
>
> A platform is erected round her bow, and standing on it is Mr. Pike and his invited guests. From her stem-head a christening bottle of champagne, suspended by a gay-coloured ribbon. And now all is ready – the dog-shore is knocked away, and as she moves almost imperceptibly at first, the bottle is broken on her bows by her sponsor, as she exclaims 'God speed the Ibis' and amidst the cheers of the vast assemblage who line both banks of the river, the 'Ibis' glides down the launch way like a thing of life to her native element.

The poet known as The Bard of the Lee was John FitzGerald (1825–1910), who was born in Hanover Street and educated at the North Monastery which he left at fifteen to be an apprentice to his brother, a cabinet-maker in London. Returning to Cork after twelve months he worked at O'Keefe's furniture factory for six years and then decided to concentrate on wood-carving.

His skills were widely recognised, as was his gift for water-colours and his ability as a historian and antiquarian. His poems were published with those of two Cork contemporaries, Thomas Condon and Daniel Casey, as *Gems of the Cork Poets* (1883); *Echoes of '98* (1898) was a centenary reminiscence of the leading figures of the Rebellion of 1798, but his name endures in Cork through the still-popular songs he left behind. 'Cork is the Eden for You Love and Me', 'The Swans of the Lee' and especially the lovely verses of 'The Green Hills of Cork':

> I have sought to discover a haven of rest,
> Where the sun sinks by night in the land of the West;
> I have dwelt with the red man in green forest bowers,

Or the wild-rolling prairie, bespangled with flowers;
I have hied to the north, where the hardy pine grows,
'Mid the wolf and the bear, and the bleak winter snows;
I have roam'd through all climates, but none could I see
Like the green hills of Cork and my home by the Lee.
Beautiful city, beautiful city,
Beautiful city, the pride of the Lee ...[49]

Michael John O'Sullivan (1794–1845) was a poet, playwright and journalist whose education began at the school in Cork run by William Maginn's father. He was for a while editor of *The Freeman's Journal* but his fame rests with his successful dramatisation of Thomas Moore's *Lallah Rookh*.

Another now almost forgotten name is that of George Savage-Armstrong (1845–1906), born in Dublin and appointed professor of English at Queen's College Cork in 1871; with his brother Edmund he produced collections of fashionable poetry.

Con O'Leary (1887–1958) was another graduate who made his name in London as a novelist and journalist and racing historian. His play *The Crossing* (1914) was produced at the Abbey Theatre in Dublin.

Katherine Mary Murphy (1840–85) was the daughter of a coal merchant who moved his family from Ballyhooley to the city centre at Pope's Quay. She wrote widely for British and American periodicals but was also published as 'Brigid' in *The Nation*. Martin Francis Mahony (1831–85) was a nephew of Francis Sylvester Mahony (Fr Prout) and wrote under the pseudonym of Mathew Stradling.

Something of Cork's heroic heritage affected Robert Brophy (b. 1865) who wrote as R.J. Ray and was one of that group of playwrights designated the Cork Realists by W.B. Yeats. His dramatic work concentrated on the prejudices, hypocrisies and savageries of Irish life to a degree which dismayed Yeats. Befriended by Lennox Robinson, *The Casting-Out of Martin Whelan* (1910) and *The Gombeen Man* (1913) were produced at the Abbey Theatre.

Another playwright was Robert Bell (1800–67) whose work in London included journalism, fiction and editing anthologies, as well as a life of George Canning (1846); his plays include *Marriage* (1842) and *Mothers and Daughters* (1843).

The contemporary writer Conal Creedon (1961–) works with two city theatre organisations as a playwright and also writes wildly comic radio scripts. Living in Coburg Street he has written a book of short stories – *Pancho and Lefty Ride Out* (1995) and a novel *Passion Play* (1999) – work which is redolent of typically Cork wit but which is strongly marked by Creedon's own literary identity.

The river Lee divides into two channels near the university buildings to the west of the city; the commercial centre is islanded, the residential areas now spread north and south of each channel. The southern marshes were drained and filled in to provide a mesh of suburbs and of these the small peninsulas to the east, bordering the estuary, rivalled the heights of the northern shore in the elegance of their locations. What Sunday's Well and Montenotte are to the north side, Blackrock, Douglas and Rochestown are to the south.

The main Blackrock Road is the home of Ashton Comprehensive School; this is the modern edition of the former merger of the Cork High School with the Cork Grammar School and Rochelle School. The appointment of Miss Harriet Martin as headmistress of the Cork High School led to the setting-up there of the league of Rose Queens, instituted among English schools by John Ruskin, whose later years were disturbed by his affection for Rose La Touch. Ruskin's letters to Miss Martin in Cork suggest that the Queen was selected from schoolgirls engaged in philanthropic work – a 'sewing bee' for clothing poor children is described. Crowned at his suggestion with dog rose, wild rose or Burnet rose, the Queen was rewarded with 'real girls' books' such as those written, says Ruskin, by Miss Edgeworth. In 1907 a letter from Ruskin is addressed to 'H.M. the Rose Queen, Miss Gladys Cunningham'. While a grammar school, Ashton was also the home of a drama group dedicated to the production of the plays of William Butler Yeats, established by the late Mrs Rachel Burrows, wife of the headmaster The Revd G.H.J. Burrows.

The peninsula of Blackrock and Mahon was the birthplace of James Cavanah Murphy (1760–1814), a brick-layer who went to Spain and became an architect and whose books, including *Arabian Antiquities of Spain* (1815) were immensely influential on the architectural fashions of the time (especially in the work of Richard Morrison); he is singled out by Thomas Crofton Croker as the only artist to whom Cork can justify a claim.

George Boole, the university's first professor of mathematics, lived near Ballintemple on the Blackrock Road; his youngest daughter Ethel Lilian Voynich (1864–1960) was born in Cork but was educated abroad, where she met and married a Polish count.

After some years in London they settled in New York, but in the meantime Ethel had had an affair with the so-called 'Ace of Spies' Sidney Reilly. This relationship influenced the plot of her book *The Gadfly* (1897), an enormously successful novel of the Italian revolutionary movement of 1848. Although two more novels were published to complete a three-part development they did not achieve much critical or popular attention, yet *The Gadfly* is still widely recognised as a remarkable historical romance.

Further along the suburban edge of the estuary opposite Blackrock is Glenbrook, birthplace of Seán O'Brien, the sculptor, painter, dramatist and novelist who emigrated to America but whose play *Duty* was a repeated success at the Abbey Theatre from 1916.

Jack (William John) White (1920–80) was born in Cork of English parents and worked for twenty years as a journalist with *The Irish Times*. He moved into television and by 1974 was controller of programmes at Radio Telefís Éireann. His three novels took the Dublin, and not the Cork, middle class as their context, and while he wrote several plays only one was published. This was *The Last Eleven*, based on his awareness of the decline of the Protestant community in Ireland; it won the Irish Life Drama Award in 1967 and was produced at the Abbey Theatre in 1968.

There was a time in Cork in which the community mourned by Jack White was vigourously influential; one of its scions was Sir Hugh Lane (1875–1915), born at Ballybrack in Douglas to a clergy family. His mother was a sister of Lady Augusta Gregory of the Abbey Theatre, but his own fame rests with his talent as an art dealer and collector.

His wish – eventually a mission – to found a gallery of modern art in Dublin became increasingly controversial, especially when his preferred site for such a gallery was to be a new bridge over the Liffey. Yeats, Lady Gregory and even the Abbey as an institution became embroiled in this campaign; Lane dangled the prospect of Degas, Pissarro, Renoir, Corot, Monet, Courbet and Manet, and several others, before their hungry eyes.

Not at all sure that modern art, especially French art, was what the citizens of Dublin needed, both Dublin corporation and the Royal Irish Academy had wavered (as had Belfast, where Lane's exhibitions included a painting in which a mother was portrayed, but without an obvious wedding-ring) to such an extent that Lane had altered his will. Perhaps he might have changed it back again – certainly a codicil indicated another change of mind – but he died with the sinking of the *Lusitania* in 1915 and left his pictures in a diplomatic limbo somwhere between Dublin and London. Fifty years or so later the matter was resolved by a tactful compromise, but what cannot be obliterated now are the verses provoked from Yeats by the controversy of the time.

The first of these was the poem with the rancorous title 'To A Wealthy Man Who Promised A Second Subscription to the Dublin Municipal Gallery If It Were Proved The People Wanted Pictures' (1912); this polemic was published in *The Irish Times* as Yeats' reaction to corporation shenanigans.

His sense of cultural betrayal, and his shame at the petty manoeuvres and mediocre attitudes of his fellow-citizens is given a historical gloss in the second poem, 'September 1913':

What need you, being come to sense,
But fumble in a greasy till

And add the halfpence to the pence
And prayer to shivering prayer, until
You have dried the marrow from the bone?
For men were born to pray and save:
Romantic Ireland's dead and gone,
It's with O'Leary in the grave ...

Was it for this the wild geese spread
The grey wing upon every tide;
For this that all that blood was shed,
For this Edward FitzGerald died,
And Robert Emmet and Wolfe Tone,
All that delirium of the brave?
Romantic Ireland's dead and gone,
It's with O'Leary in the grave ...[50]

Sir Hugh Lane is commemorated in the Church of Ireland in Douglas, a place which would have been well known to the playwright Lennox Robinson in his boyhood. Born near Douglas, Robinson (1886–1958) left the city when he was six years old, his father exchanging his life as a stockbroker for that of a clergyman. The family moved to Kinsale and then to Ballymoney near Bandon, from where Robinson began his life as writer and, through his dealings with Yeats and Lady Gregory, as manager of the Abbey Theatre.

Theatre-going was rare. Our last train from Cork left so early in the afternoon that a matinee could not be seen to its conclusion ... But occasionally, when something very special was billed, a late train would be run to Bandon and Clonakilty and there was a junction on that line only six miles from home. My sister and I would seize such opportunities, parking our bicycles at Gaggin Junction and riding home – it seems to me it was always raining and the road heavy with mud and sharp with stones and one or other bicycle punctured – and getting to Ballymoney after midnight. I was at the romantic age. Martin Harvey was my god and when some publisher – Fisher Unwin was it? – offered a big prize for a novel. I wrote one. It was all concerned with very high English life, the hero was a duke and I showed it to my father. My knowledge of the peerage consisted of an occasional glimpse of the Earl of Bandon entering or leaving the train at Bandon station. I must have written my duke in terms of Bandon for, having read my manuscript, my father pulled down some old copy of *Burke's Peerage* and showed me what the appendages of a real duke were. I burned my novel. I wrote a long play for Martin Harvey, the subject of which I have entirely forgotten nor was it ever sent to him.[51]

Robinson was to find his material, although not immediately:

We were very young and we shrank from nothing. We knew our Ibsen and the plays of the Lancashire school, we showed our people as robbers and murderers, guilty of arson, steeped in trickery and jobbery. Lady Gregory said of me years later that I 'waded in blood to write, at last, The Whiteheaded Boy'.[51]

The plays of Robinson's which have retained their popularity are those comedies of the Irish country towns and villages such as *The Whiteheaded Boy* (1916) and *Drama at Inish* (1933); his first play was the one-act *The Clancy Name* produced at the Abbey in 1908. Longer plays followed and in 1910, after the death of John Millington Synge, he was invited to become manager and director at the theatre. Dissensions – most notably about his refusal to close the Abbey as a mark of respect on the death of King Edward VII – led eventually to his decision to leave it in 1914, when he took a position with the Carnegie Library Trust. His play about Parnell, *The Lost Leader* (1918), reinstated his good name at the Abbey which he rejoined as manager and producer, being appointed to the board in 1923.

More plays followed but his life with the Abbey was not untroubled; big personalities had little room to offer one another in administrative or theatrical terms and those early years of new nationhood were rife with aspiration, disappointment and distrust.

Yet Robinson himself produced work which while light-hearted in theme or tone was structurally efficient – which is why it has lasted so well. He wrote the official history of the Abbey 1899–1951 (1951), edited *Lady Gregory's Journals* (1946) and also edited, with Donagh MacDonagh, *The Oxford Book of Irish Verse* (1958).

As a suburb Douglas is linked to the city centre first by the Douglas Road and then by the narrower alleys of Douglas Street. These are the among the precincts used by Patrick Galvin (1927–) who went first to school here at the South Presentation Convent. The many creative talents encapsulated in this single personality have made his career as colourful as the imaginary – although sometimes actual – wanderings of some of his characters. England and Israel were included in the travels of his early life, and from these he wrought poems collected in *Heart of Grace* (1957) and *Christ in London* (1960). While *The Madwoman of Cork* is one of his most locally recognised pieces, his collection *The Woodburners* (1973) emphasises the breadth of his poetic imagination.

His residency with the Lyric Theatre in Belfast on the Leverhulme Fellowship in 1973 expanded his reputation as a playwright; two plays (*And Him Stretched* and *Cry the Believers* had been produced in London in 1960 and

1961) and these were followed in Belfast by *Nightfall to Belfast* (1973), *We Do It for Love* (1976) and *The Last Burning* (1974); another play *The Devil's Own People* was produced in Dublin in 1976.

Galvin's collected poems were published in 1998; his work combines energy and intimacy with entertaining effect, and his lyricism is often subversive in tone. But he is not a comic or anarchic poet; his craftsmanship is always serious and his effects, whether light or sober, are deliberately and skillfully achieved, as in this extract from 'Plaisir d'Amour':

... My mother, who was younger by a year,
Looked young and fair.
The sailors from the port of Martinique
Had kissed her cheek.

He searched the house
And hidden in a trunk beneath the bed
My father found his second-hand guitar.
He found her see-through skirt
With matching vest.
'You wore French knickers once' he said
'I liked them best.'

'I gave them all away', my mother cried
'To sailors and to captains of the sea.
I'm not half-dead
I'm fit for any bed – including yours.'
She wore a sailor's cap
And danced around the room
While father strummed his second-hand guitar.
He made the bed
He wore his Kaftan dress
A ribbon in his hair.
'I'll play it one more time', he said
'And you can sing.'
She sang the only song they knew –
Plaisir d'Amour.

Winter

At sixty-four
My mother died
At sixty-five

My father.
Comment from a neighbour
Who was there:
'They'd pass for twenty.'
Plaisir d'Amour.[52]

Now spreading its campus across the city, UCC still offers a kind of literary bridge between the catalogues of north and south. Within its confines can be gathered, as if in a net, a shoal of writers representing different faculties: among this number are historians such as William O'Sullivan, (*c.* 1900–) author of *The Economic History of Cork City from the Earliest Times to the Act of Union* (1937) or, more recently, Joe Lee (1942–), professor of modern history at UCC and author of *Ireland 1912–1985: Politics, History and Society* (1989).

A colleague in the history department is Professor Dermot Keogh (1945–), whose titles include *Ireland and the Vatican* (1995), *Ireland and Europe 1919–1948* (1994) and *The Jews in Ireland* (1998).

Emeritus Professor of Irish History John A. Murphy (1927–) also held a senate seat for the National University of Ireland; well known as a scholarly contributor to leading academic journals and as a trenchant newspaper columnist, his major publications include *Ireland in the Twentieth Century* (1975) and the text-book series *Stair na hEorpa* (1958). He edited *De Valera and His Times* with J.P. O'Carroll (1983), and was also editor of *The French Are In the Bay* (1997). His book *The College* (1995) is a history of UCC, published to commemorate the one hundred and fiftieth anniversary of its foundation.

That history offers the reminder that Daniel Corkery's successor as professor of English at UCC was B.G. McCarthy (1904–93), a woman who may have shared Corkery's fervent nationalism but who – even by the very fact of being a professional woman in her own right – must have seemed antithetical to many of his fondest literary ideas.

Women's contribution to literature is no arbitrary or artificial distinction. However much the reformer may welcome, or the conservative lament, the growth of a harmonious sharing of ideals between men and women, that growth has been a hard-fought struggle. It has been an escape from a prison, which, when it did not entirely shut out the greater world, at least enclosed a little world of education meant for women, a literature adapted to the supposed limitations of their intellect, and a course of action prescribed by the other sex.[53]

Thus B.G. McCarthy begins her treatise on the early women writers of fiction. *The Female Pen* (1944/47 repr. 1994) is still a salutary essay on the whole business of writing – why and how it happens at all – but its burden is an assertive reclamation of vanished names, titles, lives and reputations, and an equally assertive assessment of those that have survived. She took as her starting point the questions about Shakespeare's sister raised by Virginia Woolf in *A Room of One's Own*, leading to 'a long journey backwards through the years – a journey which had for its object a consideration of those forces which affected women writers during the sixteenth, seventeenth and eighteenth centuries ...' 54

Defining McCarthy as a literary critic rather than a cultural historian, Janet Todd of the University of East Anglia applauds the originality of her approach, which advances a more daring notion than that of Virginia Woolf:

> that women are particularly associated with realism and verisimilitude ... Shakespeare's sister failed to write not only because she was maltreated by men but also because she did not much care for her brother's sort of plays ...
>
> [McCarthy] counters the absurdity displayed by men interpreting women by taking the male images and running with them towards the real women she knows. So she delightedly quotes Addison's consumerist description of the lady living to be ornamented by furs and feathers, ores and silks. Then she allows the image to self-destruct in its confrontation with the gifted Brontës, for whom not even a moulting parrot would cast a feather, with poor ugly Harriet Martineau at whose feet no self-respecting lynx would cast his skin ... 55

When Brigid McCarthy retired she gave away her library, leaving only a memory of 'an abrasive temper and an exhilarating style'; she had been married but quickly separated from her husband. She is not revered or commemorated at UCC, although graduates still remember her eccentricity of temper. What has been forgotten is the skill displayed in her play *The Whip Hand* which was produced at the Abbey Theatre (directed by Frank Dermody, with Maureen O'Sullivan and F.J. McCormick in the cast) which had a protracted run in 1942 and remains in the amateur repertoire throughout Ireland.

McCarthy was succeeded by Seán Lucy, who remained at UCC for twenty years. One of his graduates is Robert Welch, professor of English at the University of Ulster at Coleraine and editor of the *Oxford Companion to Irish Literature* (1996). Born in Cork he writes both in Irish and in English and has published several novels including *The Kilcolman Notebook* (1994) and *Groundwork* (1998) as well as a collection of poetry in *Muskerry*. His academic career has been distinguished by the publication of *Changing States: Transformations in Modern Irish Writing* (1993) among other works of criticism.

Cork-born Richard Kearney (1954–) might be included here although his college is University College Dublin where he is professor of philosophy; he has written extensively on philosophical and cultural themes but has also published the novels *Sam's Fall* (1995) and *Walking at Sea Level* (1997) and a volume of poetry *Angel of Patrick's Hill* (1991).

In a reverse process Dublin-born Colbert Kearney (1945–) is professor of English at UCC; his novel *The Consequence* was published in 1993 and his critical work includes *The Writings of Brendan Behan* (1977) and his study of the early plays of Seán O'Casey *The Glamour of Grammar* (1999).

As critic and editor Patricia Coughlan of the English department has contributed widely to academic journals at home and abroad on a wide range of subjects – from Spenser to Beckett – and produced, with Alex Davis, the critical survey *Modernism in Ireland – the Poetry of the 1930s* (1995).

The play, *The Rock Station*, by her colleague Gerry FitzGibbon was published in 1995; another colleague Éibhear Walshe, has published on Elizabeth Bowen, Kate O'Brien and modern Irish writers, and on Teresa Deevy (1903–63), the Waterford-born playwright who studied at UCC, and who despite being almost totally deaf, wrote a number of plays for radio. Several of her dramas were produced at the Abbey Theatre.[56] Walshe's study *Sex, Nation and Dissent* was published in 1997.

These and other members of the department – including short story writer Ellen Beardsley – sustain a continuing production of critical research as well as creative material; it is well to remember here that creative writing is not exclusive to the English department (Tomás Ó Canainn, formerly of the engineering department being merely one example) at the university.

Both the departments of English and Irish have been influenced in their time by teachers such as John Montague in English and Seán Ó Tuama or Seán Ó Riordáin in Irish, and a fusion has been created which has enriched literature throughout Ireland during the last thirty or forty years.

In his study of local contemporary writing *The Accents of the South* (1998), poet Thomas McCarthy (himself a graduate of UCC) notes that the melancholia of six decades of Cork prose has passed away:

In its wake have come the flashing divers and screeching gulls of young poetry. As Ó Riordáin noted in his Diary, 'Tá na tithe agus an áit go léir lán de smaointe chomh maith le duilleoga agus iad ag fás' (The houses and the whole place are as full of thought as of sparrows, both thriving.)[57]

Some of that flowering must be due of course to the cavernous brilliance of
Ó Riordáin himself; he embodied the sense of ownership of language as something which transcends what McCarthy calls the custody of one's native
place. Yet when the literary abacus of Cork life is fingered into meaning it
must become clear that the towering literary personality of these years at UCC
is that of Seán Ó Tuama, emeritus professor of modern Irish literature.

Born in Cork in 1926, Ó Tuama is a graduate of UCC where he was taught
by Daniel Corkery. From the beginning of his career he wrote in Irish and
produced in 1950 an anthology of modern Irish poetry (*Nuabhéarsaíocht*)
and from then on his critical but passionate understanding of Irish poetry
has been an important ingredient in contemporary Irish scholarship.

One ground-breaking study was *An Grá in Amhráin na nDaoine* (1960) in
which he discusses the themes and provenance of love-songs in the Gaelic
tradition; another was the collection *An Duanaire 1600–1900: Poems of the
Dispossessed* (1981) which he edited and translated with Thomas Kinsella. He
is a playwright, his dramas including *Moloney agus Drámaí Eile* (1966) and
Gunna Cam agus Slabhra Óir (1969) and performed throughout Ireland.

Ó Tuama's critical work, his lecturing in America and elsewhere, his role
on educational and other boards and commissions all contribute to a diverse
and colourful career which despite its variations has retained a driving sense
of dedication. That dedication, even above his commitment to the Irish language – which is still the language of his home – is to poetry. Admired as a
teacher, it is as a poet that he is revered. It is as a poet that he has left his signature on his native place and on its people; the shape of his seal is fluid but
not ephemeral – it emerges, for example, in his mystic 'Besides,Who Knows
Before the End What Light May Shine' (the English verses quoted here are
not translations of the Irish extracts);

Maidin ghorm ins an Ghréig
(an leathchéad scoite agam)
faoi bhíomaí buí is giolcaigh fhite –
mo chorp ar teitheadh ón ghréin ...

Liszt go glinn im chluais ag cumasc
le lapaíl shámh no dtonn,
táim síoraí anseo so bhfuarthan
idir fallaí bána an tí ...

*As soon as the piano ceases
the sea ebbs from my heart
and I think of people home in my city
who, not long ago, stood high ...*

a sage who trembled at the brightness
in the forge of ancient poets,
a druid who released our dammed-up music
and perished in the flood,

a tortured poet who fashioned for us
new Irish-language lungs,
a sculptor who set headstones dancing
with his carefree lore ...

File, ceolteóir, dealbhadóir,
is rompu an máistir-saoi,
ina measc siúd do tharlaíos-sa;
ní tharlóidh sé arís ... [58]

In this blue mid-morning in Greece Ó Tuama conjures an almost Yeatsian sense of epic; the four men from his native city who rise before him are the musician, the poet, the sculptor and before them the master-sage: Ó Riada, Ó Riordáin and Seamus Murphy and Corkery, first of all. His life happened to fall among them, a coincidence which would not occur again. Light, heat, Liszt on the piano, the lapping sea, the white walls – they are all vulnerable to the sense of presence.

That magic irradiation pulses from Ó Tuama also. It is the light which shines on a recent collection of poetry edited by Nuala Ní Dhomhnaill and Greg Delanty; the deliberately reverberant title – *Jumping Off Shadows* (1995) invokes Sean O'Faolain's statement that no man jumps off his own shadow. Cork, O'Faolain said, was dyed into him, part of his way of seeing and feeling forever. 'Somebody else who lived there, unknown to me at the same time, might well see it differently ...'

Few of these writers lived in Ireland, not to mind Cork, at the same time as O'Faolain, but they did share this city with Ó Tuama, and lived in his light. The collection is dedicated to Ó Tuama, Seán Lucy, John Montague, Seán Ó Riada and Seán Ó Riordáin and it indicates the assertive, challenging nature of the work between these covers, work which has Cork as its breeding ground and in some cases as its inspiration. These writers not only want to jump off their own shadows but do so, some with a confidence and command which has supported their status as belonging to the most important literary voices in Ireland today.

Among them are Seán Dunne and Nuala Ní Dhomhnaill; Robert Welch and Derry O'Sullivan, Paul Durcan and Ciarán O'Driscoll, Áine Miller, Maurice Riordan, Liz O'Donoghue and Catherine Phil McCarthy. Writers of stature, of reputation and complete, acknowledged, applauded arrival.

The generous allotments of *Jumping Off Shadows* mean that the choices for quotation are too alluring to allow justice or even evaluation. Perhaps in these closing paragraphs some personal favouritism is permissible – perhaps in fact such favouritism is the best arbiter in a guide such as this where preference can only be deferential up to a point. This is the point. For here enters on one side the poet Paul Durcan, and on the other the ageing pianist Charles Lynch. The gentle trajectory of their collision produced, from Durcan, 'The Late Mr Charles Lynch Digresses':

> Having sat all morning at the bay window
> Of the run-down boarding house on the bitch-bedecked hill
> Overlooking the drowned city of Cork
> With a long-stemmed wine-glass balancing on the fulcrum
> Of his ladylike, crossed knees – the deceased virtuoso
> In the threadbare black greatcoat and frayed white shirt
> Tiptoes through the urban heat
> And scrupulously digresses into the Cork School of Music
> When, from next door's crucial radio studios,
> A production technician, Evie, comes skittering –
> 'Mr Lynch, they necessitate you urgently next door'.
> Without altering the adagio of his gait, or its cantabile,
> The ghostly pianist, the master digresser,
> Perilously whispers:
> 'I'm sorry, Evie – but I'm *dashing*'. [59]

If we are hearing with the eye, what reader could resist the invocations of Roz Cowman, born in Cork in 1942, winner of the Patrick Kavanagh Award in 1985. Her subjects are myth and fairy-tale, wildlife and home; her tone is questioning but deceptively gentle – there is always the hard, inflexible bone beneath the leaf, fur or skin. But her imagery is exquisite, as in her presentation of the Annunciation late on a heat-struck day:

> Even the furniture's turned hostile.
> In what's left of air, spermatozoa
> float like pollen. She would gasp
> for breath in the rush
> of his descent beside her,
> but the atmosphere
> vacuums to him,
>
> the frail tympani of her ears
> snap like furze-pods,

and with everything still
unsaid between them,
the word is made flesh. [60]

Eiléan Ní Chuilleanáin (1942–) is a child of the college, having grown up there with her parents Cormac Ó Cuilleanáin and Eilís Dillon. Now a fellow of Trinity College where she lectures in English she lives in Dublin with her husband the poet MacDara Woods.

Widely published, her collections range from *Acts and Monuments* (1972) to *The Magdalene Sermon* (1989) and include her verses in *Cork* (1977) with the artist Brian Lalor; she has won the Patrick Kavanagh Award, the *Irish Times*/Aer Lingus Award and the O'Shaughnessy Prize for Poetry (1992).

The anthology gives a biographical note and publishing history for each poet: Limerick-born Gabriel Rosenstock (1949–) was one of the *Innti* writers gathered around Michael Davitt's enterprise at UCC; so was Nuala Ní Dhomhnaill (1952–) who edited this anthology with Greg Delanty (1958–). Louis De Paor (1961) studied Irish at UCC; twice winner of the Seán Ó Riordáin poetry prize he now lives in Galway. Pat Cotter (1963–) has produced three collections while working as a bookseller and publisher. Gregory O'Donoghue (1951–) is son of the poet, playwright and journalist Robert O'Donoghue: both still live and write in the city.

Gerry Murphy's (1952–) relaxed and anarchic style includes 'Poem in One Breath':

Not that you
would notice
but every time
you pass
up the corridor
Lenin's statue
levitates slightly
to get a better view
of the remarkable ease
with which you fill
curved space. [61]

Líam Ó Muirthile (1950–) also contributed to *Innti*; winner of the Seán Ó Riordáin prize (1988) and the Irish American Cultural Institute Award (1984) he writes a weekly column, 'An Peann Coitianta' for *The Irish Times*.

These are not local reputations. But repeatedly the theme is locality or personality. Again Cork is no exception in this; these writers make each settlement, even each visit, their own, even if for the purposes of this survey the insistence is on Cork as the Eden.

There is, therefore, a breath of recognition when reading 'stiúrthóir Coir' by Colm Breathnach (1961–), as he remembers a Cork choirmaster:

D'ardaiteá do lámh is chanadh cór cois Laoi
d'ardaiteá do lámh athuair
is chanadh cór i gCarraig na bhFear ó thuaidh,
nó arís eile sa tSeandún faoina spuaic ...

... And the torrents and currents of Cork,
the air all around the city would be filled
with the voices of throats you controlled.

At Easter Mass in Farrinferris
music spread over the sides of the mountain
and down to the Glen,
making the people below raise their heads
that white-bright Sunday morning.
You raised your hand and the whole world sang for you.

On the sickly pale hospital sheet
I watched your right hand in its weakness
I heard the noisy torrents of the river outside
and I understood why
voices need a master of choirs. [62]

The lyric insights of Theo Dorgan (1953–) cannot be confined to his native city, but his 'Nocturne for Blackpool' has all the stealthy power of ancient legend revived in a modern city:

The ghost of Inspector Swanzy creeps down Hardwick Street,
MacCurtain turns down the counterpane of a bed he'll never sleep in,
Unquiet murmurs scold from the blue-slate rooftops
The Death-Squad no-one had thought to guard against ...

Dorgan's *The Second Fortune* is due in 1999.[63] His fellow-graduate Greg Delanty (1958–) is a recipient of the Patrick Kavanagh Award (1983) and the Allen Dowling Poetry Fellowship (1986); Delanty teaches at St Michael's College, Vermont, from where he continues to publish collections, the most recent being *The Hellbox* (1998) from Oxford University Press.[64]

Cork is a city of hills, of vistas; its slopes always offer another way of seeing things, another way of looking. Delanty disputes the city's tolerance for such differences. In 'Leper's Walk' he translates the old Irish name to its modern adaptation of 'Lover's Walk', actually a bowered avenue in Montenotte:

... Lover's Walk that's the epitome of a lover's walk.
Its winding incline skirts the city, blossom-confettied,
bordered with necking nooks and arbours ...

In fact the hilly laneway was a quarantine route for lepers, or later victims of fevers from the shipping trade of the city, to a contagion hospital:

They bypassed locals, themselves infected
with the typical small town mycobacterium laprae,
the paralysis that no soul dare attempt anything
different, diagnosed as rising above one's station ...

Yet it is this very height that Tom McCarthy (born in Cappoquin, Co. Waterford, in 1959), uses as a kind of telescope, a site from which to view the world. A devotee of altitude (in 'The Classic Cinema' he watches the demolition of an old movie-theatre – 'Each exposed frame gives way completely./The projection-room fireplace gapes at the sky/Watches openly the last blue movie –...'

From his windows there he can see the railway station, the river, the loading and unloading of ships, the traffic that made Cork a city in the first place. In 'Love Like Trade' the transformation of place to mood suggests some level tier of happiness denied, perhaps, to O'Faolain; its intimate exactitude reflects a city from which escape is, at last, both easy and acceptable. And perhaps, also at last, it offers a level tier of opportunity, or happiness, from which to make that jump from one's own shadow:

Beloved, the emptied ship rises in the sunlight.
You cross the room to look. The plimsoll line
made by your pantihose is level with my eyes

When you stand beside the chair. My lips
touch your skin. Your indelible fingers
stroke my hair. Love registers the Cuban ships.
It makes a chandlery of tide-charts and cigars. [65]

Notes to Cork City

1. T. Crofton Croker, *Researches in the South of Ireland* (1824).
2. Evelyn Bolster, *A History of the Diocese of Cork, from the earliest times to the Reformation* (1972).
3. Pádraig Ó Ríain, 'Another Cork Charter: the life of Saint Finbarr' (*Journal of the Cork Historical and Archaeological Society*, 90, 1985.
4. William O'Sullivan, *The Economic History of Cork from the Earliest Times to the Act of Union* (1937).
5. From Richard Caulfield, 'The Annals of Cork', Council Book of Cork Corporation (1870).
6. O'Sullivan, op. cit.
7. Michael Davitt, 'Ar Filleadh Abhaile ó Dhún Chaoin' (On Returning from Dunquin) in *Selected Poems 1968–1984* (1987). *Ghleann ar Ghleann* (1982), *Bligeard Sráide* (1983) and *An Tost á Scagadh* (1993) are among Michael Davitt's publications.
8. Greg Delanty, *The Hellbox* (1998).
9. Sean Dunne (ed.), *The Poets of Munster* (1986).
10. Alan Titley, 'Contemporary Literature in the Irish Language' in *Hogan's Dictionary of Irish Literature* (1996).
11. ibid.
12. Augustus Young (James Hogan) verse translation of Thackeray's *Irish Sketchbook*: 'Mr. Thackeray in Cork', included in *The Poets of Munster*; Young's poetry is published regularly and collections include *Dánta Grádha: Love Poems from the Irish* (1975) and *Lampion and his Bandits* (1995). His plays include *The Bone in the Heart* (1976).
13. Theo Dorgan *A Nocturne for Blackpool* from *The Ordinary House of Love* (1991/93).
14. Sean O'Faolain: *Vive Moi!* (1963).
15. ibid.
16. ibid.
17. O'Faolain, *An Irish Journey* (1940).
18. ibid.
19. O'Faolain, letter of 1953 written to J.V. Kelleher and quoted by Maurice Harmon in *Sean O'Faolain, A Life* (1994).
20. Terence Brown: *Ireland's Literature* (1988).
21. O'Faolain, *Vive Moi!*.
22. Brown, op. cit.
23. Patrick Maume, *Life that is Exile* (1993).
24. Frank O'Connor, *An Only Child* (1961).
25. Maume, op. cit. See also Sean O'Faolain: *Daniel Corkery* in *The Dublin Magazine* (1936).
26. Daniel Corkery, *Studies*, (1920).
27. Maume, op. cit.
28. O'Connor, *An Only Child*. Cork poet, playwright and novelist Jim McKeon (1942–) has made a special study of the life and work of Frank O'Connor; his biography *Frank O'Connor: A Life* was published in 1998.
29. ibid.
30. ibid.
31. O'Connor, *My Father's Son* (1968).
32. O'Connor, *The Backward Look* (1967).
33. R.I. Best, O.J. Bergin, *The Book of the Dun Cow* (1929) note also the commentary *The Book of the Dun Cow* in Robert Welch (ed.) *The Oxford Companion to Irish Literature* (1996).
34. O'Connor, *My Father's Son*; for more on Bergin see Daniel A. Binchy *Osborn Bergin* (1970).

35. Brown, op. cit.
36. Ethel Mannin, *Rev. Francis Mahony (Father Prout)* from *Two Studies in Integrity* (1954).
37. ibid.
38. Amelia Curran, probably unsettled by events at home, travelled extensively in Europe and became a noted philanthropist. Financially independent, she was a friend of Dr Barry O'Meara of Mallow, one of the doctors attending Napoleon Bonaparte. O'Meara is said to have allowed her on board the *Bellerophon* to sketch the defeated emperor. She lived mostly near the Spanish Steps in Rome and is buried in the crypt of St Isadore's. Among her friends in Italy was Percy Bysshe Shelley, and her portrait of the poet now hangs in the National Portrait Gallery in London. Her resemblance to Rose Cuzzle, red-haired and Irish and with her portrait of Napoleon, suggests she may be the original for that character in Thomas Mann's *Lotte in Weimar*.
39. Leonard Huxley (ed.), *Letters of Elizabeth Barrett Browning to her Sister 1846–1859* (1929).
40. Mannin, op. cit.
41. *The Memoirs of Edward Vaughan Kenealy, LL.D.* (1908) were edited by his daughter Arabella and include his autobiography.
42. Blanchard Jerrold wrote a biographical introduction for *The Final Reliques of Fr Prout* (1876); Charles Kent also wrote a biographical introduction for his collection *The Works of Father Prout* (1881).
43. Quoted in M.M. Thrall, *Rebellious Frasers* (1934). For more on Maginn see R. Skelton Mckenzie (ed.) *Miscellaneous Writings of the late Dr Maginn* (in five volumes, 1855–57); Edward V. Kenealy, who seems to have been an incurable plagiarist of themes and titles, included Prout in *Our Portrait Gallery no. 34, Wm. Maginn, Ph.D.*, (Dublin University Magazine no. 23, 1844).
44. The influence of Crofton Croker on aspects of the Celtic Revival is assessed by Mary Helen Thuente in *W.B. Yeats and Irish Folklore* (1980).
45. Gerald Griffin, *The Collegians* (1829); see also Ethel Mannin, *Two Studies in Integrity*.
46. See also John Wyse-Jackson and Peter Costello, *John Stanislaus Joyce* (1998) and Colbert Kearney, *The Joycead* in *Coping with Joyce*, Maurice Beja and Share Benstock (eds.) (1989).
47. Eilís Dillon, *Inside Ireland* (autobiography) (1982)
48. See also the biography by Colin Scott-Sutherland (1973) and a musical evaluation by Felix Abrahamson (1983).
49. John FitzGerald, The Bard of the Lee, *Legends, Ballads and Songs of the Lee* (1913).
50. This controversy is described in detail in Roy Foster's *W.B. Yeats: A Life* (1997).
51. Lennox Robinson, *Curtain Up* (1941); M.J. O'Neill has written the biography *Lennox Robinson* (1964) and Christopher Murray has edited *Selected Plays of Lennox Robinson* (1982).
52. Among Galvin's other work are two volumes of autobiography, *Song for a Poor Boy* (1990) and *Song for a Raggy Boy* (1991).
53. B.G. McCarthy, *The Female Pen* (1944/1947).
54. ibid.
55. Janet Todd, Preface to *The Female Pen*.
56. Éibhear Walshe, *Other Dominions; the plays of Teresa Deevy* Irish University Review (1995).
57. Thomas McCarthy, in *Gardens of Rememberance* (1988).
58. Collections of Ó Tuama's poetry include *Faoileán na Beatha* (1961), *Saol Fó Thoinn* (1978) and *An Bás i dTír na nÓg* (1988); in 1997 he published, with Peter Denman, his selected poems *Death in the Land of Youth*.
59. From *Going Home to Russia*. Born in Dublin in 1944 Paul Durcan has published more than fifteen collections, the latest being *Greetings to Our Friends in Brazil* (1999).

60. Roz Cowman, *The Gooseherd* (1989).
61. Gerry Murphy's most recent collection is *Extracts from the Lost Log Book of Christopher Columbus* (1999).
62. Colm Breathnach (1961–) has published three books of poetry, including *Scáthach* (1994) which won the Príomhdhuais Filíochta at the Oireachtas of 1994.
63. Theo Dorgan's collections include *The Ordinary House of Love* (1991) and *Sappho's Daughter* (1998); he is co-editor of *The Great Book of Ireland* (1991) and Director of Poetry Ireland.
64. Greg Delanty won the Patrick Kavanagh Award in 1983 and the Allan Dowling Poetry Fellowship in 1986. His next collection is *Leper's Walk*.
65. Tom McCarthy, *The Lost Province* (1996). McCarthy has published several collections of poetry and two novels: *Without Power* (1991) and *Asya and Christine* (1993); his most recent publication is *Gardens of Remembrance* (1998).

Index